Berlin

Now capital of the Federal Republic of Germany, Berlin rose from insignificant origins on swampy soil, becoming a city of immigrants over the ages. Through a series of ten vignettes, Mary Fulbrook discusses the periods and regimes that shaped its character – whether Prussian militarism; courtly culture and enlightenment; rapid industrialisation and expansion; ambitious imperialism; experiments with democracy; or repressive dictatorships of both right and left, dramatically evidenced in the violence of World War and genocide, and then in the Wall dividing Cold War Berlin. This book also presents Berlin's distinctive history as firmly rooted in specific places and sites. Statues and memorials have been erected and demolished, plaques displayed and displaced, and streets named and renamed in recurrent cycles of suppression or resurrection of heroes and remembrance of victims. This vivid and engaging introduction thus reveals Berlin's startling transformations and contested legacies through ten moments from critical points in its multilayered history.

Mary Fulbrook, FBA, is Professor of German History at University College London. Her previous publications include the Wolfson Prize-winning *Reckonings: Legacies of Nazi Persecution and the Quest for Justice* (2018) and the Fraenkel Prize-winning *A Small Town near Auschwitz: Ordinary Nazis and the Holocaust* (2012). Her mother fled Berlin in the 1930s, and Fulbrook has long been fascinated by the city.

Ten Moments That Shaped

Structured around ten evocative moments in a city's past, these concise and engaging volumes allow readers to discover the rich histories of cities around the world. Our expert authors combine vivid historical detail and insightful analyses to tell the story of each city in an accessible and compelling manner.

For a list of titles in the series see
www.cambridge.org/10-moments

Berlin

Mary Fulbrook
University College London

 CAMBRIDGE
UNIVERSITY PRESS

CAMBRIDGE UNIVERSITY PRESS

Shaftesbury Road, Cambridge CB2 8EA, United Kingdom

One Liberty Plaza, 20th Floor, New York, NY 10006, USA

477 Williamstown Road, Port Melbourne, VIC 3207, Australia

314–321, 3rd Floor, Plot 3, Splendor Forum, Jasola District Centre, New Delhi – 110025, India

103 Penang Road, #05–06/07, Visioncrest Commercial, Singapore 238467

Cambridge University Press is part of Cambridge University Press & Assessment, a department of the University of Cambridge.

We share the University's mission to contribute to society through the pursuit of education, learning and research at the highest international levels of excellence.

www.cambridge.org
Information on this title: www.cambridge.org/9781009160940

DOI: 10.1017/9781009160957

© Mary Fulbrook 2025

This publication is in copyright. Subject to statutory exception and to the provisions of relevant collective licensing agreements, no reproduction of any part may take place without the written permission of Cambridge University Press & Assessment.

When citing this work, please include a reference to the DOI 10.1017/9781009160957

First published 2025

A catalogue record for this publication is available from the British Library.

A Cataloging-in-Publication data record for this book is available from the Library of Congress

ISBN 978-1-009-16094-0 Hardback
ISBN 978-1-009-16093-3 Paperback

Cambridge University Press & Assessment has no responsibility for the persistence or accuracy of URLs for external or third-party internet websites referred to in this publication and does not guarantee that any content on such websites is, or will remain, accurate or appropriate.

CONTENTS

List of Figures page x
List of Maps xiii
Preface xv
Chronology xxiii

Introduction: People, Place, Identity 1

1 **Foundational Moments** 9
   Albert the Bear, 1157 9

2 **Courtly Residence** 21
   End of the Thirty Years War, 1648 21
   The Thirty Years War 22
   The Great Elector: Peace, War, and Reform 24
   Royal Residence and Social Diversity 29

3 **Absolutism and Enlightenment** 38
   Moses Mendelssohn arrives in Berlin, 1743 38
   Garrison Town 41
   Toleration, Diversity, and Enlightenment 47
   Berlin at the Turn of the Century 52

4 **Emerging Powerhouse: From Napoleon to Unification** 57
   French Emperor Napoleon Enters
   Berlin, 1806 57
   The Impact of the Napoleonic Wars 59
   After Napoleon 62
   1848 71
   Berlin on the Eve of German Unification 76

CONTENTS

5 **World City: Imperial Berlin** 80
　Great Industrial Exposition,
　Treptow, 1896 80
　Imperial Berlin, Capital of the Reich 83
　Housing Berliners 85
　The Topography of Imperial Power 95
　The Impact of War 105

6 **Greater Berlin: The Weimar Era** 109
　Murders of Rosa Luxemburg and Karl Liebknecht, 15
　January 1919 109
　History Happening in Berlin 112
　Greater Berlin: Expansion and Transformation 118
　Refractions of Modernity and Mass Society 126
　Political Ferment and the End of Democracy 130

7 **Nazi Berlin: Performance, Persecution
　and Destruction** 134
　Ruth Andreas-Friedrich Notes the Deportation of Berlin
　Jews, 1942 134
　The Enactment of Power 137
　The Capital of the Nazi 'National Community' 144
　Destruction: Berlin at War 154

8 **Double Visions (1): Divided Berlin from the War
　to the Wall** 161
　Berliners Experience Defeat and the End of War,
　1945 161
　Occupation and Division 165
　Building Two New Berlins 176
　Cementing Division 182

CONTENTS

9 **Double Visions (2): Divided Berlin from the Wall to Reunification**   185
Luxemburg-Liebknecht Demonstration, January 1988   185
Diverging Societies   188
Divided Approaches to a Common Past   200
The End of Two Berlins   205

10 **Re-connection: United Berlin since 1990**   209
The Unification of Germany, 3 October 1990   209
Cityscapes of Transformation   212
Moving Berliners   222
Landscapes of Remorse   228
An Ever-Changing Kaleidoscope   235

Epilogue: Forever Changing, yet Always Berlin   238

Notes   241
Index   253

FIGURES

0.1 Medieval fortress and tower of Spandau *page 6*
1.1 Albert the Bear, statue from the Tiergarten 12
1.2 Nikolaikirche (Nicolai Church) 14
1.3 Medieval Dance of Death (c. 1484), Marienkirche (St Mary's Church) 15
1.4 Schloss Köpenick, as portrayed in a copper engraving by Matthäus Merian, 1652 19
1.5 Map of Berlin, c. 1600 20
2.1 Französische Dom (French Cathedral), Gendarmenmarkt 29
2.2 Zeughaus (arsenal), built between 1695 and 1706 33
3.1 Map of Berlin in 1739 40
3.2 Prussian Militarism: Statue of Frederick the Great on Unter den Linden 47
3.3 Turn of the century literary salons: Rahel Varnhagen von Ense, *née* Levin 55
4.1 Napoleon entering Berlin through the Brandenburg Gate, 1806 58
4.2 Potsdamer station, 1841 70
4.3 Friedrichshain cemetery: Graves of young demonstrators killed in March 1848 73
4.4 Porcelain plate portraying a mid nineteenth-century bourgeois house on Unter den Linden 77
5.1 Neue Wache, Unter den Linden, c. 1900 86
5.2 Wasserturm (water tower) Prenzlauer Berg 92
5.3 Slum housing: A cellar room in Grossbeerenstr. 6, c. 1905 93

LIST OF FIGURES

5.4 The Lunapark, Halensee 95
5.5 'Colonial wares' in a shop window in Köpenick 103
6.1 Architect-designed housing in Siemensstadt, 1920s 122
6.2 Potsdamer Platz, 1932 124
6.3 Advertisement for an event at the 'Ladies Club Violetta', Kreuzberg, November 1928 129
7.1 SPD demonstration against Hitler and the NSDAP, Lustgarten, 19 February 1933 138
7.2 *Schwerbelastungskörper* (heavy load-exerting body) 145
7.3 *SS-Kameradschaftssiedlung* (SS comradeship settlement), Krumme Lanke 150
7.4 Hitler youth relief on housing estate, Grazer Damm 152
7.5 Forced labour barracks, Schöneweide 156
8.1 American and Soviet soldiers in front of a portrait of Stalin, 1945 167
8.2 Layers of history: An old wartime bunker beneath a post-war West Berlin apartment block 179
8.3 Kaiser-Wilhelm-Gedächtniskirche (Kaiser William Memorial Church) and Kurfürstendamm, January 1947 181
9.1 Landscapes of power in East Berlin: Unter den Linden, 1981 196
9.2 East Berlin memorial to the 'Köpenick blood week' 201
9.3 Topography of Terror, on the site of Heinrich Himmler's Reich Security Head Office (RSHA) 204
10.1 Reichstag dome: Transparent democracy? 214
10.2 Revolutionary demonstrations by Berlin citizens in March 1848 on the site of the former Royal Palace, now occupied by the Humboldt Forum 220
10.3 Communist heroes who remain: Marx and Engels 221

10.4 Glienicke Bridge between Berlin and Potsdam   223
10.5 Memorials to victims of Nazi persecution: *Stolpersteine* (stumbling stones)   231
11.1 Tourist boat on the River Spree   239

MAPS

1 Berlin in 1798 *page* xviii
2 Greater Berlin in 1920 xix
3 Berlin in divided Germany 1945–90 xx
4 The Berlin Wall 1961–89 xxi
5 The Berlin Wall in Central Berlin 1961–89 xxii

PREFACE

BERLIN is arguably one of the most fascinating cities in the world – certainly it is my own *Lieblingsstadt*, or favourite city, not only despite but even precisely because of all the continuing ambivalence it evokes, the absolutely appalling aspects of its history and yet the wondrousness of others, and indeed the repeated and continuing efforts to overcome the worst of the past and to strive energetically towards a better future. Related to this, of course, is the fact that what a better future might look like is always strongly contested; and hence, Berlin has been and remains a forum for constant debate, controversy, and outright conflict. Innumerable visions and widely differing possibilities in practice have been played out on its stage, sometimes simultaneously, while the wider parameters of the city's very existence have been continually changing. The contrasts across time are extraordinary.

Any attempt to cram Berlin's multifaceted history into one short book must inevitably be a highly selective enterprise, and every take on this protean city will differ accordingly. The vignettes or brief 'moments' at the start of each chapter have been chosen to illustrate or open up wider aspects of the period addressed in each case. The short chapters then provide overviews of more extended 'moments' in the broader sense, as distinctive periods of time differing significantly from what came before and after. I hope that what follows will in this way provide both a stimulus and a helpful framework to assist further exploration; there is so much more that could have been included, had space permitted.

PREFACE

I cannot recall any time in my own life when a sense of a lost Berlin, accompanied by a yearning to revive an atmosphere that could never actually be recaptured, was not present. My mother was one of so many Berliners who had to leave their native city against their will; but she was lucky enough to be able to emigrate to the UK in the 1930s. When she eventually went back to visit former friends after the war, she was aghast at how the remembered city of her childhood had been so comprehensively destroyed by Nazism and war; yet she herself conveyed many traditions, tastes, linguistic quirks, and even jokes from pre-war Berlin. By the time I lived in the city for a while before beginning my undergraduate studies, it was the Wall and the Cold War that dominated the landscape; and now, since reunification in 1990, the place has radically altered again. In becoming a 'Berliner by choice', a *Wahl-Berlinerin*, and in exploring the city's history in more detail, I feel that I am picking up torn threads and reclaiming, in however limited a way, some fractured sense of continuity across generations.

I would like to express my thanks to my UCL colleagues who read an earlier draft of the book, Zoltán Kékesi and Stephanie Bird. I am extremely grateful for their insights and perceptive comments, although I have not acted on all of their suggestions, and they of course bear no responsibility for my own errors and infelicities. I would also like to thank, as always, the members of my family, who have in their own ways developed distinctive personal relationships with this extraordinary city; not only Conrad, Erica, and Carl, all of whom chose to live there for a while on quite separate endeavours, but also their partners and children. They assure me that Berlin remains 'worth a visit' not only for reasons of family heritage but primarily because the city itself is so spectacularly interesting and so many aspects of it so enjoyable. Last but never least, I would

PREFACE

like to thank Julian for his constant presence, his putting up with my interests and obsessions, and his willingness to trek around every last corner of the city in search of historical details. It helps that there is nearly always a congenial café in which to recover.

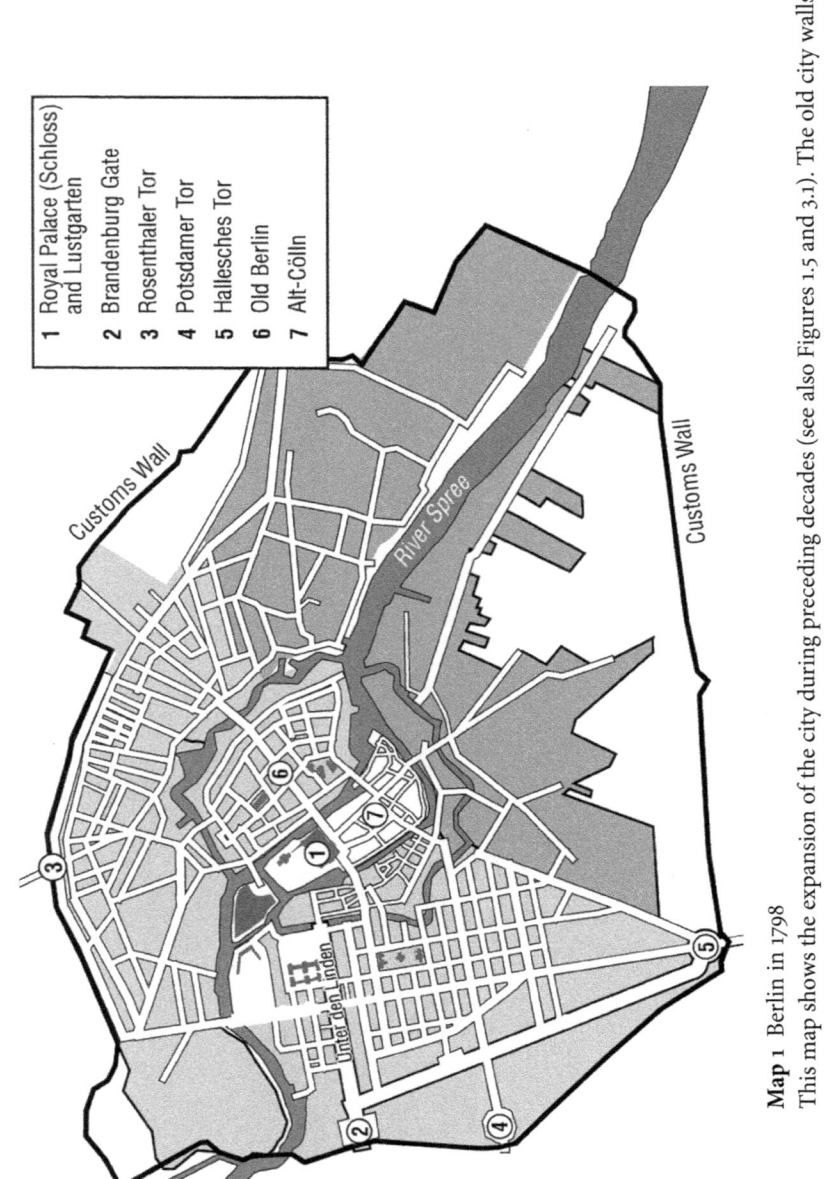

Map 1 Berlin in 1798

This map shows the expansion of the city during preceding decades (see also Figures 1.5 and 3.1). The old city walls have been replaced by waterways; the more recent customs wall shows historic city gates that remain important sites today, such as the now iconic Brandenburg Gate. Drawn by Joe LeMonnier, https://mapartist.com

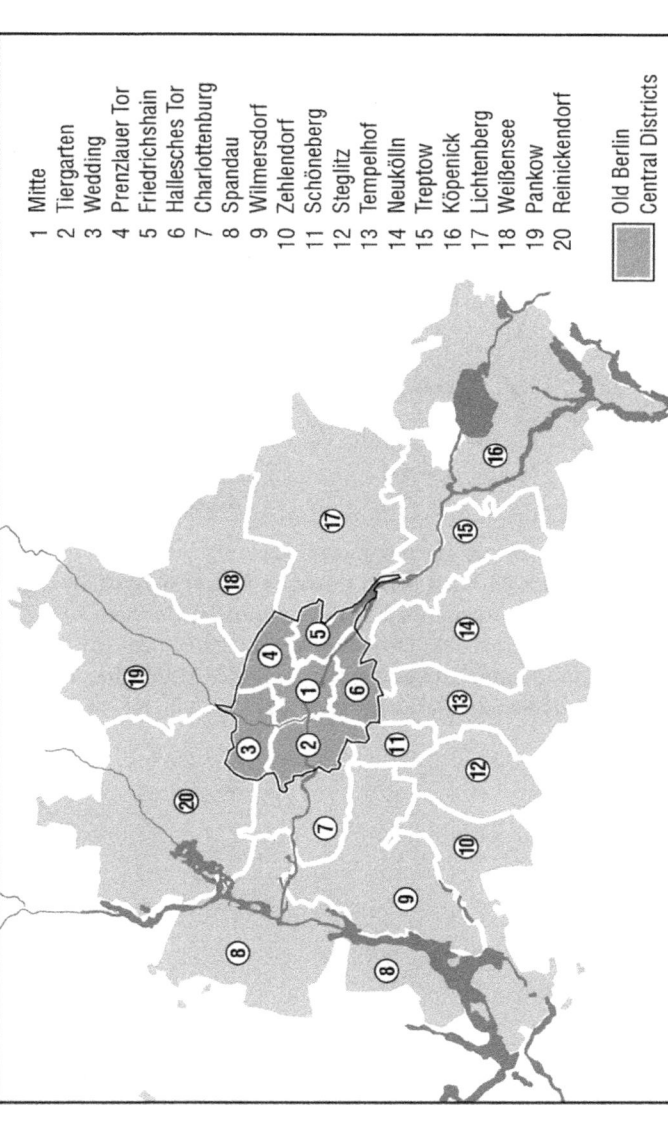

Map 2 Greater Berlin in 1920

With the incorporation in 1920 of surrounding suburbs and villages as well as formerly independent townships, Greater Berlin expanded massively in both extent and population. Movement between home and workplace was facilitated by the rapidly extended network of S-Bahn and U-Bahn trains in addition to trams and road traffic. Drawn by Joe LeMonnier, https://mapartist.com

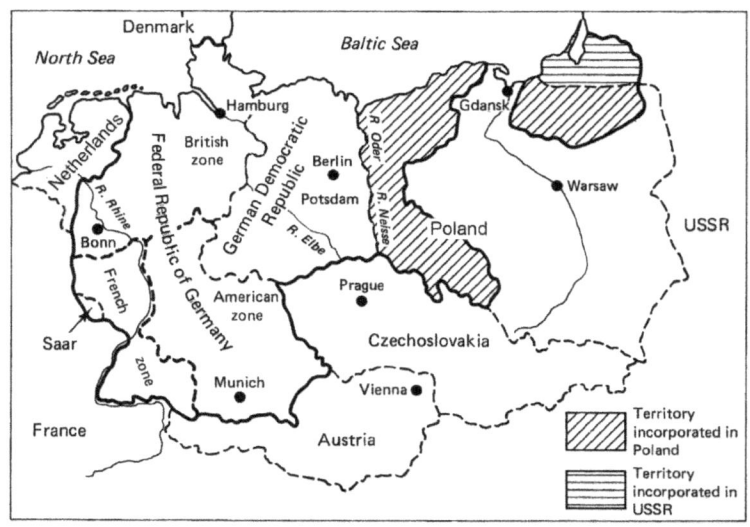

Map 3 Berlin in divided Germany 1945–90
During the Cold War, West Berlin became a remote outpost of western democracy, surrounded by the communist German Democratic Republic (GDR; *Deutsche Demokratische Republik*, *DDR*) in Soviet-dominated Eastern Europe. After M. Hughes, *Nationalism and Society: Germany 1800–1945* (London: Edward Arnold, 1988)

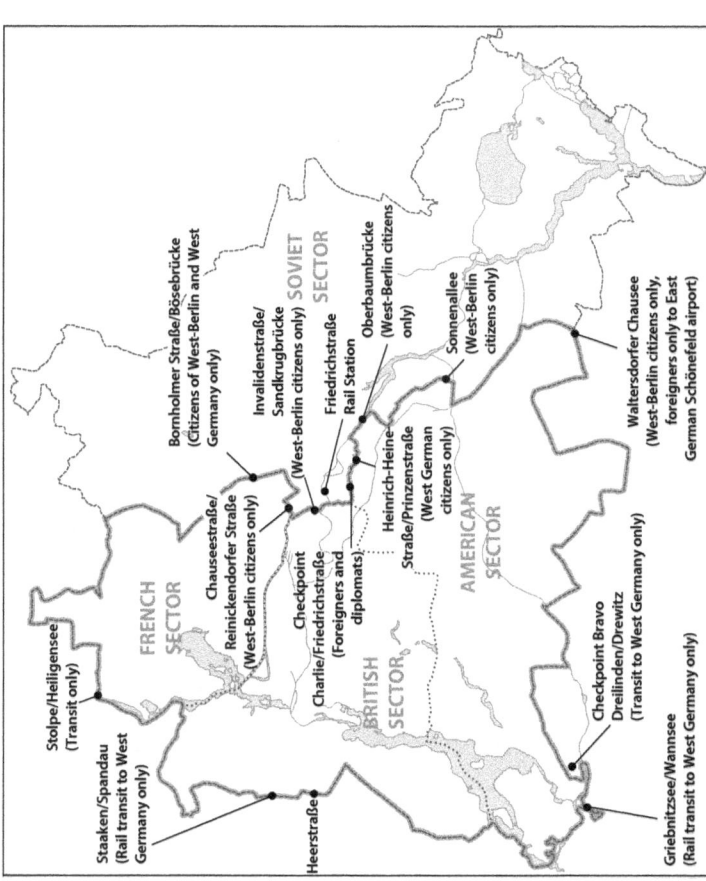

Map 4 The Berlin Wall 1961–89
This map shows the fortified border encircling West Berlin, totalling some 156 kilometres or just under 100 miles. Visas were required to cross the border for transit routes to West Germany, or for traffic between East and West.

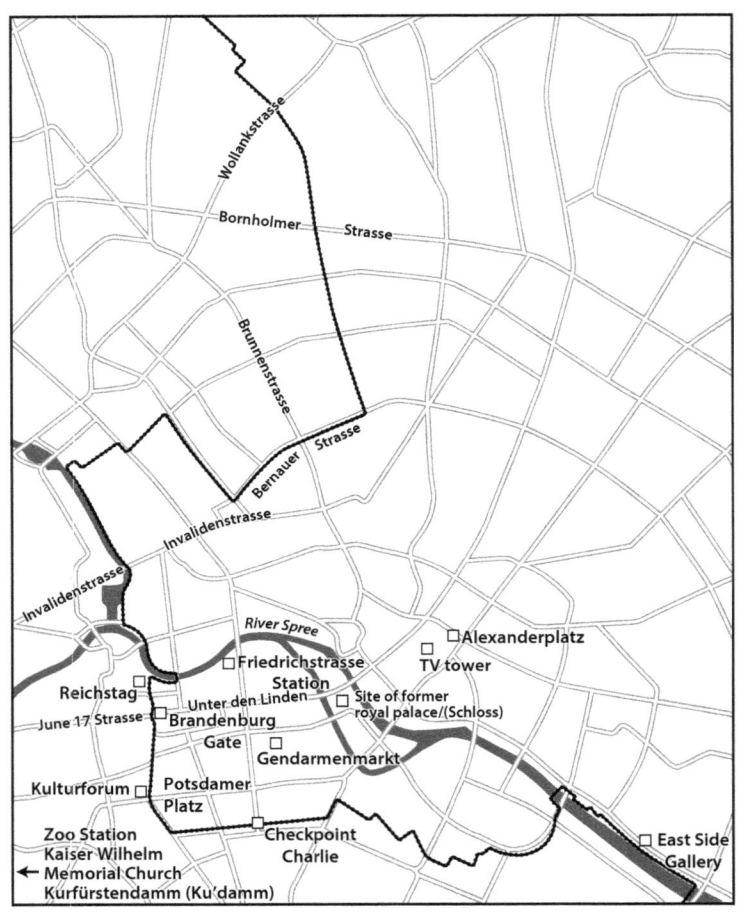

Map 5 The Berlin Wall in Central Berlin 1961–89
Roughly 27 miles of the Wall snaked through the city, cutting off streets and dividing West and East Berlin. This map shows key crossing points and the relatively few locations that have subsequently come to act as central memorial sites.

CHRONOLOGY

1157	**Albert the Bear gains control of Brandenburg**
1157–1323	Ascanian dynasty rules as margraves of Brandenburg
1237	First written mention of Cölln
1244	First written mention of Berlin
1307	Legally binding union of Cölln and Berlin with common seat of government
1323–73	Wittelsbach dynasty rules as margraves and electors of Brandenburg
1369	Berlin gains the right to mint its own coins
1373–1415	Luxemburg dynasty rules as electors of Brandenburg
1391	Berlin joins the Hanseatic League
1432	Berlin and Cölln officially merge
1415–1918	Hohenzollern dynasty rules as electors of Brandenburg, from 1701 as Kings in and of Prussia, from 1871 as Emperors of the German Empire
1442	Frederick 'the Iron Tooth' (*Eisenzahn*) of the Hohenzollerns settles in Berlin
1443	Establishment of a palace (*Schloss*) in Berlin
1446	Anti-Jewish pogrom
1447–48	Citizens' revolt, known as the 'Berlin Indignation'; burghers lose control
1510	100 Jews put to death, Jewish community banished
1538	Berlin withdraws from the Hanseatic League

CHRONOLOGY

1539	Berlin adopts the Reformation
1618–48	Thirty Years War
1619–40	Rule of Elector Georg Wilhelm
1627	Georg Wilhelm flees Berlin; Count Adam von Schwarzenberg left in charge
1627–39	Berlin periodically set on fire by imperial troops or attacked by the Swedes
1640–88	Rule of Elector Frederick William, the 'Great Elector'
1648	**End of the Thirty Years War**
1671	Jews from Vienna invited to settle in Berlin
1685	French Huguenots offered refuge in Berlin
1688–1713	Rule of Elector Frederick III, from 1701 as King Frederick I
1701	Elector Frederick III crowns himself King Frederick I in Prussia
1713–40	Rule of King Frederick William I, 'the Soldier King'
1740–86	Rule of Frederick II, 'Frederick the Great'
1743	**Moses Mendelssohn arrives in Berlin**
1786–97	Rule of King Frederick William II
1797–1840	Rule of King Frederick William III
1806	Napoleon abolishes Holy Roman Empire
1806	**French Emperor Napoleon defeats Prussia and enters Berlin**
1812	Edict of Emancipation gives Jews citizenship rights
1815	Congress of Vienna
1834	Formation of Customs Union (*Zollverein*)
1840–61	Rule of King Frederick William IV
1848	March revolution

CHRONOLOGY

1861–88	Rule of King William I, from 1871 as Emperor of Germany
1871	Unification of Imperial Germany (1871–1918)
1888	Rule of Emperor Frederick III
1888–1918	Rule of Kaiser Wilhelm II (Emperor William II)
1890	End of Bismarck era
1896	**Great Industrial Exposition, Treptow**
1914	Outbreak of First World War
1918	9 November: abdication of Kaiser, proclamation of Republic, 11 November: armistice
15 January 1919	**Murders of Rosa Luxemburg and Karl Liebknecht**
1920	Kapp Putsch
1923	Hyperinflation
1926	Joseph Goebbels appointed Gauleiter of Berlin
1929	Wall Street crash, followed by Depression
1933	Hitler appointed chancellor, 30 January. Reichstag fire. Enabling Act passed. Repressive measures against political opponents and Jews
1934	Death of President Hindenburg; Hitler unites offices of chancellor and president as 'Führer'
1935	Nuremberg Laws
1936	Berlin Olympics
1938	*Kristallnacht*, 9–10 November
1939	Invasion of Poland, 1 September, starting Second World War

CHRONOLOGY

1941	Invasion of USSR, 22 June, 'war of annihilation' unleashing genocide
1942	Wannsee conference on 20 January, coordinating the murder of Jews in Europe
1942–44	**Ruth Andreas-Friedrich notes the deportation of Berlin Jews**
1945	Closing months of war, Soviet troops enter Germany and eventually Berlin
1945	Hitler commits suicide, 30 April. Germany signs unconditional surrender, 8 May
1945	**Berliners experience the end of the war and defeat**
1945	Berlin under Allied control. Potsdam conference
1947	Dissolution of Prussia
1948–49	Currency reform in the west; Berlin airlift
1949	Foundation of the Federal Republic of Germany (in May) and the German Democratic Republic (in October). Berlin under four-power control but western and Soviet sectors divided
1953	Uprising in East Berlin, 17 June
1961	From 13 August, Wall built to separate East Berlin and GDR from West Berlin
1972	Basic Treaty eases travel restrictions from West to East Berlin
1987	Berlin's 750th anniversary celebrated in both East and West Berlin
January 1988	**Luxemburg-Liebknecht demonstration, East Berlin**
1989	Demonstrations, challenges to GDR government; Berlin Wall breached, 9 November

CHRONOLOGY

1990	Collapse of communist rule in the GDR
3 October 1990	**The unification of Germany**
1991	Bundestag vote to move the seat of government to Berlin
1994	Allies leave Berlin
1999	Reichstag re-opened for German parliament
2020	BER opened as international airport for Berlin

Introduction
People, Place, Identity

BERLIN is one of the world's most vibrant and interesting cities. Now capital of the Federal Republic of Germany, and playing a leading role in Europe and the wider world, Berlin has risen from insignificant origins in two small medieval trading centres on swampy soil at the confluence of two rivers, the Spree and the Havel, in the Brandenburg marches (or Mark) in the centre of Europe. Facing both west and east – with bitter winter winds blowing from the Urals, and hot continental summers to be enjoyed at its many lakesides and woodlands – Berlin has always been something of a frontier settlement.

Periodically undergoing radical changes of regime, it is also a highly self-reflexive city. Berlin today is not merely a centre of political power and social experimentation, but also in effect a historical kaleidoscope, selectively reflecting changing facets of an ever-present past. Traces of quite different periods are discernible – whether Prussian militarism and enlightenment, industrialisation and imperialism, experiments with democracy, or repressive dictatorships of both right and left. Statues have been erected and demolished, plaques and memorials displayed and displaced, and streets named and renamed, in recurrent cycles of repression or resurrection of heroes and remembrance of victims. Berlin is, and has long been, a wilfully self-conscious city, ever debating its continually contested past.

What then can we select as 'ten moments that shaped Berlin'? The meaning and length of a 'moment' can vary immensely, from a matter of minutes to an epoch. Whether brief or extended, moments are always in some way significant: they are discrete, distinct from what came before and what followed. Yet they also form part of a wider entity, contributing to its development and transformation. Here, I treat the notion of moment in the broadest sense: a distinctive period which might persist over years, decades, or centuries. Each chapter addresses a longer moment, a defining period of significant transformation in the character and shape of Berlin; but at the start of each chapter I have added brief vignettes that may serve to illustrate, symbolise, or crystallise specific issues within the wider moment.

What are the selection criteria for defining historical periods? At first glance, it might appear that political regimes and particularly wars were most significant in shaping Berlin. But these were not anonymous forces outside of history: decisions were made by significant individuals, social actors, and organisations, in the context of changing power constellations, and informed by cultural assumptions and ambitions. Moreover, there are distinctive longer-term patterns. Key social and economic changes affected who were 'Berliners' – and indeed how many people were what sort of Berliners – as well as the conditions in which they lived. And cultural shifts informed the ways in which people conceived of 'Berlin', past and present, as well as their conflicting aspirations for the future. While choosing distinct periods largely according to significant changes of regime, this book therefore revolves around three interrelated elements that are integral to underlying continuities as well as radical change: people, place, and constructions of identity.

First of all, the people. Those we may like to think of as an enduring collective identity, 'Berliners', were repeatedly constituted and continually reshaped by changing social and economic structures and cultural conceptions. Throughout its history, Berlin's population has been marked by diversity. For centuries,

INTRODUCTION

indeed from its earliest traceable origins, Berlin has expanded from two original small settlements on the River Spree, Berlin and Cölln, through waves of in-migration from elsewhere. Many people came in the hope of making a better future for themselves; and periodically, minorities who were perceived as economically useful were actively encouraged to immigrate, contributing significantly to the religious, cultural, and linguistic diversity of the city. Such communities range from the Dutch in the medieval period, when the German Ascanians suppressed the pagan Slavs and brought in agricultural expertise from the Netherlands, or the Rhineland colonisers who may have given Cölln its name, through the Huguenots, Jews, and Bohemians of the late seventeenth and eighteenth centuries. In the later nineteenth and early twentieth century, workers from the provinces came seeking better economic prospects in the rapidly expanding industrial city, eastern European Jews fled pogroms in the Russian borderlands, and White Russians sought to escape the Bolshevik revolution, while the supposed attractions or greater freedoms of city life played a major role for other immigrants. By the later twentieth century, the foreign forced labourers of the Nazi era were replaced by Turkish 'guest workers' (Gastarbeiter) in the west, and international workers from socialist countries in the east. Over the centuries there were changing patterns of immigration and degrees of integration; 'Berliners' were never an ethnically or culturally homogeneous community, even if certain communities were variously privileged or marginalised at different times, and frequently subjected to severe restrictions.

In this long history of diversity, the Nazi era presented a striking contrast. Berliners of Jewish descent, and Roma and Sinti ('gypsies'), were variously forced to emigrate, or were deported and murdered; people with physical and mental disabilities were killed; and others who did not fit in with Nazi ideals, such as gay men, were brutally persecuted, often with fatal consequences. During the war, foreign forced labourers were brought in to work, replacing men at the front. Post-war Berlin had a very different social profile from just a couple of decades earlier. But in the early twenty-first century, Berlin reverted to long-standing traditions, officially welcoming refugees from war-torn regions and informally attracting incomers from around the world.

Being a Berliner has often been as much a matter of choice as of descent. The notion of being a 'Berliner by choice' (*Wahlberliner*) has a long history, claimed even for incomers to East Berlin in the 1950s, while others were trying to escape at least the communist half of the city.[1] Yet alongside continuing diversity, there has also long been a sense of a distinctive Berlin identity, of what it means 'to be a Berliner'.

Constructions of this essence vary. US President John F. Kennedy famously implied, in his 1963 speech from Schöneberg Town Hall in West Berlin, that anyone committed to western notions of freedom and democracy must stand in solidarity with the population of this walled-in outpost, and could in this sense claim, as he did himself, to be a Berliner. Others have sought to identify supposedly defining characteristics of Berliners, highlighting their legendary sharp humour and 'cheekiness' (the *Berliner Schnauze*), which was ambivalently combined – at least according to the nineteenth-century novelist Theodor Fontane – with warm-heartedness and a tendency to irony and self-deprecation.[2] The art historian Karl Scheffler pointed to the wit, self-irony, and lack of sentimentality of ordinary Berliners.[3] Features such as quick-wittedness and intellectual curiosity could challenge class distinctions; and newcomers could rapidly adapt to the abrasive manners of Berliners, developing a capacity for directness and assertive repartee as an essential survival tactic.

INTRODUCTION

Incomers might however have more trouble acquiring the distinctive Berlin accent or speech patterns. Since the eighteenth century, upper-class Berlinese has incorporated a smattering of French words, but ordinary people widely indulged in distinctive local pronunciation: for example, a 'j' or 'y' sound replacing 'g', such that words like 'good' (*gut*) would be pronounced more like 'yoot' (*jut*); a hard 'ck' replacing the softer 'ch', such that 'ich' (I) would become 'ick'; or a 't' replacing 's' in words like 'das' ('the' or 'that'), which would become 'det'. Berliners often enjoy speaking *Berlinerisch* even when in perfect command of High German, or use it with affectionate humour and delight as a mark of common collective identity – suggesting that Heinrich Heine had perhaps overstated it when, in the early nineteenth century, he claimed that 'no city has less by way of local patriotism than Berlin'.[4]

Secondly, people and place need to be considered together. Not only the population but also the key sites and size of Berlin, and its relations with the wider world, were closely interrelated. Integral moments in Berlin's history are defined by changing functions – fishing village, trading centre, princely residence, garrison town, sequentially capital of radically different modern states, eventually divided pawn and then ambiguous heart of Europe. Distinctive too is its pattern of expansion, not only through urbanisation with industrialisation, but also as a conglomerate of separate localities. Many districts of today's Berlin were formerly townships in their own right, with their own castles or palaces, town halls, and idiosyncratic local history museums (*Heimatmuseen*), as in the charming old building in Köpenick or the medieval citadel in Spandau (Figure 0.1). Even in its origins, Berlin was formed by conjoining two separate settlements, Berlin and Cölln; this pattern of amalgamation continued, most notably with the incorporation of surrounding areas into the metropolis of Greater Berlin (*Groß-Berlin*) in 1920. And

Figure 0.1 Medieval fortress and tower of Spandau
In medieval times, Spandau was an independent fortified town that was far more important than Berlin.
Photograph by the author

class differences between districts were already marked well before the Cold War division between communist East and capitalist West fostered further striking contrasts.

Thirdly, and deeply significant for Berlin, are the multi-layered traces and ubiquitous representations of historical developments. From the earliest days to the present, a self-reflexive engagement with aspects of Berlin's past has been key to changing aspirations for the future. Representations of heroes and villains, from Albert the Bear or Frederick the Great to Adolf Hitler, contrast with remembrance of martyrs and victims, whether 'fallen soldiers' in war or groups persecuted under National Socialism. What is truly unique about Berlin is buried in the parts of this sentence referring to villains and victims; while communities everywhere memorialise heroes and martyrs, no other city displays, to such an extent, such visible remorse and responsibility for the legacies of its villains, or engages in comparable degrees of remembrance of the victims of its own former misdeeds. Moreover, much of this activity is in some way a recuperation, a re-valuing and an attempt to return to Berlin what has been lost.

These aspects too cannot be separated from people and place; descendants of the persecuted often return, for example, to explore landscapes inhabited by their forebears, trying to reconstruct lives before destruction; or they settle and attempt, in some way, not so much to 'make good again' (as in the wholly inappropriate German word for compensation, *Wiedergutmachung*, in principle utterly impossible after the Shoah or Holocaust) as to pick up strands of lives that were not lived and to create a new strand in their own lives that allows a sense of reconnection with the truncated or displaced lives of ousted ancestors.

But there is so much more to Berlin's past than the dozen years of Nazi rule, overwhelming though this was in its shattering impact and lasting legacies. Reflections on historical layers of identity have long preoccupied observers and residents of this fascinating city, well before Hitler took it over and nearly destroyed it. Over the last few centuries, innumerable residents, visitors, diary and memoir writers, journalists, scholars, and creative writers have made variously lengthy or pithy contributions to the project of distilling and conveying the ever-changing character of Berlin, even before we get anywhere near the preoccupations with Nazism, the Cold War, and contemporary issues that have dominated engagement with Berlin's history and identity since the mid twentieth century.[5] Visual representations of Berlin's complex history abound: reproductions of Heinrich Zille's cartoons and photographs of Berlin working-class life more than a century ago adorn the walls of some underground stations; cinematic classics from the Weimar era, including Walter Ruttman's *Berlin: Symphony of a Metropolis* (1927) and Fritz Lang's *Metropolis*, or novels by Alfred Döblin, Hans Fallada, and Christopher Isherwood, variously inform current popular perceptions of Weimar and Nazi Berlin; spy thrillers, detective fiction, and popular films play on fascination with deception and subterfuge both under Nazism and in a divided city at the flashpoint of the Cold War, while others portray the East German secret police, the Stasi, or the transgenerational legacies of Holocaust persecution. Many recent films and novels, interestingly, explore the experiences of immigrants and refugees as well as the darker sides of life in the city.

Meanwhile, tourism – so essential to modern Berlin's economy – has not merely highlighted its dark past, but also plays on reconstructing some supposed 'essence of Berlin', whether symbolised by the ubiquitous and now remarkably benign representations of the 'Berlin bear' emblem and the Brandenburg Gate, or portrayed in re-imaginings of Imperial Berlin or the 'golden twenties'. All these portrayals are selective reconstructions, and always contested, from a wide variety of perspectives. This concern with self-representation and reflection is, too, of the essence of Berlin.

In what follows, I have sought both to present an outline (necessarily sketchy) of key moments in Berlin's history, and a flavour of some of the ways in which the people, the places, and conceptions of identity, have evolved and shifted over time.

1
Foundational Moments

Albert the Bear, 1157

Was there in fact any foundational moment in the history of Berlin? Myths abound, and turning points are, as always, a matter of selection and interpretation.

In the twelfth century, a Saxon 'Count of Ascanien and Ballenstadt' known as Albert the Bear after the symbol on his shield, not his appearance, wrested control of the frontier territory or 'march' (Mark) of Brandenburg from the Slavic Wends.[1] Following a period of protracted fighting and temporary retreat, he regained control in 1157 and took the title of Margrave of Brandenburg, choosing the town of Brandenburg west of Berlin as his residence. Albert's military victory over a pagan people not only signalled German and Christian domination of the area, but also elevated the status of Brandenburg to that of an Electoral territory in the Holy Roman Empire, one of the few territories with a politically significant vote in the election of Holy Roman emperors. Furthermore, the conquest increased the ethnic diversity of the area; defeated Slavs and victorious Germans intermingled and intermarried, while Albert pursued a policy emulated by many of his successors of attracting immigrants, particularly from the Netherlands, to encourage agricultural production and economic growth.

Albert the Bear's fame persisted over the centuries. In the view of the nineteenth-century historian Thomas Carlyle: 'None of Albert's wars are so comfortable to reflect on as those he had with the anarchic Wends; whom he now fairly beat to powder, and either swept away, or else damped down into Christianity and keeping of the peace.' Carlyle considered that now the Wends 'could not but consent more and more to efface themselves, – either to become German, and grow milk and cheese in the Dutch manner, or to disappear from the world'. Carlyle concluded that this was, 'for posterity', Albert the Bear's most 'memorable feat': 'After two-hundred and fifty years of barking and worrying, the Wends are now finally reduced to silence; their anarchy well buried, and wholesome Dutch cabbage planted over it.'[2]

The moment that Albert conquered the Wends was clearly significant, but it neither constituted the foundation of Berlin, nor did it immediately enhance the status of the place. Other towns were at this time far more important, particularly the fortified town of Spandau to the west, controlled by Albert, and from 1241 also Köpenick to the southeast, under one of Albert's successors – both of which would eventually be incorporated as suburbs into the expanded Greater Berlin of the twentieth century. At the time they received their first written mentions in 1237 and 1244, the settlements of Cölln and Berlin were simply convenient river crossing points for trading routes on the waterways of the Spree and Havel. Three quite contrasting twentieth-century regimes – Nazi, communist, and democratic – nevertheless found it convenient to celebrate anniversaries of the supposed 'founding' of Berlin in 1237. In 1937, Nazi Berlin marked 700 years of the city's history, dating this to the first written mention of the settlement of Cölln, a crucial part of the central area of what we now know as Berlin. The settlement on the other side of the river, Berlin, which eventually gave the city its name, was first mentioned in a document of 1244. The date of 1237 was marked again in the competing 750th anniversary activities in East and West Berlin in 1987.

Yet the origins of Berlin go back well before Cölln and Berlin were first recorded in writing; and leaving historical heroes and celebratory reflections aside, it is not so easy to identify a precise date of origin. The related ambiguity about place of origin is also oddly apposite: the city's double foundations in Cölln and Berlin continued to be reflected in the multiplicity of districts across subsequent centuries.

• ● •

Archaeological evidence of human settlements in this swampy area of lakes and waterways, set in a wider landscape of sandy soil, go back for centuries before the Christian era. This was border territory never conquered by the Romans, populated by those they considered 'barbarians'. During the long medieval period, movements of peoples across Europe from both west and east contributed to a mixed linguistic and ethnic heritage, again a continuing feature of the city's history. Berlin lay in one of the last areas of central Europe to be Christianised, with rivalry for control from both Germans to the west and Polish Catholics to the east, while pagan Slavs or Wends held much of the region in between.

This ethnic and cultural diversity created some later sensitivity with regard to specifying foundational moments. Two eighteenth-century chroniclers, Johann Christoph Müller and Georg Gottfried Küster, who compiled a lengthy history of *Old and New Berlin* running to several thousand pages, remained mystified about Berlin's origins; yet, noting that waves of immigrants had contributed to the city's development over the centuries, they perceptively commented that many contemporaries 'would prefer to credit a German, rather than a foreign people' with founding Berlin. Even so, they added with some candour, 'it is hard to discover the truth in the darkness of the past'.[3]

A key turning point clearly came with Albert the Bear's conquest of this frontier territory, and Albert may or may not have lent Berlin its name and its emblem, the bear (Figure 1.1). Müller

Figure 1.1 Albert the Bear, statue from the Tiergarten
Statue of the legendary twelfth-century Albert the Bear (standing), created in 1898 for Emperor Wilhelm II's 'Victory Avenue' in the Tiergarten and now on display in Spandau's Citadelle Museum.
Photograph by the author

and Küster, like many others, speculated that 'Berlin' was based on the word for bear (*Bär*). The eighteenth-century publisher and author Friedrich Nicolai, writing in 1769, also considered the origins of the city to be lost 'in the darkness of history', and mentioned the historical significance of Albert. As far as Berlin's name was concerned, however, Nicolai thought a reference to water was more likely, since 'from olden times' the word 'Bäre' referred to 'a dam or water building designed to stop or hold the flow of water for purposes of a mill or a fishery' (as in 'barrier').

There were two such places in Berlin, and in Nicolai's view the Mühlendamm was probably the origins of the settlement. Yet ethnic and linguistic diversity suggested other possibilities too; many now think the name quite likely originated in the Slavic word for swamps, marshes, or boggy ground, 'Brl': Berlin would be the settlement in the swamp. The name Cölln very likely derived, in Nicolai's view, from the influx of colonial settlers – 'Christians from the Rhineland, Holland, Flanders and the Netherlands' – giving it the name of 'colony', as in Cologne (from where many immigrated). Berlin was indeed in some sense always a somewhat colonial outpost, as Karl Scheffler too noted in the early twentieth century.[4]

In the twelfth and thirteenth centuries, the 'germanisation' of lands east of the river Elbe continued, spearheaded not only by military force but also by the economic and cultural power of Christian churches and religious institutions. People from west and east, Slavs and Germans, intermingled and intermarried, and the ethnic mix was further enriched by settlers from further afield, such as the Flemish, attracted by prospects for economic productivity and well-being. Migrants also came from the Rhineland, and later, with the advent of the Hohenzollern dynasty in the fifteenth century, from Swabia in southwestern Germany. All these influences affected the language, with what became known as High German eventually predominating over the Low German dialects of northern Germany, but with the admixture of some words of Slavic derivation, as in place names ending in 'ow', such as Rudow, Treptow, and Pankow, or in 'itz', as in Lankwitz, Steglitz, or Wandlitz.

Whatever the origins of the population, the place or the name, during the middle ages the double settlement became more firmly established, leaving traces that persist into the twenty-first century. The locations of roads in the oldest part of the centre, and even some of their names, are still recognisable on maps of Berlin today. The foundations of the Nikolaikirche (Figure 1.2) date from

BERLIN

Figure 1.2 Nikolaikirche (Nicolai Church)
The foundations of the Nikolaikirche date from approximately 1230. Following major destruction of the historic Nikolai quarter during the Third Reich, the East German communist regime reconstructed it for the 750th anniversary celebrations of Berlin in 1987.
Photograph by the author

approximately 1230, and many other Berlin churches and religious orders can trace their origins to the Middle Ages. In the Marienkirche, which remarkably survived both Second World War bombing and communist demolitions in the post-war ruins, a terrifying mural depicting the 'Dance of Death', dating back to perhaps 1469–70 or to the plague in 1484, can still be seen (Figure 1.3). A white skeletal figure dances between well-dressed burghers, who may be plucked from life at any moment, while

Figure 1.3 Medieval Dance of Death (c. 1484), Marienkirche (St Mary's Church)
A fresco more than 22 metres long and 2 metres high depicts the Dance of Death in the late thirteenth-century Marienkirche. The skeletal white figure of Death is depicted dancing with citizens who can be snatched away at any time, while the verses below are among the earliest surviving Berlin literary works. Photograph by M-Verlag Berlin/Hansmann reproduced courtesy of United Archives GmbH/Alamy stock photograph

verses below represent the oldest surviving written piece of Berlin literature.

Like other medieval towns, Berlin experienced varying fortunes. It was afflicted by periodic bouts of plague and pestilence, with the Black Death decimating the population in 1348; and fires destroyed flimsily built housing, particularly in 1376 and 1380. Jews had lived in the area from around the year 1000, and other residents often targeted them as scapegoats for misfortunes. Pogroms erupted in the aftermath of disease and mass death, as in 1354, precipitating the flight of many Jews eastwards to Poland. In 1510, around one hundred Jews were put to death in Berlin, and

Jews were banished from the city and March of Brandenburg.[5] More broadly, this was an era marked by ubiquitous violence, when robber barons raged across the countryside, and horrific physical punishments were meted out to citizens found guilty of sometimes entirely spurious offences.

With the growth of trade, Berlin and Cölln began to challenge the economic ascendancy of nearby towns. Increasingly cooperating, Berlin and Cölln entered a legally binding union in 1307, and established a common centre of local government and joint town hall on the 'Long Bridge' (*Lange Brücke*) that connected them. In 1369, Berlin gained the right to mint its own coins, and in 1391 it joined the Hanseatic League of mercantile free cities. In 1432, Berlin and Cölln officially merged; and by the early fifteenth century, the city enjoyed a degree of independence and self-government. Yet even if gaining in regional importance, Berlin nevertheless remained relatively small and insignificant in comparison with Europe's great medieval cities. It might, on this trajectory, have simply developed like other trading towns with their ups and downs, periods of growth and prosperity, and times of trouble, like others in the Hanseatic league (of which Hamburg remains perhaps the most significant example). But, in the context of wider power struggles over control of the territory, the autonomy of Berlin as an independent trading town was not to last.

Key changes took place in the early fifteenth century, when the fiercely ambitious, energetic, and autocratic Frederick 'the Iron Tooth' (*Eisenzahn*) of the Hohenzollern family, from southwestern Germany, took over as Elector of the March of Brandenburg – which held some importance as an electoral state in the 'Holy Roman Empire of the German Nation'. In 1442, he established his base in Berlin. It was not an easy start, and conflicts between city and ruler rumbled through the 1440s. In 1447–48, in an incident known as the 'Berlin Indignation', a citizens' revolt was put down by the superior military force of the ruler – establishing a pattern of dynamics between forceful ruler and repressed if insubordinate ruled that would be repeated frequently in future centuries.

This too is often singled out as a foundational moment in the longer history of Berlin. Territory that the town had acquired was rapidly taken over by the Elector; rights which burghers had won over previous decades were rescinded; and city self-government soon gave way to princely control, backed by military power. By the early sixteenth century, Berlin was no longer just a trading town situated conveniently on the waterways of central Europe; it was also a significant base for both courtiers and soldiers, attracting wider interest across Europe.

From one perspective, the defeat of the citizens and their claims to self-government might be interpreted as a backward step in Berlin's history, with diminished power for the previously dominant burghers and the four most weighty medieval guilds. But viewed another way, the establishment of Berlin as a *Residenzstadt*, a courtly residence where the Hohenzollern dynasty would be based for centuries – indeed until the abdication of the Kaiser following military defeat in 1918 – set Berlin on another historical course entirely. Rather than remaining a self-governing trading centre like many other small towns across the 'Holy Roman Empire of the German Nation', Berlin was now set on the path to becoming a seat of significant political power, potentially a capital city in the making: first of the Electorate of Brandenburg, with additional territories acquired over time through both conquest and marriage; then of the Kingdom of Prussia; eventually of the German Empire, the Weimar Republic, and the Nazi Third Reich; and finally, following the Cold War era of national division, capital of the united Federal Republic of Germany. Viewed from this longer-term perspective, the setback to local autonomy in the late 1440s could be seen as switching the tracks to a political trajectory characterised by centralisation of power based largely on military might. This moment could be interpreted as prefiguring and symbolising the tensions between autocratic rulers and subservient people that would characterise so much of Berlin's history over the following centuries.

But nothing in history is predetermined. However much later observers may want to identify foundational moments, the future is always open, always contested, and always subject to competing visions of what might be possible or desirable under changing and unpredictable wider circumstances. These moments may have opened up particular paths; but nothing predetermined the whole route.

With the advent of Hohenzollern rule came not only the loss of self-government, but also a significant reshaping of the character of the city. The royal palace, or Schloss, was established in 1443, and the centre of Berlin began to take shape in ways that remain recognisable today. The Schloss opened onto the Lustgarten, or pleasure gardens, where Berliners could stroll and watch the public enactment of symbolic power by members of the court and significant citizens. Hunting lodges and little palaces were built on the outskirts of the city and in princely estates that were readily reachable by horse and coach, such as the *Jagdschloss* 'in the Green Forest' by a lake to the west, built in 1542–43 and giving Grunewald its name, or the palatial hunting lodge in Köpenick by the Müggelsee lake to the southeast, built in 1558 on the foundations of an earlier fortress (Figure 1.4). In 1538, Berlin withdrew from the Hanseatic League, marking the end of that alternative possible path of development, and became ever more oriented to becoming a courtly residence. In 1539, Berlin adopted the Reformation, becoming predominantly Lutheran.

The character of the population changed with the growth of court administrative functions as well as professions ranging

FOUNDATIONAL MOMENTS

Figure 1.4 Schloss Köpenick, as portrayed in a copper engraving by Matthäus Merian, 1652
One of several hunting lodges around Berlin, like the Jagdschloss Grunewald, Schloss Köpenick illustrates how the power of the rulers was beginning to shift to symbolic displays of status and indulgence in leisure pursuits – although not at the expense of military might.
Matthäus Merian, copper engraving, 1652. public domain.

from alchemy, astrology, and architecture, through finance, law, and music. As the residential areas grew, churches and religious buildings were augmented by locations for more secular pursuits, including the first performance of a play in 1541. People were increasingly attracted to come to Berlin from far and wide, seeking a productive and interesting life, in what would become a long tradition of being a *Wahl-Berliner*, a Berliner by choice rather than birth.

Berlin was nevertheless very far from being anything like a significant European city, and remained relatively small

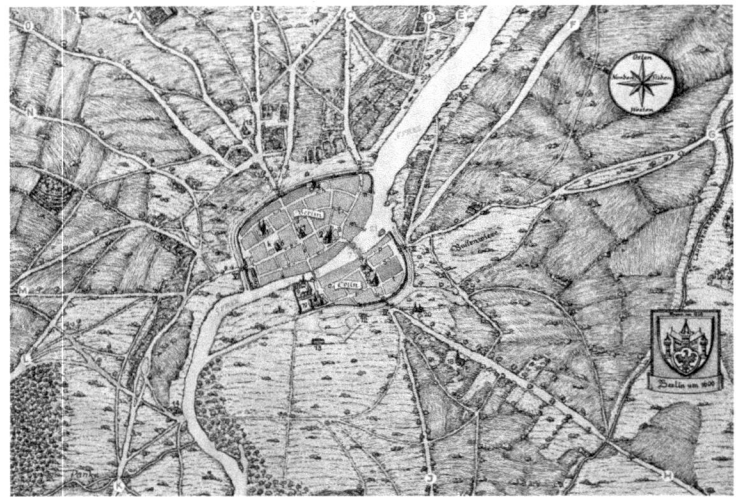

Figure 1.5 Map of Berlin, c. 1600
This map shows the two original settlements on either side of the River Spree: Cölln and Berlin. Note: the north/south points of the compass are not as conventionally displayed today.
Public domain

compared to other major cities at the time (Figure 1.5). In the late sixteenth and early seventeenth century, Berlin had a population of only around 10–12,000, at most only around one-fifth of the size of Vienna, and in stark contrast to Paris with 200,000 inhabitants, let alone Shakespeare's London, which had a population of around 300,000. Most residents lived not in the finer houses of the elites and courtiers but rather in crowded and unsanitary conditions, their short lives marked by hard work, poverty, and disease as well as the ever-present threat of fires rapidly destroying their homes. The future of Berlin as a capital city of major world-historical significance was far from given in its humble and somewhat obscure origins.

2
Courtly Residence

End of the Thirty Years War, 1648

In 1648, what became known as the Thirty Years War (1618–1648) nominally came to an end with the signing of the treaties that made up the Peace of Westphalia. By now, Berlin was little more than an overgrown village in ruins. The subsequent course of Berlin's history was radically transformed by the consequences of what had been a continent-wide series of interrelated military campaigns. The responses of Berlin's rulers to the destruction wrought by the Thirty Years War would prove immensely formative, shaping the Berlin we still know today – in terms not only of its physical topography, militaristic, and political traditions, but also, curiously, its continuing patterns of immigration and associated religious and cultural diversity.

Out of poverty and devastation was, extraordinarily, born a wholly new courtly city: one that combined symbolic power and fine buildings with growing military power and administrative efficiency; and one that welcomed immigrant minorities in the interests of economic productivity. It was not so much the war itself that shaped Berlin's future as the responses of its highly proactive rulers, which had an enduring impact over subsequent centuries. This too was a recurring feature of Berlin's history.

• ● •

The Thirty Years War

For a whole generation, central Europe was engulfed in overlapping waves of conflicts – between Protestants and Catholics, between the Austrian Habsburgs and their continental rivals, between specific rulers and their nobilities, and between emergent states variously competing for enhanced power and enlarged territories in a complex maelstrom of cross-cutting issues. Mercenary soldiers changed sides according to relative risks and profits, with little or no loyalty to one flag or another. They had equally little heed for the well-being of local people, seizing their livestock, taking or tearing up crops, setting fire to housing, and leaving mass death by communicable diseases as well as military violence and material devastation in their wake. In every region touched by war, there was an impact on trade and industry; agricultural productivity declined, and hunger or starvation was rife, with widespread reports of cannibalism among the desperate and destitute. The military conflicts raged across central Europe, moving from the south and southwest to the northeast, with periods of apparent respite punctuated by decisive battles or interventions, and complicated by the shifting involvement of differing powers. Some places in the German lands were particularly badly affected, including Magdeburg, which was devastated by an attack in May 1631 in which around 20,000 people were killed, more than Berlin's total pre-war population.

Berlin itself was hard hit on several occasions over a protracted period. The Elector at the outset, Georg Wilhelm, first sought to stay entirely out of the war. In 1627, he fled to what he hoped would be greater safety in the far-distant Königsberg (now Kaliningrad) in the eastern Duchy of Prussia. His representative left in charge of Berlin, Count Adam von Schwarzenberg, retreated behind the walls of the medieval fortress of Spandau, and subsequently distinguished himself by singularly mismanaging the defence and government of Berlin. The city was set on fire by imperial troops in 1627 and again in 1633, destroying much of the housing stock and precipitating the flight of many residents. It was then repeatedly beset by the invading Swedish army in 1636, 1638, and 1639, and the by now deeply unpopular Schwarzenberg helplessly sought to defend only the central core of Berlin while ceding the suburbs to the Swedes.

In 1640, the clearly ineffectual Elector Georg Wilhelm died, and his place was taken by Elector Frederick William (Friedrich Wilhelm), who later became known as the 'Great Elector'. The royal castle or Schloss, abandoned by his predecessor, was in such a state of disrepair that Elector Frederick William considered it uninhabitable for three years after coming to power. And even after peace had been declared in 1648, the wider situation remained precarious. There were significant social and economic legacies of the decades of warfare. In 1618, the city had counted some 12,000 inhabitants; by 1638 this had fallen to 7,500, many having died from bouts of plague or other illnesses exacerbated by malnutrition.[1] By 1648, at the end of the war, Berlin had further shrunk to 6,000 inhabitants, around half of its pre-war population. Much of Berlin's housing lay empty, having been abandoned or rendered uninhabitable; what remained was deeply undesirable. Regulations issued in 1660 complained how the unpaved alleyways readily filled with mud and excrement, both animal and human, and ordered that 'muck, dung and similar rubbish' had to be removed in such a way as not to block the gutters.[2] The surrounding areas of Brandenburg had been massively laid waste by warfare too, and not only peasants but also members of the landowning nobility were severely impoverished.

After decades of sporadic fighting, there was a persisting sense of the ever-present danger of recurrent warfare even after apparent lulls. Relations between citizens and ruler, already exacerbated by the behaviour of the late Count von Schwarzenberg, were riven by continuing tensions. Strong rulership appeared, in this situation, the only way forwards. Moreover, citizens who had survived decades of warfare and destruction were powerless to raise much by way of a voice of protest; and within a matter of years, Frederick William seized the opportunity to enhance the power of the ruler, paving the way for the notorious Prussian absolutism of the eighteenth century.

The Great Elector: Peace, War, and Reform

Elector Frederick William, who had been brought up as a Calvinist and educated in the Netherlands, transformed challenges into opportunities. Using the threat of continued warfare as a pretext, he took advantage of the weakness of both the landed nobility and urban burghers to impose new taxes in order to maintain a standing army. This was precisely the issue on which the English parliament had refused to budge in 1642, precipitating the English Civil War, and the beheading of King Charles I in 1649. Although the interregnum in England eventually ended with the return of the monarchy, the upheavals did ultimately confirm the power of provincial representatives in parliament to give or withhold their assent to taxation, in this way restricting the monarch's capacity to rule without the consent of those responsible for raising taxes. The development in Brandenburg-Prussia was very different, paving the way for absolutist rule. Direct excise taxes and what was effectively a property tax known as the 'contribution' were hugely unpopular, but gave Frederick William a degree of independence and the leeway to introduce new policies.

Berlin was not what we would now think of as a capital city of a specific state, let alone a nation state. Frederick William ruled over what might be called a 'composite state', an assortment of territories from Cleves in the west to Königsberg and East Prussia, outside the Holy Roman Empire, in the east. He brought to this inheritance a determination to ensure the future of his own family's fortunes, acting in a variety of capacities and under different titles according to the disparate territories over which he ruled. His policies were not consciously aimed towards building a Prussian future – which he could not have predicted – but rather to the betterment of current conditions in the interests of the Hohenzollern dynasty.[3] Yet, with his focus on enhancing productivity and stimulating economic regeneration, the reforms that the Great Elector introduced would stamp a lasting mark not only on Prussia, as the composite state eventually became known, but more specifically on Berlin's character, topography, economy, and society.

Having enhanced his resources through increased taxation, the Great Elector was able to maintain a standing army from 1653, and also began to set up the basis of a modern administrative system. With the growing emphasis on military power, around 2,000 soldiers were quartered in the houses of citizens, beginning to give Berlin the air of a garrison town for which it would subsequently become famous. Frederick William also established an elite officer corps, which would prove a crucial force over the following centuries. The princely palace was extended, with new quarters for different branches of an increasingly centrally-organised state. The grounds around were expanded and parks established, lending an aura of greater spaciousness to the centre of the city. Along with his Dutch first wife, Louise Henriette of Orange, whom he married in 1646, Frederick William brought in not only artists, manufacturers, and traders from the Netherlands, but also architects who had a decisive influence on the rebuilding of Berlin and surrounding areas. Even the new fortifications that were constructed around the perimeter in the early 1660s were influenced by Dutch styles. Despite having negotiated peace settlements, he engaged in further military campaigns and won a decisive battle over the Swedes at Fehrbellin in 1675, earning him the title 'Great Elector'.

Regeneration of the economy was a key task. During his formative years in the Netherlands, Frederick William had gained an interest in waterways and ship-building. Water-based trade routes had suffered not only as a result of warfare and foreign control of north German ports but also, already from the later sixteenth century, because of a broader reorientation of European trade to the Atlantic seaboard. Frederick William now supported the construction of canals linking the river Elbe to the Havel and the Oder rivers, facilitating the regeneration of shipping in the waterways around Berlin and reconnection with ports to the north, leaving traces still in the canal landscape around Berlin today. Thomas Carlyle particularly praised him for these pursuits: 'He drains bogs, settles colonies in the waste-places of his Dominions, cuts canals; unweariedly encourages trade and work.'[4]

Less often commented upon was Frederick William's involvement in overseas colonialism and the nascent slave trade of the time, first unsuccessfully in India and then with particular interests in West African 'Gold Coast' territories. The Brandenburg-Africa Company (BAC) was established in 1682, again under Dutch influence in the person of the trader and shipowner Benjamin Raule. The BAC itself suffered from financial problems and lack of adequate markets for luxury goods such as ivory and gold; and it was wound up in 1711 by the Great Elector's successor, King Frederick I, who rejected this as much else of his father's interests. Yet although colonialism was a short-lived failure at this time, the memory of these early exploits was revived when colonialism reappeared on the German agenda in the 1880s, leaving traces on the street landscape of Berlin. The Gröben-Ufer, for example, was named in 1885 after Friedrich von der Gröben, who in 1683 had built both a factory and a fort, Gross Friedrichsburg, on the Gold Coast of Africa, through which some 30,000 African slaves passed on their way to Europe or the Caribbean. In a symbol of changing times and values, the street was renamed in 2010 after the female activist, writer and educator May Ayim, an Afro-German resident of Kreuzberg.

More significantly both at the time and for the long-term future of Berlin, the Great Elector engaged in active immigration policies to repopulate devastated lands and stimulate manufacturing and trade. In particular, he persuaded economically productive minorities to immigrate to Berlin and the surrounding region. People came from all across Europe, including the Low Countries, Denmark, Sweden, Scotland, and Bohemia. The influx of foreigners did indeed serve to stimulate the economy, with the introduction of new technologies and methods. They also contributed significantly to the linguistic, cultural, and social diversity of the city. Some groups are particularly notable in this respect.

In 1671, Frederick William invited in a group of Jews who had been desperately searching for a new place of refuge after being persecuted and thrown out of Vienna. Although they were placed under considerable restrictions, and were not allowed to build their own synagogue, this was a first step towards the religious toleration for which Prussia would subsequently be praised – and more significantly for the history of Berlin, a first step in the development of a German-Jewish community that would, over the following two and a half centuries, make immensely significant contributions to the intellectual, cultural, social, and political life of the city. It would take decades for Berlin Jews to overcome the restrictions under which they were initially placed, while other minorities were treated with a degree of privilege from the outset.

The most privileged immigrants were the French. In 1685, the Great Elector offered refuge to Huguenots, a Calvinist religious minority who faced persecution following the revocation of the Edict of Nantes. Around 170,000 Protestants had fled France in the 1680s; of these, around 20,000 Huguenots settled in Berlin under the terms of the 1685 Edict of Potsdam. Making up around 20 per cent of the city's population, they had a significant impact not only on the immediate state of the local economy, but also left long-lasting traces in Berlin's architecture, language and customs, as well as shaping identities and cultures of remembrance over the following two centuries.[5] With their expertise in trade and handicrafts, and particularly textile manufacturing, they gave a significant boost to productivity. The French Cathedral, the Französische Dom in the Gendarmenmarkt, still stands resplendent in Berlin today (Figure 2.1); a French high school, the Französische Gymnasium, also still operates to considerable renown; and other physical traces of the French immigrants include institutions such as an orphanage, churches, and housing communities. The Huguenots intrinsically affected the language of Berlin, with a significant French-speaking minority introducing French words and expressions into Berlinese German, traces of which lingered over the following centuries. In all of this, the Huguenots were greatly aided by the fact that they were a privileged minority whose culture, language, and productivity were greatly valued by the Hohenzollern rulers. But their privileged status and the competition they posed to indigenous manufacturers also aroused local envy; the prestige of these newcomers, and their own sense of superiority, significantly affected their relations with other Berlin residents. In the longer term, the Huguenots' gratitude to the rulers and determination to make a success of settling in Berlin informed their repeated emphasis on being loyal to Prussia as their new home. This too could be variously reappropriated, with the regeneration and resuscitation of traditions under new circumstances in the nineteenth century.

COURTLY RESIDENCE

Figure 2.1 Französische Dom (French Cathedral), Gendarmenmarkt
The influence of French immigrants is evident not only in buildings such as the French Cathedral, but also in language, including the name 'Gendarmenmarkt': the 'Gens d'Armes' – literally, 'men-at-arms' – refers to the regiment whose stables were based in this square.
Photograph by the author

Royal Residence and Social Diversity

An unbroken line of Hohenzollern rulers – with four long-lived undisputed male heirs in succession – presided over the startling rise of Brandenburg-Prussia between 1640 and 1786, and significantly transformed the character of Berlin in the process. Frederick III, who took over as Elector on his father's death in

1688 and crowned himself King in Prussia in 1701, is often written off as the 'least impressive' in this chain from the Great Elector, through Frederick William I 'the Soldier King' (1713–40), to Frederick the Great (1740–86).[6] It is also notable that Frederick III/I is the only one not to have received some kind of additional name-tag implying military success, although he did himself add the royal title in front of his name in 1701. Yet the alleged insignificance of Frederick III/I can only be argued from a perspective according primary historical value to military might and conventional state building. If looked at another way, in terms of contributions to Berlin's appearance and status, the evaluation turns out very differently. During the quarter century of his rule from 1688 to 1713, Frederick III/I transformed the built environment of Berlin in ways still visible today, and shaped courtly culture and symbolic power in a manner that stamped a less visible yet persisting mark over succeeding decades. His reign shaped Berlin in crucial ways that may have been eclipsed by the militarism of his successors, but cannot be simply dismissed or sidelined because it is seen as irrelevant to the story of growing Prussian military power.

In January 1701, when Elector Frederick III crowned himself King Frederick I in Königsberg, 30,000 horses were apparently required to transport the ruler and his sizeable retinue along the arduous twelve-day journey to this outlying corner of the Hohenzollern lands that made up the sprawling territory of Brandenburg-Prussia. And no expense was spared in the profligate ceremonies, which cost roughly twice the annual state revenue. Nearly four months later, on 6 May 1701, the newly crowned King Frederick I returned to Berlin, where he celebrated his regal status with further pomp, ceremony, and expense. He had in fact delayed the date of his return, lingering in an assortment of castles along the way, in order to give time for Berliners to make appropriate preparations and to deck out both the town and themselves in their best finery. The nineteenth-century historian of Berlin, Adolph Streckfuß, tells us that when the king finally entered the city through a specially constructed series of 'gates of honour', he was greeted by the pealing of bells, the thundering of more than 200 cannons, and the firing of shots and flaming torches from turrets and towers. The royal parade lasted for four hours before the king reached the palace; festivities in the city continued for several days thereafter, ending only with fireworks on 9 May. The whole of central Berlin – the royal palace, the newly built Zeughaus (arsenal) on Unter den Linden, the surrounding bourgeois and noble villas – was 'illuminated from top to bottom', while there were 'innumerable lights and lamps lit up in all the windows' giving the town centre 'a marvellous appearance'. In front of a couple of noble residences – those of Count von Schwerin, and privy councillor Stephani – fountains were installed from which, for several hours, flowed not water but wine, while many members of the resident French refugee community set up tables outside their houses with bottles of wine, offered freely to all. The 'common people', we are told, availed themselves of this free-flowing wine to the full, and spent the next couple of days in a drunken stupor crying out variations on 'Long live the king!' according to degrees of language ability (and presumably hangover).[7] Given the desperate poverty of most Berliners at the time, this must have been a truly memorable occasion.

The coronation was an unusual event in many respects. First of all, Frederick set the crown on his own head before being anointed by bishops, eschewing the usual religious authorisation of a coronation; and secondly, the ceremony took place in East Prussia, outside the borders of the Holy Roman Empire, since within the Empire it was not permitted to hold a monarchical title. Moreover, at this stage Frederick could be only King *in* Prussia, not *of*; this would later change, as landgrabs were made in the course of the eighteenth century. (The Emperor had given his permission for this unusual coronation only on payment of considerable sums of money and promises of military support.) At the time, however, these constitutional niceties seem to have made little difference to Frederick I, who set about transforming the physical appearance and symbolic topography of Berlin with little regard to expense.

This moment, a symbolic culmination of significant longer-term changes over a far larger canvas, was perhaps all the more surprising because it arose out of a period of protracted warfare, economic devastation, and dramatic population decline. But the influence of the wider shift from military to symbolic power on the landscape of Berlin was immense.

The urban scenery was reconstructed on a grand scale. The royal palace was expanded from 1699 and then significantly rebuilt under the guidance of the architect Andreas Schlüter, taking on aspects of the majestic appearance that it maintained until its destruction in the Second World War and eventual demolition under communist rule in 1950. A sense of its dimensions and former magnificence has been conveyed to twenty-first century audiences through the curiously hybrid construction of the contested Humboldt Forum, with three external walls faithfully following the earlier design while the interior spaces serve entirely modern notions of museum construction. Further west, in what was still an outlying village at the time, a beautiful baroque palace was built for Frederick's wife, Sophie Charlotte, named Charlottenburg in her memory after her death in 1705. Although a number of architects including Johann Arnold Nering and Johann Friedrich Eosander were central to its design and construction, here too Schlüter played a significant role. The wider landscape of princely power began to change, as the spacious avenue running from the palace towards the Tiergarten, Unter den Linden, began to take form with the construction of significant buildings. The Zeughaus, which now houses the permanent exhibition of the German Historical Museum, was built between 1695 and 1706, with evidence of Schlüter's handiwork here in the gruesomely sculptured masks of dying soldiers on the façade (Figure 2.2).

The cultural topography of Berlin was also massively transformed. Influenced more by the French court of Versailles than the Dutch ideals of his father, in 1697 Frederick founded an Academy of Arts, followed in 1700 by an Academy of Sciences, of which the first president was the philosopher Gottfried Wilhelm

Figure 2.2 Zeughaus (arsenal), built between 1695 and 1706
The Zeughaus on Unter den Linden, close to the Lustgarten and royal palace (Schloss), was built for Elector Frederick III, who in 1701 crowned himself King Frederick I. It illustrates the architectural display of symbolic and military power characteristic of this era.
Photograph by the author

Leibniz. The expanding numbers of new posts at court, and the attractions of courtly culture alongside a lively intellectual and social life, stimulated the building of grand houses as well as the proliferation of trade and manufacturing, including fine clothing, wigs, and jewellery. The king, living well beyond his means, resorted to a variety of ways of raising revenue, including the sale of offices and taxation on luxury items; but this did little to dampen enthusiasm for the new spirit of conspicuous consumption and mundane enjoyment of life, particularly in the long aftermath of the devastations of the Thirty Years War.

Although the emergence of a courtly culture marked a significant change in style, many developments around the turn of the century nevertheless continued initiatives that had begun in the Great Elector's reign. This was the case with respect to the influence of the immigrant communities, particularly the French Huguenots, whose Gendarmenmarkt church was inaugurated in 1705. The Huguenots contributed not only to the rapid growth of manufacturing, particularly in textiles, silk, and jewellery, but also affected fashions and everyday habits. Indeed, in the view of the eighteenth-century Berlin historian Georg Gottfried Küster, 'although the inhabitants here had been very much brought down by the Thirty Years War, they were now craving for new fashions'. Küster went on to observe, with a degree of evident distaste, that while the Great Elector had given them peace, under Frederick I 'previous clothing styles were no longer good enough for Berliners, but rather they had to dress according to the most resplendent French styles'; and on special occasions, such as 'weddings, baptisms and funerals, they knew no boundaries', so special regulations were required to ensure Berliners observed some moderation.[8] Küster treats his readers to detailed descriptions of 'the laws that have been issued against finery in clothing, and excesses in eating and drinking', with differing rules according to social class, gender, and marital status under different circumstances.⁹ But the influence of French fashions and customs in Berlin would not disappear so easily.

Other minorities did not at this time have such impact beyond the borders of their own communities. In 1697, more than a quarter of a century after they had been permitted again to settle in Berlin, Jews were finally allowed to have a dedicated building in which to hold religious services. These premises were however too small, and in 1700 Jews were given permission to build a new synagogue, which was eventually inaugurated on the sabbath before the Jewish New Year in 1714 (just after Frederick I's death, at the start of the reign of his son Frederick William I). In the view of Müller and Küster, this luxurious synagogue proved to be 'one of the most beautiful religious school buildings in the whole of the Roman Empire' [sic], and the Berlin Jews were accordingly grateful to the king, expressing their loyalty as his subjects.¹⁰ They also now had their own Jewish hospital, poor-house, and graveyard. But they were still placed under severe restrictions, including even a ban on reciting the prayer starting 'Olenu lefchabbeach' (sic), which was held to be in some way potentially blasphemous. Müller and Küster hastily end these reflections by adding that they have insufficient space to discuss 'whether Jews should be tolerated in Christian states'.¹¹ This question, with variations over time, would continue to affect the status and identity of the growing Jewish community in Berlin over the following two centuries, before the Nazis – hardly guardians of a Christian state – gave their fatal final answer. In the meantime, however, this marked the beginning of an extraordinary period of cultural and social symbiosis.

Under the Great Elector, the population of Berlin had more than trebled in size. Most of this dramatic increase took place in the last two decades of his reign, rising from still only around 6,000 in 1670 to more than 20,000 by 1690. In the following two decades under Frederick III/I, the population more than doubled again, reaching over 50,000 by 1710 – roughly ten times as many inhabitants as during the worst troughs of the Thirty Years War.[12] Berlin had in this time been transformed from a ruined and half-deserted town into a magnificent courtly capital. The leaps in population size were rooted in the planned stimulation of the economy, the growing liveliness and associated attractions of urban life, and the influx of immigrant communities. By the early eighteenth century more than a quarter of Berlin's population were *Wahl-Berliner*, foreign immigrants who became Berliners by choice; all made a significant contribution in shaping the character and culture of Berlin – although in constant tension with the increasingly militaristic and absolutist policies of the rulers in the decades that followed.

By the time the eighteenth-century Berlin chroniclers, Johann Christoph Müller and Georg Gottfried Küster, proudly compiled their history of this 'very beautiful city', they were certain that the 'royal residential city' of Berlin could claim to be 'not only the capital of the Mittel-Mark, but also of the whole of the Electorate and Mark of Brandenburg, since it is the permanent residence of His Most Serene Highness the King in Prussia and Elector of Brandenburg'.[13] Moreover, in the opinion of Müller and Küster, by the early eighteenth century Berlin, 'due to its size, sumptuous and beautiful palaces and houses, its splendour, and the great number of its inhabitants, unquestionably surpasses all other towns in the Electorate of Brandenburg'.[14]

Foreign visitors also commented positively from a wider perspective. In 1702, the Irish philosopher, free-thinker, and polemicist John Toland reported back to England that he had found much to impress him in this 'city, which is indifferently spacious, but extremely fine'. He noted that the 'streets are very large and noble, much better pav'd than is usual in Germany, and planted in most parts of the town with rows of trees'. He went on:

There are fine canals that cross and separate the several wards, with draw-bridges after the model of those in Holland, and as handsome. The new houses are mostly built after the best taste of architecture, being generally beautify'd on the outside, and not always ill-furnish'd within; the few old houses that remain, being in respect of the others as ragged and deform'd dwarfs compar'd with gentile and proper men.[15]

Moreover, in Toland's view like that of so many subsequent visitors, there 'are in this city many things worthy the curiosity of strangers'.[16]

Yet for all the praise bestowed by visitors, and the pride of the city's own chroniclers, it is notable too that, even by the early eighteenth century, there was little to suggest that a town that stood out as a courtly residence in the flat, sandy, politically unimportant Brandenburg Mark would ever rise to being the metropolitan capital of a European state, let alone a globally significant power. It was the use made of this heritage by Frederick I's immediate successors, his son and grandson, that would set it on those tracks.

3

Absolutism and Enlightenment

Moses Mendelssohn arrives in Berlin, 1743

In 1743 Moses Mendelssohn, the later renowned German-Jewish philosopher but at this time still only fourteen years old, is said to have entered Berlin through the Rosenthal Gate, an entrance reserved exclusively for cattle and Jews. He had walked all the way from his home town of Dessau. When interrogated at the customs post, he supposedly assured the gatekeeper that he was coming not to peddle wares but rather to acquire learning. This indeed he subsequently did, not only devouring works of scholarship but also developing facility in a number of foreign languages in addition to the versions of Hebrew and Yiddish with which he had grown up.[1]

This moment, small enough in itself, encapsulates key aspects of the history of eighteenth-century Berlin. For one thing, this garrison city was surrounded by walls designed not only to control incomers and extract taxes, but also to prevent Berliners who were subject to military service from fleeing the city. For another, Jews were still treated with a degree of prejudice and suspicion. The arrival of Moses Mendelssohn, his subsequent friendships and influence, and the wider cultural and social processes in which he would participate, signify the inauguration of nearly two centuries of what has been termed the 'German-Jewish symbiosis', that uniquely creative intertwining of intellectual currents that marked Berlin society and German culture more broadly in ways that would only be destroyed by the devastating rule of the Nazis.

ABSOLUTISM AND ENLIGHTENMENT

In the meantime, however, there were innumerable hurdles and constraints imposed on Berlin's Jews – not least by the supposedly enlightened and tolerant ruler himself, Frederick the Great. Regulations included restrictions on permission to get married, since Frederick did not want the Jewish population to reproduce and grow significantly, and limited rights of residence, with Jews allowed to reside in only forty houses in total in the city, later raised to seventy. Among innumerable ways of trying to make money out of Jews – for many seemed to prosper, despite all – they were forced not only to purchase quantities of royal porcelain, but also to buy up unprofitable manufacturing concerns and invest in turning them into more productive enterprises. Moreover, as the nineteenth-century Berlin historian Adolph Streckfuß observed, while some individual Christians were prepared to consort socially with Jews, most people still despised them.[2] This was, then, not only a quite distinct community, like the French Huguenots, but one that was, unlike the French and other immigrant Protestants, also socially ostracised at the time.

Despite all, the Jewish community of Berlin – only achieving citizenship rights in 1812 – managed to develop and flourish, playing a crucial role in the intellectual and social as well as economic life of the city over the following century and a half. Their fate in some ways also illustrates the wider ambivalences and contradictions of this period in which absolutist rule was combined with enlightenment thinking.

• • •

The era of enlightened absolutism in the eighteenth century was a moment that decisively shaped Berlin in all senses: topographically and architecturally; socially both at the time and subsequently; and in the cultural imaginary, in terms of what we think of as 'Berlin' today (Figure 3.1). Most obviously: under the two

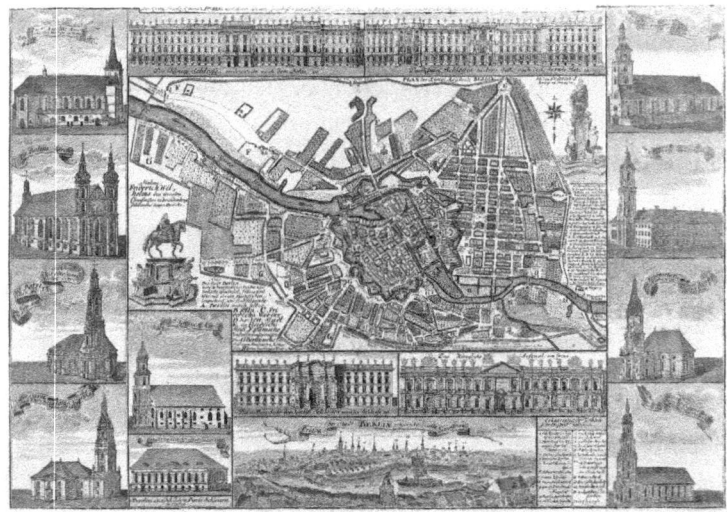

Figure 3.1 Map of Berlin in 1739
This map, again showing the original settlements of Berlin and Cölln, but now also expansion beyond the fortified walls surrounding the city, is enhanced by portrayals of the royal palace, the Zeughaus, churches, statues, and a panorama of Berlin's spires and the River Spree viewed from afar.
Public domain

monarchs who ruled for nearly three-quarters of a century, Frederick William I (1713–40), often dubbed the 'Soldier King', and his son Frederick II (1740–86), widely known as 'Frederick the Great', Berlin was transformed from a small courtly city into a significant European capital, a garrison town in a Prussian state that became infamous for its militarism, with reverberations well into the twentieth century. Equally obviously, but appearing at first glance to be heading in a quite different direction: throughout the century, Berlin was a centre of what historians have come to term 'enlightened absolutism', which is not as oxymoronic a concept as it might first seem.[3] Under strong rulers, reforms were not merely debated and discussed by intellectuals; policies could also be effected in practice. In Berlin, religious toleration and cultural diversity were related to policies of fostering economic growth through population expansion. Perhaps less immediately evident, but absolutely fundamental to the shaping of Berlin, were the ways in which Berliners – including the immigrant minorities who did so much to fuel the growth of the city – engaged with each other and the wider world. From the contributions of leading philosophers, through the culture of debate and lively discussions in clubs, reading groups, and salons, to the everyday cheekiness or wit for which Berliners would become renowned, this was a key moment in the formation of distinctive Berlin traditions and mentalities. Meanwhile, the urban landscape was changing with the growth of the city and the development of trade and industry. While the period of military ascendancy came to something of a temporary reversal during the Napoleonic wars following the French revolution, the undercurrents of social and intellectual development persisted into the nineteenth century, fundamentally shaping the character of Berlin well into the present.

Garrison Town

Berlin had, by the early seventeenth century, become a significant courtly centre which had grown well beyond the original two medieval settlements. In 1713, when Frederick William I came to the throne, Berlin housed around 61,000 inhabitants – already ten times as many as at the end of the Thirty Years War – and was expanding from its core around the court. The by now five constituent districts – Berlin, Cölln, Friedrichswerder, Dorotheenstadt, and Friedrichstadt – were formally joined together as an administrative entity in 1709, confirming what was already the case in practice. By the early eighteenth century, immigrant communities made up around one quarter of Berlin's population; over the following decades, more followed, attracted by new opportunities in this growing city. The influence of immigrant minorities was evident in language and architecture, well beyond notable buildings such as the French Cathedral or Potsdam's 'Dutch quarter', and now including for example rustic Bohemian Rixdorf (today's Neukölln, still housing significant new immigrant populations). By the end of Frederick the Great's reign in 1786, the population had risen to 150,000; and in 1800, Berlin was home to some 170,000 people, making it the sixth largest city in Europe at this time (London, Paris, and Vienna were the top three, trailed by Amsterdam and St Petersburg).[4]

Population growth was important not only for the social and economic policies of the monarchs but also their militaristic interests and ambitions. Frederick William I reacted strongly against what he saw as the spendthrift style of his father, but nevertheless continued some of his predecessor's policies – exhibiting the tense cycle of difficult father–son dynamics that would soon be repeated across the next generation. The state bureaucracy, developed by the Great Elector in the late seventeenth century, was further expanded and streamlined with the establishment of a General Directory and separate administrative branches; policies for fostering population growth were continued, and economically productive religious minorities still encouraged to immigrate. The purpose now, however, was different: not to maintain a luxurious court characterised by conspicuous consumption and symbolic power, as under Frederick I, but rather to support the growth of the military.

Under Frederick William I, the 'Soldier King', there was a massive increase in the size of the army, which more than doubled from 40,000 to 83,000 men. Parade grounds became a feature of Berlin's topography; even the Lustgarten, formerly a pleasure garden opposite the Palace, was transformed into a space for military exercises, and marching soldiers were everywhere to be seen. This had an impact on Berlin society: according to contemporary reports, off-duty soldiers still marched in unison, and even civilians began to adopt military habits, manners, and topics of conversation, or take up roles more commonly seen in the environment of military encampments during an active campaign.[5] For young men, the consequences were particularly unsettling. Frederick William I had a penchant for 'tall fellows' as soldiers (*lange Kerls*), putting at extra risk any men who were over six feet tall and might have preferred a life pursuing anything other than a military career. But all young men were exposed to recruitment against their will. Army recruiting officers even forced their way into Berlin high schools, occasioning incidents where students tried to defend themselves by hiding behind barricades of chairs and tables. Apprentices and workers also sought to avoid being drafted, resisting violently when recruiters came to take them out of their places of work, or fleeing Berlin entirely. Whether workers were recruited or absconded, these developments caused sudden and often severe labour shortages. Even some of the French settlers began to feel they might be better off elsewhere, and left for England or Ireland.[6] In the later 1720s, as Berlin expanded well beyond the city walls, the previous military fortifications around its perimeter were torn down and the old gates were replaced by open squares, some of which were used for military exercises; but in place of fortified walls to keep the enemy out, Frederick William I chose to have a new wall erected, now conceived as a 'customs wall' (*Zollmauer*) not only to control the passage of goods and raise taxes, but also to prevent people leaving in an attempt to escape military service. This would not be the last time that Berlin was notable as a place where city walls were designed more to keep unwilling citizens in than to keep the enemy out.

Moreover, while rapidly becoming a garrison town, Berlin did not have anything like sufficient barracks to accommodate rising numbers. In 1721, as many as 12,000 soldiers and their families were put up in private quarters, making up around one fifth of the Berlin population; and by 1735, some 18,257 of Berlin's by then 79,000 inhabitants belonged to the garrison.[7] The necessary compensation for billeting soldiers was paid out of a tax known as the *Servis*, occasioning discussion as to whether even normally tax-exempt privileged classes should be required to pay.

So virtually the entire population of Berlin was in one way or another affected by this dramatic growth of the army. By the end of the Soldier King's reign, jokes abounded about Prussia being 'not a state with an army, but rather an army with a state'.

Despite his obsession with military matters, the Soldier King did not seem to have much practical use for his army. This was left to his son, Frederick II, commonly known as 'Frederick the Great'. Caught in a deeply troubled relationship with his overbearing father, in yet another cycle of the father–son tensions that bedevilled this family, Frederick was a French-speaking, music-loving, flute-playing, and clearly gay intellectual who both reacted against his father and yet felt compelled to fulfil in practice the mission for which the frugal Soldier King had laid the practical groundwork. Throughout his youth, Frederick was subjected to numerous privations, humiliations, and punishments, including most horrifically being forced to watch the beheading of his lover, Hans Hermann von Katte, with whom he had intended to abscond. The death of his father finally gave Frederick the opportunity both to throw off some of the compromises he had made – not least, being forced into an unwanted marriage – but at the same time to prove himself in ways that would show he was better than his father.[8]

Frederick was fortunate in having a considerable financial inheritance that he could use not only to indulge his musical and cultural passions but also to engage in military campaigns abroad. Within months of his father's death, in December 1740 Frederick had already deployed the sizeable Prussian army to invade Silesia, opportunistically taking advantage of a momentary weakness in Austria at a time of the disputed right to succession of Maria Theresa following the death of her father, the Habsburg Emperor Charles VI. There followed a series of wars over Silesia in 1740–42 and 1744–45, in which Prussia ultimately emerged successful in its challenge to Austria. This land grab did not necessarily secure Prussia's position, however, and the following years from 1756 until the end of the Seven Years' War in 1763 were marked by periodic and sometimes prolonged warfare. At times, the impact on Berlin was deeply damaging. During the winter of 1740–41, with many men called up to fight, a great deal of Berlin's economic activity – the building trade, textiles production – ceased, and contemporary reports describe how women and children were left to live on water, falling ill and dying of starvation. During the Second Silesian war, in late November 1745 there was a general panic about an impending Austrian invasion; the flimsy city walls, essentially a customs border, were hastily fortified and furnished with cannons; wealthy and powerful citizens hid their valuables and papers; and the poor who lived in unprotected suburbs outside the city walls sought to find safety within.[9] In the event, the Austrians did not arrive on this occasion; but in October 1757, with renewed fighting, the Austrians did manage to enter the city and demanded a considerable sum of money before they would withdraw. In 1760, Berliners were again subjected to invasion, this time by a more significant combined force of Austrians and Russians. In addition to demanding an enormous sum of money, the troops looted and plundered palaces and houses, leaving Berlin devastated and bankrupt.

While the military campaigns might have appeared successful, by the time of their conclusion in 1763, the city of Berlin itself was in a poor state. Its population had declined by more than one-fifth, industrial and agricultural production had suffered, and people were starving. Yet this would, in the longer term, come to be seen as less significant than the implications for Berlin's status as capital of a growing European state. Prussia was beginning to rival both Austria and Russia as one of the great central European powers. After annexing Polish Prussia from the Polish–Lithuanian Commonwealth in 1772, in the first of three partitions by Prussia, Austria, and Russia that would swallow up Poland by 1795, Frederick II changed his title from the previous 'King *in* Prussia' to 'King *of* Prussia'. Through his militaristic policies, Frederick II had not only earned himself the epithet 'the Great' but also unleashed the rivalry between the Austrian Habsburgs and the Prussian Hohenzollerns that would shape the following century. Ultimately, rather than Vienna dominating a larger Reich, in 1871 it would be Berlin that became capital of the German Empire.

Militarism was undoubtedly a significant force in shaping Berlin's topography and society, with ultimately immense significance for Germany and the world. And it was this emphasis on military strength for which the Soldier King and Frederick the Great were largely remembered, in portraits, texts, and statues, including the magnificent statue, designed by Christian Daniel Rauch, of Frederick the Great on his horse, facing eastwards on Unter den Linden, first erected in 1851 (Figure 3.2). Prussian militarism proved to be a complex and deeply contested legacy – and after the Second World War the statue was for a time removed by the East German communist regime, only being reinstated in the centre of Berlin with the resurrection of Prussian traditions in the 1980s. But there were other ways too in which this period was deeply formative for Berlin.

Figure 3.2 Prussian Militarism: Statue of Frederick the Great on Unter den Linden
This statue of King Frederick II, known as Frederick the Great, was designed by Christian Daniel Rauch and first erected in 1851; following removal in post-war East Berlin, it was returned to its place facing eastwards on Unter den Linden in 1980.
Photograph by the author

Toleration, Diversity, and Enlightenment

The policies of enlightened absolutism were not all about military might and territorial expansion. Berlin was also becoming a centre of education, science, and culture, renowned too for its unusual degree of religious toleration.

Significant initiatives had begun already under Frederick I, including the foundation of the Academies of Arts and Sciences. The Charité hospital was established in 1710 on the banks of the Spree, just outside the then city borders, to deal with an expected wave of the bubonic plague; it subsequently became a great university teaching hospital as well as a centre of scientific research, still renowned today. Universal primary education was introduced across Brandenburg-Prussia by the Pietists, particularly by August Hermann Francke, a pupil of Philipp Jakob Spener, preacher at Berlin's Nikolaikirche. Both Frederick I and Frederick William I, for different reasons, supported the Pietist movement, which preached the virtues not only of literacy, Bible-reading, and a pious lifestyle, but also subservience to worldly authority – at least in Prussia, where they were dependent on state support. Other religious minorities, who had also been attracted to immigrate, similarly repaid the gift of freedom of religion with political loyalty to the ruler of the day, as in the case of the Huguenots.

Members of the French Colony were awarded particular privileges, including for many decades subjection only to their own courts of law and not those of Berlin. More broadly, French manners, customs, and language were highly regarded, and set the tone for behaviour and clothing styles well beyond the Huguenot community. Other minorities, such as the Bohemian Protestants who arrived from 1732, were not awarded the same degrees of privilege, but integrated into Berlin society. Although not confined to a ghetto as elsewhere, Jews in Berlin led far more restricted and segregated lives. Their numbers grew steadily from the fifty families admitted in the 1690s; when Frederick William renewed their 'Privilegium' in 1714, a total of 119 families were mentioned by name. By 1769, when the publisher Friedrich Nicolai compiled his account, there were around 400 Jewish families in Berlin. They were subjected to constraints and regulations, limiting their freedom of movement as well as profession. Most were engaged in trade, and some in banking; but it also struck Nicolai that among Berlin Jews were to be found significant scholars, as well as 'many people of taste and lovers of the fine arts and sciences'.[10] Moses

ABSOLUTISM AND ENLIGHTENMENT

Mendelssohn, who had arrived as a penniless teenager in 1743, eventually gained the right to permanent residence in the city, and became close friends with the writer and dramatist Gotthold Ephraim Lessing (1729–81), who had chosen (between stints elsewhere) to make Berlin his home.[11] Lessing's play pleading for religious toleration, *Nathan der Weise* (Nathan the Wise), was in part modelled on his friend and colleague Mendelssohn. Nicolai also collaborated with Lessing and Mendelssohn in writing literary commentaries.

These developments were related to wider cultural currents and social changes. Education was increasingly important, with a number of older and prestigious high schools, including the Joachimsthaler Gymnasium (high school) and the Graues Kloster, complemented by the more recently established Friedrichswerdersche Gymnasium and the Französisches Gymnasium. All of these academically oriented schools offered a broad curriculum of languages, humanities, and sciences. In 1747, a *Realschule* (technical school) was founded, oriented towards the more practical education of young people aiming for a future in trades and production. There were also a variety of smaller so-called 'free schools', supported by donations from wealthy benefactors, where the children of poor parents might be taught reading, writing, arithmetic, and religion.

In the course of the eighteenth century, increasing numbers of Berliners engaged in lively discussions of literary, religious, and philosophical ideas. With the growth of an educated bourgeoisie came the expansion of new reading publics, including women, eager to discuss ideas informally among themselves, beyond the confines of organised institutions, academies, or churches. Reading circles and societies sprang up; people regularly met up to talk in cafés, on walks through the Tiergarten, in private houses, or in libraries and reading rooms. Newspapers, pamphlets, and works of literature and philosophy were subjected to intense scrutiny and debate.

Religious toleration and enlightenment thinking were supported in principle by Frederick II – even though he was openly critical of Jews, in contrast to his positive attitudes towards the French. He invited the French philosopher Voltaire to stay at his princely palace of Sanssouci in Potsdam, modelled on Versailles. Here, Frederick the Great indulged in entertaining friends, playing the flute, and famously conversing in the court language of French to his equals while, it was said, reserving German for servants and horses. While critical of religious orthodoxy, Frederick II equally famously felt that 'everyone should be free to pursue their own path to salvation', and certainly indulged in his own forms of spiritual life. He was particularly passionate about music, encouraging German composers, and inviting French and Italian singers and musicians to Berlin. One of his major projects was the construction of the magnificent Royal Opera House (now known as the State Opera), long in the planning and designed in conjunction with the architect Georg Wenzeslaus von Knobelsdorff. This was one of the largest and most impressive opera houses in Europe, with a seating capacity of 2,000, and among the first to be free-standing rather than embedded within or attached to a palace.[12] The Opera, along with the Catholic St Hedwig Cathedral, built from 1747 to 1773, and the Royal Library (*Königliche Bibliothek*, now known as the *Alte Bibliothek*), built from 1775 to 1780, combined to form what was known as the 'Forum Friedericianum' on Unter den Linden, dedicated to the combination of religious toleration, music, and scholarship that were the cultural hallmarks of Frederick II's reign. The Royal Library, along with the Library of the Academy of Sciences as well as a proliferation of bookstores and publishers, made ever more works available to Berlin's avid readers. It was on the open square of the Forum Friedericianum that, on 10 May 1933, Goebbels orchestrated the public burning of books by Jewish authors and others of whom the Nazis disapproved. A memorial to this event consists simply of a transparent pane in the ground above empty bookshelves.

Frederick II was committed to reform of the administrative system, leading to a proliferation of state offices and growth in numbers of civil servants and other salaried professionals. He remained concerned to support and regenerate the economy, introducing policies to foster trade, industry, and agricultural production. He notoriously promoted the benefits of the humble potato, an undervalued but highly nutritious crop that could alleviate shortages of grain and other foodstuffs; potatoes even gained a place of honour on his grave. Far less humble was Frederick II's support for the production of luxury goods, including porcelain – establishing the Royal Porcelain Factory in 1763 – as well as textiles and silk. Silk production was further fostered by the attraction of further immigrant communities from around Europe, who were offered incentives to settle in 'colonies' in outlying villages, where they specialised in growing mulberry trees, using the leaves to feed the silkworms, and creating copious home-grown supplies of costly silk. Developments in technology were harnessed both to feed the masses and sustain the elites in the latest fashions and lifestyles.

In a variety of ways, then, Frederick II combined paternalism with despotism, militarism with intellectual, sensual, and cultural pleasures. Acquiring great power status through military exploits had not been entirely at the expense of domestic developments; and it had even enhanced the status of the capital city. While courtiers and the military might still seem to dominate the city's streets, and distinctive religious minorities attracted attention, the wider population of small producers and manufacturers was also growing, as was a lively intellectual and cultural life.

Berlin at the Turn of the Century

In 1783, just three years before Frederick II's death, the *Berlinische Monatsschrift* published a vivid description of the city written by an outsider, prefaced by editorial comments on the value of such a perspective, since a visitor might notice things that residents took for granted or thought barely worthy of comment. The writer, a self-designated 'stranger' (*Fremder*, in the sense of being 'foreign to these parts') began with a good dollop of praise, saying that 'Berliners are proud of their city, and rightly so, since it is the most beautiful in Europe'. Berlin shone out, for this visitor, through its wealth of impressive buildings, even more in number than in Paris or London, as well as its wide streets and many squares. Berlin was far from being monotonous or uniform in style, but rather was varied, with different districts each having their own character, their own distinctive mixtures of old and new, sumptuous and meagre. The oldest parts in the original two medieval centres were marked by narrow, crooked, dark alleyways, while the more recently built districts were spacious and regular in layout, with well-designed houses for the bourgeoisie. Particularly notable was the size and number of military barracks; our visitor notes with some astonishment, for example, that the four-storey building for the Third Artillery Regiment took up the whole width of a street block and had as many as fifty-five windows on this side. Other buildings worthy of note for their size or their beauty included the palace built for Frederick II's brother, Prince Heinrich, which would later become what is now the Humboldt University of Berlin, as well as the Zeughaus, the Opera House, and surrounding private houses. The visitor was also impressed by the many open spaces, some garnished with statues and others with trees, including the Linden or lime trees that gave the central boulevard of Unter den Linden its name.

ABSOLUTISM AND ENLIGHTENMENT

With no fewer than thirty-six bridges, the river was itself a source of pleasure, lit up on winter nights when coaches drove past with torches alight; passing boats, busy quaysides, and pretty pathways added to the visitor's enjoyment of the scene. Moreover, the city was still in many places quite agricultural or rural in character, with animals, gardens, fields, and orchards, even vineyards (traces of which still echo in the name of the Weinstraße, or 'wine street', by the Volkspark Friedrichshain). All this provided a welcome contrast to the 'jostling of soldiers [and] the extraordinary quantity of factories' in the city. In short, the stranger concluded, in Berlin 'more or less everything that is useful or enjoyable is squashed together, in order to be sufficient unto itself'.[13] This was, in many ways, a remarkably perceptive summary of Berlin at the end of Frederick the Great's reign.

Dying childless, Frederick the Great was succeeded in 1786 by his nephew Frederick William II, and from 1797 Frederick William III, neither of whom were as forceful rulers as their predecessors. Frederick William II's most visible legacy was to commission what has now become a widely recognised emblem of Berlin, the Brandenburg Gate, designed by Carl Gotthard Langhans and built between 1788 and 1791. Situated at the end of Unter den Linden on the way to the Tiergarten, it was topped with Johann Gottfried Schadow's famous Quadriga, or four-horse chariot triumphantly driven by Victoria, Roman goddess of victory (as her name suggests), although the gate was intended to symbolise peace. It would do little to ensure either peace or victory for Berliners in the short term.

The city was in a transitional state at this time. In 1808 Friedrich von Cölln, comparing Berlin with Vienna, was far less positive in his description than the 'Foreign Visitor' had been a couple of decades earlier. Friedrich von Cölln did indeed appreciate the distant sight of the magnificent buildings of the city;

having arduously travelled across the sandy soil and swamps of the Brandenburg Mark, the visitor 'is delighted when one finally espies the turrets of Berlin' – perhaps more of a reflection on the disagreeable character of the surrounding countryside than the distant sight of the city's towers. But when the city itself was reached, von Cölln continued, 'the traveller is greeted by a frightful stink, since Berliners dump all their waste products just outside the city gates'.[14]

By the beginning of the nineteenth century, Berlin was finding it hard to accommodate its growing population of, by now, around 170,000. It was still a garrison town, but increasingly industrial. There were around 19,000 ordinary soldiers in the city, without counting officers, wives, or children. The most important single branch of industry was textiles, employing around 28,000 workers, while some 36,000 people worked in the gold and silver trade, or with tobacco and leather goods, or in sugar refineries, beer breweries, and brandy distilleries.[15] Despite the beauty of the major buildings, living conditions in the backstreets and alleyways were poor, with impoverished residents suffering overcrowding, illness, ubiquitous violence, and drunkenness.[16] This was no great world city or significant capital.

Yet culturally and intellectually, Berlin continued to thrive, with notable scientists, thinkers, and creative writers as well as wider publics with a keen interest in the life of the mind. More generally in the German-speaking world, this was an era when the *Sturm und Drang* (storm and stress) movement associated with Johann Wolfgang von Goethe, based in Weimar, began to challenge the prevailing Enlightenment influence of French culture; this eventually gave way to Romanticism, with immense impact on creative writing and the visual arts as well as inflecting a growing sense of German nationalism.[17] Some significant developments were more specific to Berlin – most notably perhaps the

ABSOLUTISM AND ENLIGHTENMENT

Figure 3.3 Turn of the century literary salons: Rahel Varnhagen von Ense, *née* Levin
Rahel Varnhagen was one of a number of intelligent and independent-minded women in Berlin, including Henriette Herz, who ran literary salons, or informal discussion circles, in their homes.
Gottfried Küstner (Lithograph), *Gallerie der ausgezeichnetsten Israeliten,* ed. Eugen von Breza, Stuttgart 1834, Bild-PD-alt; public domain

prominence of salons run by women, especially those run by highly intelligent Jewish women such as Henriette Herz and Rahel von Varnhagen (née Levin, who converted to Christianity on marriage; Figure 3.3).[18] These were, in effect, initiatives deriving from an educated and engaged citizenry, fostering habits of lively intellectual engagement that, in many ways, have endured as a striking aspect of Berlin society across multiple changes of regime through to the present.

But what made a crucial difference to the further development of the city was the impact of events elsewhere. The turn of the century was dominated by revolutionary France and the Napoleonic wars of expansion, which would radically transform the shape of Berlin, Prussia, and Europe.

4
Emerging Powerhouse
From Napoleon to Unification

French Emperor Napoleon Enters Berlin, 1806

On 27 October 1806, having defeated the Prussians in a decisive battle in his military crusade across Europe towards Russia, the French Emperor Napoleon rode through the Brandenburg Gate at the head of his troops (Figure 4.1). He was in no great hurry; he even spent a while in Potsdam on his way to Berlin, paying his respects to the deceased Frederick the Great by visiting Frederick's favourite palace of Sanssouci and his grave in the Garrison Church. After a moment of silent contemplation. Napoleon allegedly expressed his admiration for this military hero by uttering the words 'If you were still alive, I would not be here.'

In Berlin, the French were met with no resistance. The Prussian king and his wife had already fled for safety, as had many senior officials. Berliners who remained were enjoined to 'keep calm' as their 'primary duty to the state' – 'Ruhe ist die erste Bürgerpflicht', a proclamation pasted up all over the city. One civil defence guardsman, indeed, having been found sleeping while on duty, apparently replied with Berlinese wit, playing on the double meaning of the German word *Ruhe* as both 'calm' and 'rest': 'Rest is the highest duty of the citizen; I obey!'[1] It was not only the Berlinese cheekiness and ready repartee of this resting guard that was supposedly typical; later, the injunction was seen as encapsulating the alleged German proclivity for obedience to authority.

Figure 4.1 Napoleon entering Berlin through the Brandenburg Gate, 1806
Despite the earlier build-up of the Prussian army and military successes under Frederick the Great, Berlin was unable to fend off the invading French troops under Napoleon in 1806. Defeat nevertheless inaugurated a series of reforms within Prussia itself. Painting by Charles Meynier, 1810; public domain

Yet a supposed tendency to obey authority is far too simple a judgement. In the revolutionary uprising of 1848, hundreds of Berliners were prepared to risk their lives, demonstrating on the streets – as they were again in 1918–19. Rather, political divisions and control of the means of force always made a crucial difference to eventual outcomes. The significance of military power would echo throughout the decades that followed, eventuating in a series of wars under the leadership of Bismarck, architect of the unification of the German Reich in 1871.

Napoleon's entry into the city precipitated a period of transformation; and in the longer term, this moment would reshape not only Berlin but also the place of Prussia in Europe – and indeed the place of Berlin in the wider world.

• • •

Following military defeat and domestic reforms in the Napoleonic era, Berlin became capital of a larger and more important Prussian state, stretching from eastern outposts by the Baltic to western provinces in the Rhineland. As trade and industry grew, Berlin began a further striking transformation: from being primarily a princely residence and garrison town to a rapidly expanding industrial city. The eighteenth-century traditions of militarism and enlightenment would continue to inflect the character of Berlin; but the Napoleonic wars inaugurated a wholly new era in the city's history.

The Impact of the Napoleonic Wars

Despite its previous military prowess, Prussia was ill-prepared to face the self-designated Emperor Napoleon's expansive campaigns across Europe. Germans had initially watched the revolutionary overthrow of the old regime in France from 1789 with distanced detachment; there was even some initial enthusiasm for the ideals of liberty, equality, and fraternity. As events developed, however, opinions altered, and military involvement became an issue. Prussia became involved in the struggle against revolutionary France, along with Austria, but from 1795 retreated into indecisive neutrality. A decade later it was however rudely jolted out of any hope of remaining quietly on the sidelines. In 1806, having conquered and occupied the western provinces of Germany, Napoleon formed the Confederation of the Rhine; and in August 1806, he abolished the Holy Roman Empire, which had served as the loose framework for the patchwork of German lands for just over one thousand years. The Prussians under King Frederick William III had for a while been dithering; in 1806, just days after the abolition of the Empire, they finally joined the anti-French coalition and mobilised their troops. But barely two months later, on 14 October 1806, the French inflicted a massive defeat on Prussia at the battle of Jena-Auerstedt – the preface to Napoleon's victorious entry into Berlin. By the end of 1806, the iconic Quadriga had been seized by the French from the Brandenburg Gate and taken to Paris, symbolising the ignominy of defeat. There it languished in storage for several years, more or less forgotten, before eventually being returned to Berlin.

Prussia lost a great deal of territory in the humiliating Treaty of Tilsit in 1807, and was faced with massive financial payments to France. Berlin itself was entrusted with accommodating and feeding thousands of French troops, who were quartered with local residents or in makeshift barracks rapidly erected to the west of the city. And Berliners had to raise a significant 'contribution', initially bleeding the local economy almost to the point of destruction.

Both the necessity of reform, and the opportunity to initiate significant changes, were not lost on senior members of the government; and ideas that had already been long in the planning but previously blocked by the monarchy could now be more readily effected. Two individuals in particular, Karl Freiherr vom Stein and Karl August von Hardenberg (whose views differed considerably, and who apparently did not like each other personally) designed and spearheaded a series of measures that went a long way to dismantling long-standing structures and outdated practices in order to modernise the economy. They were not alone; the need for reform was now widely recognised in a whole variety of spheres, and the state bureaucracy assumed ever greater significance.

City government was reformed, with an elected council, a central municipal authority (*Magistrat*), and a city mayor

(*Oberbürgermeister*), even if the electorate was restricted to a small minority of privileged citizens. The power of the medieval guilds was broken, and customs and taxes were reformed. Serfdom was abolished, although the now formally 'free' peasants were still economically subjugated and politically disadvantaged. Taken together, even despite limitations in practice, these reforms did a lot to remove restrictions on economic development over subsequent decades.

Alongside other reforms went a recognition of the significance of education, science, and technology. In 1810, Wilhelm von Humboldt founded a university based in Prince Heinrich's palace on Unter den Linden; known as the Friedrich Wilhelm University until the Second World War, it was subsequently renamed the Humboldt University, after both its founder Wilhelm and his brother Alexander, an avid explorer and scientist. The university pioneered work across the faculties, including medicine in conjunction with the Charité hospital founded a century earlier.

In 1812, an Edict of Emancipation finally gave Jews full rights of citizenship; yet Jews were still subjected to significant restrictions, and had to care for their own poor, sick, orphaned, and elderly. The need to emphasise their German patriotism would continue to be a feature of the remarkably productive yet continually fragile 'German-Jewish symbiosis' of the coming century. Two decades later, the Jewish artist Moritz Oppenheim painted a striking domestic scene representing German Jews as patriotic citizens, portraying a Jewish soldier being welcomed home by his clearly religious family on returning from fighting for his German fatherland in the Napoleonic wars.[2]

Defeat at the hands of the French had also made clear the urgency of reforming the Prussian army, previously the glory of the state. Military reforms were introduced under the leadership particularly of General Gerhard von Scharnhorst, along with others such as August von Gneisenau; they sought to foster individuals on merit, and challenged the privileges of the nobility in the officer class, as well as building up reserve troops and involving ordinary residents in the Landwehr or local defence force. Some members of the army were nevertheless critical and even refused to accept responsibility for military defeat; according to one contemporary French report, they 'had not lost their proud, supercilious spirit', and were trying 'to cloak their downfall by saying they had been betrayed rather than defeated' – prefiguring similar claims about a supposed 'stab in the back' a century later.[3]

The military reforms made a difference when it came to fighting alongside Austria and Russia in the Wars of Liberation that finally ended Napoleon's domination over Europe. And with the defeat of Napoleon in 1815, the Quadriga was finally returned to Berlin to sit once again atop the Brandenburg gate – symbol now of national victory and a new sense of identity.

The Congress of Vienna in 1815, dominated by the reactionary Austrian Chancellor Metternich, had major long-term implications for Prussia, Germany, and Europe, and inaugurated a period of widespread political repression. Significantly for the longer term, state borders were redrawn; medium-sized and larger states replaced the patchwork of multiple principalities, duchies, independent city states and larger electoral territories that had characterised the Holy Roman Empire. And Prussia emerged as one of the largest and most powerful states, with the acquisition of substantial and economically significant territories, particularly in western areas of Germany.

After Napoleon

The Napoleonic era fostered a new sense of German nationalism, expressed in the philosopher Johann Gottlieb Fichte's 'Speech to the German nation' of 1807–8. There was an all-pervasive militarism in Berlin's cityscape and society. The importance of sport and gymnastics in developing bodies fit to fight and die in service of the nation was fostered particularly by Johann Friedrich Ludwig Christoph Jahn, popularly known as 'Turnvater Jahn' – 'gymnastics father Jahn' – with his open-air exercise field in the Hasenheide, while nationalist student associations (*Burschenschaften*) fostered militaristic values.

Not everyone was as enthusiastic. The poet Heinrich Heine made fun of the numbers of men who would walk down Unter den Linden wearing military uniforms and displaying all their medals.[4] And on visiting Berlin, the Swedish Romantic poet and Professor of Philosophy Per Daniel Amadeus Atterbom commented that, having got used to the sand-storms constantly swirling through the streets, and having admired both the magnificent buildings and the diligence of Berliners in tending their gardens, the visitor would eventually tire of all the straight lines, geometric shapes and curious decorations; in his view, Berlin's 'monotonous' architecture eventually conveyed an impression of just 'walking through a series of barracks'. This was 'hardly an illusion', Atterbom continued, since 'it is almost impossible to turn a corner or look in any direction without bumping into soldiers, parades, marches and manoeuvres'.[5]

There were long-lasting physical testaments to the new spirit. A substantial monument designed by Karl Friedrich Schinkel was erected as a National Memorial to the Victories in the Wars of Liberation against Napoleon. Sited on a little hill in what became Victoria Park, it was topped with a cross visible from afar, eventually giving the district of Kreuzberg its name. Schinkel also designed the Neue Wache, or Guardhouse, on Unter den Linden, with marble statues of General von Scharnhorst and Friedrich Wilhelm von Bülow guarding its sides. This continued to function as a central war memorial site with significant shifts in political values and meanings through changes of regime over the following two centuries. The contentious memorialisation of selected opponents or victims of war and dictatorship would eventually displace the celebration of national military heroes.

Gratitude to the Russians for opposing Napoleon also affected Berlin and its environs. A visit from Tsar Alexander I in 1805 occasioned the re-naming of what became Alexanderplatz in his honour; and in the later 1820s, following his death, the Russian colony of Alexandrowka in Potsdam was founded, with Russian-style farmhouses set in gardens and orchards designed by landscape architect Peter Joseph Lenné. Russians inhabited these picturesque wooden farmsteads throughout the nineteenth century, and despite being marooned for forty years in the communist GDR, when buildings and land were repurposed, the area has been preserved as a UNESCO World Heritage site and remains an attractive spot conveying images of a bygone era.

Even in the later nineteenth century, street names in the expanding suburbs of southern Berlin were chosen to recall the Wars of Liberation. The so-called '*Generalszug*' was a sequence of roads running all the way from Breitscheidplatz in Charlottenburg, through Schöneberg, to Südkreuz in Kreuzberg. Streets and squares along this route emblazoned the names of famous generals, such as Yorck, Bülow, Tauentzien, and Gneisenau, and commemorated victories, as in Wittenbergplatz. Even Nollendorfplatz, which from the 1920s was more readily associated with Berlin's gay scene, originated in this excess of enthusiasm for military heroes and battles. U-Bahn stations along the way still bear these names, and few of the streets have been renamed; entrenched in Berlin's everyday topography, their nationalistic and militaristic origins are now largely forgotten.

Not everyone experienced the city in the same way; and there was more to Berlin than the military aspects. Heinrich Eduard Kochhann, for example, enjoyed the beauty of the crossings over the River Spree, or excursions further afield by horse-drawn coach on sandy or muddy roads, even if this was not very comfortable; he also vividly remembered the gallows in Berlin and how public executions attracted large audiences.[6] The writer Karl Gutzkow, who grew up in some poverty in northern Berlin, recalled the 'terrifying' if renowned Charité hospital 'that appeared to all Berliners to be the antechamber to death'. He was also deeply affected by the sight of 'a garden where the mentally ill ran back and forth' or were 'laughing maliciously, disdainfully measuring up others and grimacing at them, or quietly digging around in the ground with a spade and singing secular or religious songs'. Even more scary, he felt, was passing the Work House where 'beggars, vagabonds and reprobates beyond salvation' hung around.[7] Adolph Streckfuß, meanwhile, was impressed by the provisions made for the poor by Christian Koppe, a local politician who had acquired a plot of land to be used, from 1704, as a burial ground (eventually closed around 1840) for the totally destitute who could not afford a grave in a churchyard, and those who had committed suicide and were excluded from religious burial; attached to this plot was 'Koppe's Poor House' where people eked out their lives on charity.[8] The square named after him, Koppenplatz, now hosts a memorial to deported Jews under Nazism; a table with two chairs, one of which has been overthrown in haste, is surrounded by verses from a poem by Nelly Sachs.

The wealthier classes lived in substantial mansions or 'palaces' around the city centre or near Unter den Linden – such as Wilhelm Straße, later the centre of government. Yet even for the better off, Berlin was not always a pleasant environment. A contemporary, Hugo Wauer, recounted that in Leipziger Strasse – a magnificent street in the core of old Berlin – most wastewater was simply tipped out into the gutters and gullies along the sides of pavements; only entrances to the grander houses had little bridgeways or walkways over the gulley between street and sidewalk. Outside the butcher's shop, wastewater ran red with the blood of slaughtered animals. People also threw out human waste products, despite being against regulations. Better houses were fitted with privies or 'closets', but without facilities for waste disposal. Every night, waggons came by with a team of ten to twelve women armed with covered buckets and lanterns; they marched into the houses to collect full buckets and replaced them with empty ones for the following day. The stench, according to Wauer, was unbearable for anyone passing by. Meanwhile, the less well-to-do and the servants had to tip their waste products into a communal trench, which was emptied every couple of months by local peasants who took the contents to use as fertiliser. Again, the stench was intolerable; and the peasants' carts were far from watertight, so that trails of human waste products were leaked along the streets as they slowly creaked and bumped their way to the villages around the city.[9]

In the 1830s, comfortable residential quarters for the professional and upper middle classes were being constructed in western areas of Berlin, particularly around the Tiergarten, based on plans drafted already in 1816 by Peter Joseph Lenné. Lenné also redesigned the Tiergarten itself as a place for leisure and pleasure for all social classes. Friedrich Hitzig and David J. L. Hansemann continued this approach by designing villa-style houses in the increasingly important area around Potsdamer Platz.[10] But while these spacious new villas provided accommodation for the growing urban bourgeoisie, there was no way such developments could meet the housing needs of the expanding urban working classes; this would only be seriously – and inadequately – addressed in the latter half of the century.

With the expansion of the middle classes came the development of bourgeois culture. Buildings such as Schinkel's new theatre (Schauspielhaus, 1818–21) on the Gendarmenmarkt, and the Altes Museum (1822–30) on Museum Island, expressed a new sense of national pride. King Frederick William IV, who came to the throne on his father's death in 1840, decided to donate his father's curious collection of animals and birds on Peacock Island (Pfaueninsel) in the Wannsee to the city of Berlin, forming the basis for Berlin Zoo, which opened in 1844. He also supported the development of the National Gallery and other museums. Collections and exhibitions flourished, reflecting the growth of interest in science, the past, and the cultural and natural worlds. Theatre, opera, and concerts were increasingly popular, with romantic operas such as Carl Maria von Weber's 'Der Freischütz' being particularly beloved. The music of Johann Sebastian Bach was introduced to Berliners, and Felix Mendelssohn Bartholdy began to make his name as an extraordinarily precocious composer, holding regular Sunday matinées.

Reading groups, discussion circles, and regular salons had already been a feature of Berlin in the later eighteenth and early nineteenth century; these continued to flourish. One estimate suggests that there were more than ninety active salons between 1780 and 1914, fostering lively literary and philosophical discussions; Berlin salon culture was, for more than a century, unparalleled in both quality and scale, even if there were isolated salons elsewhere. While literary salons initiated by women enhanced their freedom and space for expression, and gave privileged women some access to education and the public sphere, they also offered men valuable experiences of intimacy and friendship. These encounters were important at a personal level, at a time when religion was changing its meaning, and significance was attached to notions of 'authenticity'.[11] Personal accounts and letters reveal spirited and lively intellectual exchanges, as well as critical companionship and mutual support, with persisting friendships that could flourish in relatively unconstrained domestic contexts.[12]

By the 1830s, Berlin held many attractions, particularly for people living far afield, such as the young Fanny Lewald, who grew up in a Jewish family in the East Prussian outpost of Königsberg. Lewald's first journey out of her native city was a trip to Berlin with her father in 1832. She was shocked by the many 'ugly little Jewish towns' they passed on the long journey through the Polish countryside by horse-drawn coach – three days and three nights squashed in with six people, unable to rest or change clothing, but at least no longer the two week journey of her grandparents' day – and then amazed and exhilarated by her first impressions of Berlin. Spending the first night in a hotel near the Palace, Lewald was overwhelmed by the beauty of the city. She was less enthusiastic about the ten days spent with relatives in the 'horrible, noisy Münz Strasse'. Although delighted by Berlin's cultural offerings, from theatre visits to admiring the sculptures in the Altes Museum, Lewald realised with dismay that an underlying purpose was to find her a suitable husband. She hated how her aunt and others fussed over her appearance, criticising her clothing, hairstyle, and manners, and saying she needed to catch a man through her looks because she had no large inheritance; and she was not impressed when introduced to a prospective bridegroom. On attending the theatre on her final evening in Berlin, Lewald caught a glimpse during the interval of the now elderly Rahel von Varnhagen, formerly hostess of one of Berlin's most significant literary salons; Lewald later wished she had visited Varnhagen at home, an opportunity she and her father had not taken up.[13]

Many Berlin Jews were impatient with limitations imposed by both gentile society and Jewish customs. Henriette Herz, like Lewald, had cavilled at gendered expectations about covering her hair, marriage to a partner not of her own choosing, and limited freedom to pursue her own interests.[14] Some restrictions – on both men and women – could be circumvented by converting to

Christianity, and there were growing numbers of conversions, as well as intermarriages.[15] Moreover, wider social changes provided Jews with new opportunities; many developed more prominent roles in the economy and professions, as attested by the magnificent range of graves and inscriptions in the Jewish cemetery in Senefelder Platz on Schönhauser Allee, on land bought in 1824.[16]

Despite economic developments and significant social changes, however, Berlin society remained dominated by the court. As Streckfuß commented, many people aspired to courtly connections, even by adding the word 'court' (Hof) to the name of their business; ordinary traders, for example, wanted to be known as *Hoflieferanten*, 'deliverers to the court'. In his view, 'the striving for glitter and external appearances' was threatening bourgeois family life, and despite the experiences of the Napoleonic era, French manners and language still carried a certain *cachet*. 'If a bachelor today wants to gain ground with a young woman', Streckfuß complained, 'he has to make his advances suitably attired in French hat, vest, gallant stockings, and so on', and he 'must be and remain a *Monsieur*, if he can *parley* even a little French'. French manners and expressions had, Streckfuß thought, so permeated Berlin life 'that virtually no one can do without these if he wants to advance in society'.[17]

Yet even if the courtly manners and French expressions still retained some cultural capital in certain circles, massive changes were underway. In Berlin as elsewhere, early industrialisation was beginning to make its mark. Closer economic cooperation and abolition of tolls across northern Germany led to the formation of a Customs Union (*Zollverein*) in 1834, further strengthening the Prussian economy. Already specialising in silk, cotton, textiles, and clothing, Berlin's manufacturing base now expanded into machine, steam-engine, and locomotive building. In 1838, the first railway line between Berlin and Potsdam was opened, its initial journeys garnering enormous public attention, marked by a mixture of enthusiasm and consternation.[18] Soon, the benefits of speedy travel between otherwise distant places became evident, and movement of both goods and people increased with the expansion of the railway network. Entrepreneurs such as August Borsig seized the new opportunities: Borsig's iron foundry in Moabit, established in 1836–37, grew in the early 1840s to become Europe's biggest locomotive factory, while the 'Potsdamer station' and Potsdamer Platz became a significant node of both transport and social interactions across the following decades (Figure 4.2).

Figure 4.2 Potsdamer station, 1841
The first steam train ran from Berlin to Potsdam in 1838. Rail travel would revolutionise transport, while the Borsig iron foundry in Moabit would become Europe's largest locomotive factory, powering German industrialisation.
Steel engraving by C. Schulin, based on a drawing by Emil Henning, 1841; public domain

Nationalist ideas had already been articulated during the Napoleonic era; but emergent cultural currents were given a new twist by economic developments. As manufacturing and commerce became increasingly important, closer economic cooperation among German states began to foster notions of political unification. The combination would first erupt in the revolutionary year of 1848.

1848

The 1830 revolution and toppling of King Louis Philippe in France did not occasion immediate political unrest in neighbouring German states; and Frederick William IV's accession to the throne in 1840 appeared to be ushering in a more liberal era in Prussia. But failed harvests and increasing poverty in the 1840s created growing unrest. In early 1844, there was an attempt in Berlin to assassinate the king; and in June, desperate Silesian weavers rose in revolt, resulting in brutal repression and some fatalities. In February 1847, a Berlin newspaper reported a case of a man who had deliberately committed a minor offence in order to spend six weeks in prison, where he hoped he would at least be given something to eat; he pleaded that he could no longer feed his wife and children, and would like them to be handed over to the care of poor relief.[19] Failures of the harvest later that year created further distress and hunger.

Poverty alone would not have created a revolution in Germany; but political eruptions in France in February 1848 sparked unrest across central Europe, including Vienna.[20] Eager for news about developments there – including the toppling of Chancellor Metternich – Berliners began to gather in open spaces and on street corners. Rattled troops now made their presence felt, often massively outnumbering locals who only wanted to talk about the day's news;

on occasion, half a dozen people would suddenly be confronted by ten or twelve armed and apparently bloodthirsty young grenadiers.[21] On 17 March, emboldened Berliners gave the king a list of demands, including withdrawal of troops, freedom of the press, calling of parliament (*Landtag*), and the establishment of an armed citizens' militia (*Bürgerwehr*). The king seemed initially willing to consider these demands; but the following day, things turned violent. When a crowd appeared in front of the Palace, soldiers appeared and two shots were fired; a moment of confusion led to panic and open street battles erupted, with barricades rapidly erected across the city centre. In the escalating violence, around two hundred people were killed. Many were young working-class Berliners demonstrating for greater freedoms; a few were shot by soldiers as they fled for safety, even after reaching the courtyards of their own homes. The simple coffins of those who had been killed were subsequently paraded through central Berlin to the Palace, in a moving funeral procession, before being buried in a dedicated cemetery in Friedrichshain, at that time outside the city boundaries (Figure 4.3).

Shocked at the violent turn of events, on 19 March the king ordered his troops to withdraw, and agreed to demands for freedom of the press, freedom of association, and the establishment of a citizens' militia. When the king himself rode through the streets with a flag bearing the revolutionary colours, the people's challenge to his authority seemed to have been met with success. Yet even so, Berliners were unsure about what to do with their new-found power. Fanny Lewald, who had just returned from Paris, was struck by the contrast in self-confidence and attitudes in the two cities. She observed that, in contrast to Parisians, Berliners were 'as frightened and at a loss as children who have been using a walker too long and are finally set on the ground to walk by themselves. They do not trust their own feet, because they are not being supported any more.'[22]

Figure 4.3 Friedrichshain cemetery: Graves of young demonstrators killed in March 1848
The Friedrichshain park harbours a small cemetery devoted to the graves of those who had been killed during the 1848 demonstrations. Simple gravestones indicate that many were only teenagers, apprentices, or young workers.
Photograph by the author

During the following weeks, changes in government were accompanied by the politicisation of the wider population. Quite apart from organised movements and political parties, there were informal discussions in public spaces. The 'Linden Club', for example, met regularly at the corner of Friedrichstraße and Unter den Linden, costing participants nothing but their time. Here, as Streckfuß observed, curious passers-by and ever-changing audiences could be entertained by 'ordinary speakers from the people who related and criticised the latest political developments with penetrating Berlin wit'. Often, too, more seasoned politicians 'did not disdain the opportunity to mix with the ordinary people, in order to agitate successfully for their own purposes'. A popular location for such events was the area in the Tiergarten known as 'Under the Tents' (roughly where the *Haus der Kulturen der Welt* now stands), where big rallies would gather to listen to potentially incendiary speeches. Such meetings took place at least twice a week, on Wednesdays and Sundays, and speeches were augmented by fliers and newsletters, peppered with what was becoming increasingly renowned as 'Berlin wit'.[23]

Social differences were ever present, and the challenges to prevailing manners and cultural norms all too evident. Men in working clothes and hob-nailed farmers' boots could walk on the polished floors of ballrooms and debating chambers that were previously the sole preserve of the privileged. And yet, even the challenges were tentative and incomplete. In Lewald's view, 'the spirit of subservience of a people which has lived under absolutism, the fear of many of the moneyed class of possible losses, and the caste mentality of the vast far-reaching bureaucracy have still not been overcome'.[24] Moreover, those who had been used to basking in the reflected glory of the monarchy and aristocracy, even if only from a distance in a menial capacity, retained a strong sense of social deference and felt discomfited by the new order.

As the months went by, it became clear that there had been no secure transfer of power. On 14 June there was a further moment of violence with an attack on the Zeughaus; and following this, the mood began to change. As the ever-perceptive Lewald put it: 'Agitation and tension, bitterness and despair, grip the wealthy more and more. They are tired of the restlessness, the excitement of the revolution, which offers them no reward.' Rather, they would like to be able to 'stroll on Unter den Linden again, unhindered by the Linden Club on the corner of Friedrichstraße and the countless posters on the trees'.[25]

Concerned about potentially anarchic conditions, there were growing splits between moderates and more radical factions. The conservatives in particular felt it was going too far when, in September 1848, radicals in the Prussian Assembly demanded the abolition of the nobility and the removal of the words 'by God's Grace' in the royal title. A period of reaction ensued, and in November royal troops re-entered Berlin, surrounded the Assembly, and declared it illegal. Royal authority backed by military might had been restored.

Yet there were nevertheless key changes. Even though parliament was dissolved in December 1848, the king declared Prussia a constitutional monarchy with limited voting rights for adult males. The following year these recently granted rights were amended to become the infamous Prussian three-class voting system: this enshrined the political power of the landowning class, whose economic decline relative to the growing bourgeoisie was masked in this way, while effectively disenfranchising the vast majority of the population. Even so, it was no longer quite the political absolutism that had prevailed before 1848.

There were also upheavals on a wider level, as representatives from the German states convened in a national assembly in Frankfurt am Main. But their protracted discussions failed to produce a mutually acceptable plan for national unification, with or without Austria. After the Prussian king had refused to accept the crown of a 'small Germany', liberal attempts at unification seemed to be at an end. A previously relatively unknown diplomat by the name of Otto von Bismarck would now seize the opportunity for Prussian aggrandisement by quite other means. Authoritarianism backed by military might would soon win out over liberalism in a new period of reactionary conservatism.

Berlin on the Eve of German Unification

When Bismarck arrived in Berlin, following service in St Petersburg and Paris, he was apparently out of tune with the spirit of Berliners.[26] Bismarck lost little time in overriding local political processes and imposing his own views; and Berlin and Prussian representatives eventually acceded to his policies. The longer-term impact of Bismarck's domination of Prussian politics was not immediately evident, however.

Looking back at the days of his youth from the vantage point of 1913, the writer Felix Philippi painted a nostalgic picture of the two decades before unification. He recalled the salons held in his parents' home in the *Geheimratviertel*, the villa quarter close to Potsdamer Platz inhabited by senior civil servants and professionals; and he remembered how Fanny Lewald effectively held court as a revered and highly spirited intellect. He had also been stimulated by the salon hosted by Heinrich and Bernhardine Friedeberg in their house on Unter den Linden, where 'the most burning questions of politics, art and knowledge would be discussed with spirit and verve and deep understanding' by leading figures of the day, in an atmosphere of 'warmth and joyful pleasure', continuing the traditions set by Henriette Herz and Rahel Levin Varnhagen decades earlier (Figure 4.4). He described too the variety of social types to be observed in the Tiergarten, variously courting, displaying their status, selling their wares, or begging.[27] But these were the last vestiges of a society that would soon be radically altered.

Berlin was rapidly expanding with the growth of industry. In 1849, the population was 412,154; it more than doubled in the next two decades, reaching 825,937 in 1871, largely due to the influx of workers from beyond the city borders. Around two-thirds worked in industry and commerce, one third in the service sector. The street

Figure 4.4 Porcelain plate portraying a mid nineteenth-century bourgeois house on Unter den Linden
This plate portrays a house on the tree-lined boulevard leading from the Brandenburg Gate to the Palace. Produced by the Royal Porcelain Factory, it symbolises an era that was rapidly disappearing, overtaken by industrialisation and population growth.
Photograph by the author

markets and stalls of earlier decades were giving way to established shops and covered market halls, as at the Schiffbauerdamm (now the Friedrichstadt Tränenpalast, or Palace of Tears, embodying an exhibition on divided Cold War Berlin). The central boulevard, Unter den Linden, was becoming not only a place for promenading under the famous lime trees, but also a centre of commerce, where Jewish and non-Jewish Berliners intermingled. The Jewish jewellers to the court (Hofjuwelier) established their premises on the block next to the university, close to the Palace, while other commercial outlets were established heading westwards towards Friedrichstraße and the Brandenburg Gate. New parks and leisure facilities were established, as in Humboldthain to the north, or Treptower Park to the southeast. For those with the necessary means, there were numerous places to eat and drink, to relax and socialise, to engage in debates or courtships. Berliners met up and talked in cafés such as Café Josty and Café Kranzler, or notable restaurants and wine bars such as Lutter and Wegner on Gendarmenmarkt.

Population growth precipitated significant changes in the size, shape, and character of the city. The most powerful role within the municipality was that of the Police President, who was responsible not only for law and order but also social policy and housing. In view of the rapidly expanding population, in 1853 the Police President issued a Building Order that authorised construction of massive apartment blocks. These turned out in practice to be rather different from the vision intended by architect James Hobrecht.[28] Hobrecht's plan, approved in 1862, proposed radial through routes to facilitate movement in and out of Berlin, with new residential neighbourhoods around the existing circumference of the city, with blocks marked out to accommodate housing schemes. Hobrecht hoped that his design would ensure a good social mix, with upper-class and bourgeois families living in close proximity to the less well off; he hoped that small acts of upper-class charity and bourgeois examples of good behaviour might rub off on the underclasses living at the rear of the building, providing both material and cultural benefits. The reality proved to be rather different: developers constructed multi-storey apartment blocks with numerous receding inner courtyards, designed to squeeze in the maximum number of inhabitants into dark and confined spaces. These buildings soon became known as 'rental barracks' (*Mietskasernen*), with well-to-do residents enjoying spacious accommodation along the gracious street frontages while large working-class families lived cramped together in single room dwellings or cellars out the back. Little sunlight could penetrate into the deep wells of the courtyards, which often also accommodated workshops, and where unattended children played among garbage.

Needless to say, the overcrowding in cramped housing, both new and old, had a deleterious impact on public health. Most people still relied on candlelight, and poorer households restricted themselves to only one candle in the evening. Sanitation was a constant problem, and varied only slightly with class. The Police President introduced regular cleaning of gutters, and presided over the opening in 1853 of a waterworks. From 1856 the English-owned 'Berlin Waterworks Comp.' at Stralauer Tor was tasked with cleansing Spree water before Berliners drank it.[29] In the 1860s the first radial canalisation system for sewerage was introduced. This certainly led to some improvements in the removal of waste products from the centre of Berlin, although the lack of indoor sanitation and increasing overcrowding continued to plague public health and well-being for decades.

Berlin was clearly becoming a significant industrial city. But it remained relatively small, still something of an outpost. Far more radical changes would come with the unification in 1871 of 'small Germany' under Prussian domination. This development was by no means predetermined; rather, it was engineered by felicitous demonstration of Prussia's military superiority in conflicts partially created and certainly manipulated by Bismarck: first a war in 1864 with Denmark over Schleswig-Holstein; then a war with Austria in 1866, over the disputed administration of these territories; and finally, most importantly, a war against France in 1870 which brought the large southern German states into alliance with the North German Confederation that had been established in 1866. In this way, with the somewhat sullen acquiescence of the rulers of formerly independent states, Bismarck brought about the unification of 'small Germany', excluding Austria, by 'blood and iron'. Berlin's new role as Imperial capital would fundamentally reshape its status and historical significance – for Germany and the wider world.

5
World City
Imperial Berlin

Great Industrial Exposition, Treptow, 1896

In 1896, a Great Industrial Exposition was mounted in the expansive grounds of Treptow Park, on the banks of the River Spree. Lasting from 1 May to 15 October, it symbolically marked Berlin's precarious and not entirely self-assured transition 'from fishing village to world city'. The exhibition followed years of controversy, with conflicting views on whether Berlin could or should mount an international trade fair along the lines of those in major cities such as London in 1851, Paris in 1855 and 1867, Vienna in 1873, or Chicago in 1893. The new Emperor of Germany, Kaiser Wilhelm II, was firmly opposed to the venture, managing to combine pejorative remarks on Paris – with its reputation as 'the greatest whorehouse of the world' – with equally derogatory views on his own capital city, Berlin, which in his view had little beyond 'a couple of museums, castles, and soldiers' to attract the international visitor's attention for more than a few days. In the Kaiser's summary verdict on the proposal in 1892, using Berlin dialect, 'Ausstellung is' nich': the 'Exhibition ain't gonna happen'.[1]

But it did. Pressure by groups of businessmen, financiers, and industrialists brought about what initially appeared to be a compromise: a trade fair on a grandiose scale, not explicitly claiming to be a world exhibition but effectively presented as such. A little legal footwork even allowed international producers to exhibit their wares. And in the event, in May 1896 the Great Industrial Exposition was opened by the Kaiser himself, attended by his wife and one of his sons, as well as numerous courtiers and visiting dignitaries. Over the months that followed, nearly seven and a half million people visited it, despite the fact that it rained on no fewer than 120 of the 165 days that it was open.[2]

Carefully designed to cover an extensive area close to the Treptower Park station on the newly opened Stadt-Bahn or S-Bahn – the height of modern technology and urban transport – the exhibition included numerous trade pavilions, an artificial lake, facilities for eating and entertainment, and even a reconstructed Egyptian pyramid. Elaborate reconstructions of exotic places required entry tickets, costing visitors not only significant sums of money but also considerable expenditure of time, since it took hours to get around even a fraction of the exhibits.

Taken as a whole, the exhibition gestured not merely towards displays of trade, industry, and modernity – even through the then still novel use of electric lighting – but also to contrasting all this with supposedly 'more primitive' parts of the world, as well as constructions of an imagined 'Old Berlin' past. 'Natives' were shipped in and dressed up to provide the requisite local colour. The spectacle was staged with full consciousness of its artificiality, as journalist and writer Alfred Kerr noted: 'All these eastern men and women, from yellow to deep black in facial colouring, have been transported directly to Berlin from the Orient. Well aware that their task is to be exhibited, they show off endlessly.'[3] Kerr witnessed a brief encounter between a former colonial master and some 'natives' whom the master knew from an earlier context; the evident embarrassment necessitated a degree of dissembling on both sides.[4] At the other end of this exhibition of performed exoticism, Kerr tells us, was a display depicting 'Old Berlin', something of a caricature of old inns (*Kneipen*) and commoners. The historic Berlin invented in this display proved highly popular. So too did the contrast with the modernity of German technology that was everywhere evident.

In this way, visitors were effectively invited to inform themselves about the wider world, while also constructing a sense of Berlin identity through (invented) traditions, and reinforcing their own sense of modernity and cultural superiority. Yet while displaying a degree of pride and new-found self-confidence as a 'world city', the exhibition curiously also underlined the fact that Berlin was in fact a late-comer, a *parvenu*, still not quite on a par with cities such as London, Paris, or Vienna. The event betrayed both aspirations and uncertainty; ambitions and ambivalence.

And, like so much else in Berlin's history, it was spectacularly temporary. Despite all the effort and material that had gone into the construction of the imagined worlds, after the exhibition closed it was entirely demolished, and the artificial lake filled in. That area is now covered by the massive Stalinist-era Soviet war memorial, constructed in East Berlin after the Second World War to celebrate its 'liberation' by Red Army soldiers, with graves decorated by Stalin quotes holding around 200 of the 5,000 or so Red Army soldiers who had died there in the final days of the war.[5] Treptow Park now bears all the signs of the more recent communist past, and no trace of the extensive event of 1896, which sought through spectacle to put Berlin onto the world stage. The exploitation of human beings in the newly acquired colonies would only be explicitly challenged and critically addressed some 125 years later, in a small exhibition in the Treptow local history museum entitled 'looking back', which sought to restore faces and names to some of the people who had been exhibited in the 1896 exhibition.[6]

Yet the exhibition was symbolic of so much more than just the physical event. It left less visible traces, as we shall see, both in the fascination with acquiring colonies and colonial goods, and in the determination to acquire great power status. And it symbolised so much of Berlin's precarious transformation during an extraordinary period of unprecedented expansion.

• • •

Imperial Berlin, Capital of the Reich

With the foundation of Imperial Germany in 1871, the status of Berlin as a capital city was transformed. The King of Prussia now also became Kaiser Wilhelm I; Berlin, a former provincial backwater, now became the capital of an increasingly significant Empire, or Reich. Becoming Reich capital certainly enhanced Berlin's status; but it also brought complications.[7] Bismarck designed the constitution of the Empire to enshrine his own role in a triumvirate of power, which effectively revolved around the Emperor, the Chancellor, and the army leadership. They operated within a field of tensions: in the Reich, between Prussia and the other constituent states, some of which, such as Bavaria, were substantial monarchies in their own right; and in Prussia, between the conservative landowning *Junker* class, which had in-built political dominance through the state's three-class voting system, and a growing moneyed bourgeoisie, as well as the swelling ranks of the working classes, generally drawn to left-wing politics.

Unification precipitated an economic boom over the following 'founder years' (*Gründerzeit*). Everywhere, businesses were founded, villas constructed, railway lines extended, in a feverish swirl of activity and development. Many people speculated and a few became rich very quickly. One such was Bethel Strousberg, who had long been active in the years prior to unification and soon became known as the 'railway king'. He masterminded a rapidly growing network fostering not only investment in property development, but also the expansion of railways right across Europe, particularly towards the east, further stimulating economic growth. At a personal level, Strousberg was apparently remarkably abstemious, generous, and philanthropic. However, the economic bubble soon burst and the stock markets crashed in 1873, and with this the fortunes of many entrepreneurs; Strousberg's empire was merely one of the largest and most visible among the many that collapsed. Members of his family suffered illnesses and premature death, and he too died in poverty, in rented accommodation, just over a decade later.[8] Strousberg was of course far from the only Berliner to benefit from the extraordinary economic bubble and then be devastated by the crash; but prominent Jewish financiers and speculators, including Strousberg, were used to scapegoat 'the Jews' for misfortunes in a period of rapid economic and social change. Rising political antisemitism became a feature of the era, even despite – or perhaps in part because of – the remarkably extensive assimilation and successful integration of Berlin's long-resident Jews. The foundations for new forms of antisemitism were being laid.

Even after the initial bubble had burst, industry continued to expand, with an exponential growth of the population through immigrants seeking work in the new capital. The construction of new housing estates and transport links continued apace, with city planners and property developers gobbling up land and obliterating previously agricultural areas. Within a couple of decades, the city was becoming one of the largest and most vibrant in Europe, at the forefront of new technologies including the development of electrification, the telephone, and the motor industry; and its political and military leaders were also harbouring far more grandiose ambitions on a world stage, seeking an imperial 'place in the sun' that would ultimately contribute to the outbreak of the first World War. All this had a major impact on Berlin – as place, as people, as contested cultural imaginary.

As Bismarck engaged in recalibration of policies from the mid-1870s, often termed the 'second foundation' of the Reich, so those who had previously been liberal became increasingly conservative, while new political and social currents were emerging. By the 1880s, perceiving not only social problems but also the potential political threat posed by the growing working class, Bismarck introduced social welfare policies that he hoped would both ameliorate conditions for the sick, injured, or unemployed, and also take some of the steam out of left-wing political movements. Juggling enemies, Bismarck also concentrated on a 'battle for culture' targeting Catholics. The political spectrum was volatile, with the emergence of new currents and voices, including not only a growing socialist party, but also women's movements.

Under Kaiser Wilhelm II from 1890, Bismarck's successors would find it hard to sustain his balancing act, both at home and abroad. In the later nineteenth and early twentieth centuries, moreover, European states were jostling for place and position across the globe, informed by nationalism and imperialism. The delicate equilibrium Bismarck had designed began to implode, paving the way for the political destabilisation and military machinations that eventually contributed to the First World War and ultimately the collapse of the German Empire. Meanwhile, rapid population expansion and continuing industrialisation fuelled exponential urban growth alongside radical social changes, massively reshaping the city in ways that still mark Berlin today.

Housing Berliners

In the half century following unification Berlin's population quadrupled, from around one million in 1871 to what would be nearly four million in the expanded metropolis of Greater Berlin in 1920. As throughout Berlin's history, population

Figure 5.1 Neue Wache, Unter den Linden, c. 1900
Designed by Karl Friedrich Schinkel, and built in 1816–18 as a guard house for the royal palace, it initially celebrated the Wars of Liberation against Napoleon and subsequently the military victories leading to German unification in 1871; its symbolism has remained contentious. This image illustrates characteristic traffic in turn-of-the-century Berlin, including private carriages and a horse-drawn bus (*Pferdebahn*). Photographer unknown. Library of Congress; public domain

growth was driven largely by immigration, now massively speeded up by industrialisation and economic growth, as people from further afield streamed into the capital in search of a better life. There were visible contrasts between the old Berlin, as incorporated in Schinkel's Neue Wache (Figure 5.1), built in the wake of the Napoleonic wars, and the new Berlin with its increased pace of life and ever-swelling population. Heavy industry and electrical engineering became increasingly important, affecting the urban landscape not only through the expansion of manufacturing but also the relationships between transport, industry, and housing.

Transportation radically altered the dynamics of the city, increasingly separating residential areas and workplaces. The circle line (Ringbahn) connecting Berlin's main train stations was first mooted in the form of a 'Royal Station Connection Railway' in 1851, and the first stations of a circle route were opened in 1871, expanding over the following years until it finally encircled Berlin. It was eventually linked to the S-Bahn (*Stadt-Bahn*, 'city rail') network, which opened in 1882, and was electrified in the 1920s. The S-Bahn was augmented from 1902 by the 'underground railway' or U-Bahn network, which initially assisted people from the wealthier western districts of Berlin to travel into the city centre; over time, further lines enabled workers from less affluent areas to commute to work. Motor traffic too began to grow, displacing individual horse-drawn carriages, while trams and buses initially complemented and eventually phased out the horse-drawn buses known as the *Pferdebahn*. At first, workers lived close to their places of work, as in Wedding and Moabit; but as transport links improved, people could live further away. Major industrialists relocated accordingly: Borsig northwest to Tegel, and Siemens westwards out towards Spandau.

Population growth was unevenly distributed between the city's older centre and the outer areas. From 1871 to 1890, the population of central Berlin nearly doubled, growing from 823,000 to 1,575,000; yet at the same time the population of the more sparsely populated suburbs more than tripled, from 109,000 to 385,000. In the following twenty years, from 1890 to 1910, while the central area grew to 2,071,000, the suburbs expanded dramatically, more than quadrupling in size to reach a total of 1,663,000.[9] In short: ever-increasing overcrowding in the centre was accompanied by exponential urbanisation of the previously more rural suburbs.

An extraordinary building programme to house this rapidly swelling population stamped an indelible mark on the city's domestic architecture, still visible in the twenty-first century. Three features in particular made their mark. First, there was continuing construction of the large apartment blocks with a series of inner courtyards, despite their poor reputation as 'rental barracks' (*Mietskasernen*), in central districts. Secondly, substantial villas were being built in more affluent areas further out, affecting a degree of grandeur. These already existing trends were increasingly complemented, thirdly, by the emergence of property development companies rapidly throwing up new estates and engulfing previously distinct villages or townships within an ever larger conurbation.

The 'rental barracks' that had started with Hobrecht's plan continued to spread, maximising population density. Many workers were barely able to afford even the smallest apartments in these slums; whole families were squeezed into a single room or a cellar, while some individuals even rented bed space by the hour. Particularly in working-class districts such as Wedding, Moabit, and Friedrichshain, where there was little or no space at home, the streets and the local pub (*Kneipe*) became the centre of social life. Aspects of the working class 'Milljöh' – as Berliners pronounced 'milieu' – was vividly captured in photographs and caricatures by Heinrich Zille. Even in relatively well-to-do areas, a sense of loyalty to a particular 'quarter' or *Kiez* often developed. But here, the more spacious apartments at the street fronts housed the better-off, with separate back exits and stairs for the use of servants, as well as smaller apartments in the side wings and back. Buildings constructed during the heyday of Imperial Germany were often garnished with decorated facades and ambitious ornamentation, including playful figurines around windows.

Neighbourhoods soon ceased to be as socially mixed as Hobrecht had intended; and the Hobrecht plan of 1862 only applied in central areas of Berlin.[10] Increasingly, the wealthy were moving out, first to the 'villa quarter' around Potsdamer Platz and the Tiergarten, and increasingly further west and southwest.[11] Bismarck was particularly keen on extending the city westwards along a spacious boulevard heading towards the Grunewald, with its charming lakes and Renaissance hunting lodge (*Jagdschloss*). The outcome was the Kurfürstendamm, or 'Ku-Damm' as it became known, enhanced by shopping facilities, glitzy cafés and restaurants, and apartments for the wealthy. In the view of the journalist Alfred Kerr, the apartments were 'often outwardly tasteless – but inside wonderful, and immensely comfortable'. Fitted out according to the latest technical know-how, they afforded new levels of hygiene and luxury, such that residents felt 'that Berlin is a "new city"; everything is constructed with the latest "achievements"'. But, according to Kerr, while on the Ku-Damm luxurious if outwardly ugly apartments were standing empty, 'what was lacking in northern Berlin was not good housing, but any housing at all'. Kerr playfully toyed with the idea that the city council could forcibly take over some of the still empty properties on the Ku-Damm to house the poor.[12] But this was not the way politics or the property market worked, and the social division of Berlin continued, with marked contrasts between the impoverished and overcrowded northern and eastern districts and the affluent west-central districts of Charlottenburg, Wilmersdorf, and beyond.

From the 1870s onwards, property developers formed businesses known as *Terraingesellschaften*, and speculators bought up large tracts of land to build private housing as well as shops, restaurants, and institutional buildings, stamping a distinctive mark on an area. One such was the Berlinische Boden-Gesellschaft under Georg Haberland, a Jewish property developer whose influence remains visible in the Rheinische Viertel and the Bavarian Quarter, to the south of the Tiergarten, as well as the Südwestkorso linking Friedenau and Wilmersdorf.[13] Further out, 'garden suburbs' were developed in the leafy environs of the Grunewald, Dahlem, and Zehlendorf, as far as the Wannsee to the southwest. These developments were in striking contrast with the predominantly working-class districts in northern and eastern Berlin; but even there, further out in areas such as Weißensee and Mügglesee, somewhat better residential quarters were also being developed. Many increasingly important outer suburbs were still beyond the then city borders but within the growing conurbation and subject to discussions about incorporation.

Former villages were linked together in the growing conurbation, as new estates sprang up on former agricultural land. In Theodor Fontane's novel *Irrungen Wirrungen* (translated as *On Tangled Paths*), set in the 1870s, a market garden is located on the then fringes of the city near the Zoological Garden; from here, the socially ill-matched lovers – he a baron, she a seamstress – can walk across fields towards the village of Wilmersdorf, whose church spire can be spied on the horizon. By the time of the novel's publication in 1888, these fields were disappearing under the new landscape of bourgeois villas. Older properties, or tumble-down cottages with thatched roofs, were also being replaced by new housing, as on Schöneberg's Hauptstraße, where the last home with a straw roof was torn down in 1889. Among the wealthier classes, former landed estates were adapted to new bourgeois lifestyles. Schloss Britz, for example, was originally built in the eighteenth century on the grounds of an older half-timbered building; under Frederick the Great it was a significant farm, with mulberry trees in the orchard for the production of silk. In the later nineteenth century the mansion was renovated and adapted to the tastes of what became known as the *Gründerzeit* or 'foundation period' of Imperial Germany; its interior furnishings variously displayed changing aspirations and marks of status, providing glimpses of upper-class tastes in the 1880s and 1890s. By the 1920s, much of the surrounding grounds of Schloss Britz would be taken over for architect-designed municipal housing estates, obliterating the rural landscape.

These developments were taking place at a pace that startled contemporaries and prompted a great deal of criticism. The new property development companies were, like the *Mietskasernen*, highly controversial. Invidious comparisons began to be drawn with London's suburban sprawl and Paris's densely concentrated urban population. On some views, new debates represented a shift from criticising inhumane living conditions for workers to a more fundamental critique of the 'big city' as such.[14] Reformers at this time favoured green spaces and clean air, and sought to find some way between the escape to the suburbs exemplified by London, and the wilfully urban lifestyle in high buildings and boulevards embodied by Paris. These debates in urban planning and architecture would come to the fore again in the post-war period, with the focus on 'modernity' in the 1920s.[15] At the same time, social commentators began to theorise the distinctions between what they saw as more traditional forms of 'community' (*Gemeinschaft*) and a new, more individualistic 'society' (*Gesellschaft*). The ever more visible emergence of the 'masses' in industrial society and the big city evoked fears of both the loneliness of the atomised individual, and the potentially terrifying power of the collective – a psychologically significant and politically combustible combination in the era of Freudian psychoanalysis and Marxist-inspired political movements. Awareness that there was a sea change in social conditions did not necessarily bring with it agreed strategies for designing a liveable future.

The challenges posed by a rapidly growing population led to growing concern about public health. The first state-run hospital was opened in Friedrichshain in 1874. Following the start

Figure 5.2 Wasserturm (water tower) Prenzlauer Berg
As Berlin's population grew, overcrowding and insanitary conditions caused major public health problems. The city's sewerage system and water supplies began to be improved from the mid nineteenth century. This water tower was constructed in 1877 and remained in use until 1952.
Photograph by the author

made in the 1860s, a comprehensive city sewerage system was developed, while a beautifully designed water tower was erected in Prenzlauer Berg in 1877 to provide Berliners with cleansed water from the Spree (Figure 5.2). In the first two decades of the twentieth century, the impact on health of overcrowding, with people squeezed together in small and airless rooms, often beset with damp and mould causing chronic respiratory infections, led a local insurance agency to engage in an extraordinary effort at

Figure 5.3 Slum housing: A cellar room in Grossbeerenstr. 6, c. 1905
The cramped and miserable living conditions for many working-class Berliners are vividly portrayed in photographs for an official investigation into the links between poverty, health, and housing. This cellar room was typical of the conditions in which many Berliners lived at the time. Unknown photographer, Firma Heinrich Lichte und Co., 1905, for the Berliner Wohnungsenquête, reproduced in Gesine Asmus (ed.), *Hinterhof, Keller und Mansarde. Einblicke in Berliner Wohnungselend 1901–1920* (Reinbek: Rowohlt, 1982); public domain

documentation complete with a detailed photographic record of cramped conditions in Berlin's tenement slums (Figure 5.3).[16]

Since very few apartments had their own toilets or bathrooms, Berliner *Badeanstalten* or public bathing facilities were initially constructed to ensure people could take a bath intermittently, perhaps even once a week. At first, customers were issued with a towel and soap, and there was a twenty-minute time limit. Then growing emphasis was put on fitness and bodily health; the Alte Halle in Charlottenburg was built in 1896–98 and opened as Berlin's first real swimming pool, designed not just for cleanliness, with its public showers and baths, but also for lap-swimming. At the turn of the century, swimming for sport and exercise began to take over as the priority for the new public baths under construction.

The social pleasures as well as health benefits of exercise and leisure were apparent not just among those involved in the assorted 'life reform' movements that proliferated around the turn of the century, but across society. Boating on the waterways around Berlin had long been popular. So too was the pastime of ice skating on lakes frozen over during the long cold winters so typical of Berlin's continental climate. For some classes, ice-dancing was not merely a sport but also an occasion for courtship rituals under the watchful eyes of mothers or chaperones, echoing the dance classes in which so many young upper-class Berliners were enrolled.[17] In summertime, far wider circles of society enjoyed the open-air Lunapark leisure facility that opened fully in 1909 at the Halensee lake (Figure 5.4), with all the latest technology for waves and water slides in addition to a 'Bavarian' beer garden, periodic fireworks displays, and other 'attractions' partly modelled on New York's Coney Island. Allotment gardens (*Schrebergärten*) became popular for those living in urban apartments and lucky enough to gain a small plot. Others used the expanding transport network to get out to the lakes and woods surrounding Berlin. And the Tiergarten remained a place where

Figure 5.4 The Lunapark, Halensee
Opened in 1909, the Lunapark leisure park represented modernity and mechanisation, the Americanisation of culture, and pleasure and leisure for the masses, with its combination of fun and frolics, beer and bathing. Its popularity declined with the economic troubles of the 1920s, and it was closed down shortly after Hitler came to power.
Paul Kaufmann, Wilmersdorf-Berlin. Zeno.org, ID-Nummer 2000057953X, https://commons.wikimedia.org/w/index.php?curid=64841337; public domain

people of quite different social classes could variously promenade, engage in rituals of social display, indulge in childhood pranks, or meet up with lovers after work, according to age and social status.[18]

The Topography of Imperial Power

Despite the extraordinarily rapid pace of expansion and social transformation, older social hierarchies and militaristic traditions persisted, with a significant impact on both the physical and symbolic landscapes of Berlin. Victories in the wars of unification, as well as the earlier Wars of Liberation against Napoleon, were commemorated in a variety of forms, while military traditions – a pervading theme in Prussian history – continued not only to colour the social environment, but also to shape German politics in fundamental ways.

The *Siegessäule*, or Victory Column, has become one of Berlin's key landmarks. Construction of this towering monument initially began in 1864 on the Königsplatz, the square just outside the iconic Brandenburg Gate, to celebrate Prussian victory over the Danes in 1864; its significance was augmented by the victories over the Austrians in 1866 and the French in 1870; and following unification, it was completed and inaugurated in 1873. Atop the great column a shining sculpture of the winged goddess of war, Victoria (colloquially known to Berliners as 'golden Elsie'), wearing a helmet with the Prussian eagle, bears laurels in one hand and an iron cross in the other, facing the Victory Avenue (*Siegesallee*). In 1899–1901, this avenue was garnished by thirty-two pompous marble statues portraying previous margraves and electors of Brandenburg and kings of Prussia, in poses symbolising military prowess, surrounded by semicircular benches adorned by further figures. Unimpressed Berliners rapidly dubbed this the *Puppenallee* (alley of puppets).[19] In 1938–9, the Nazi regime decided the Victory Column stood in the way of Albert Speer's grandiose plans for building Hitler's 'Germania', and the column was moved westwards to its current location at the *Grosser Stern* (Great Star), an intersection in the middle of the Tiergarten. This was not entirely a demotion: the column gained an extra few metres in height with the addition of a whole new section in the process. Visible from afar, the Victory Column managed to survive two world wars, radical changes of regime, and repeated controversies over the most appropriate fate for such an obvious monument to militarism and nationalism. Meanwhile, the statues were moved westwards under Nazi plans for rebuilding the city; many survived Allied bombing, dismantling, removal, and even burial after the war; and some were eventually put on display in Spandau's Citadelle Museum. These surprisingly ugly and anachronist remnants of a previous era may provoke reflections not only on Germany's militaristic past but also just how much mentalities and tastes have changed. The Victory Column however continues to soar over central Berlin, functioning as a focal point and tourist attraction, integrated into a city that largely denounces the values the column was intended to celebrate.

By the square where the Victory Column first stood, a mansion was demolished to make way for the construction of the Imperial Parliament, the Reichstag. The fact that a building designed specifically as a debating chamber for the people's elected representatives was only constructed in the later 1880s and opened in 1894, nearly a quarter of a century after the founding of the Reich, reflects conflicting visions of the time; but in any event, real power did not lie with the parliamentary deputies, whose speeches had little effect on political decision-making, but rather with the Emperor, the Chancellor, and close advisers. In 1916, in the midst of the First World War, the Reichstag was explicitly dedicated 'to the German people' with an engraving across its front portal in large lettering (*Dem deutschen Volke*). Rendered both unusable by an arson attack in 1933 and unnecessary in view of Nazi dictatorial rule, the building then suffered devastation in the Second World War and dereliction under Allied occupation, although West Berlin eventually repurposed it for exhibition space. It was only in the late 1990s, more than a century after it was first opened, that this building began to fulfil its original purpose when the government of the newly unified Federal Republic of Germany moved to Berlin. The Reichstag too has now become a tourist landmark, with tours to the top of a transparent dome designed by British architect Norman Foster, offering panoramic views across the city as well as bird's-eye sightings of parliamentarians going about their business below. Meanwhile, the former seat of the parliament in Leipziger Strasse gave way to rapidly growing commercialisation. The journalist Alfred Kerr noted that the establishment of the massive new department store, Tietz, on a spot where Bismarck had been a frequent and notable figure, somehow symbolised the transformation of the times.[20]

At the other end of Unter den Linden from the Reichstag, another building symbolised the ways in which political and religious power were closely intertwined. The Protestant Cathedral, or Dom, harbouring the family vault of the Hohenzollern dynasty over generations, had long been located by the Lustgarten on Museum Island across from the Royal Palace. In 1893, the old cathedral was torn down, and a new one, designed in the heavy ornate style of Imperial Berlin, and somewhat hampered by the decision of the Prussian deputies to halve the requested funding, was erected in its place and opened in 1905. This remnant of Imperial Germany's grandiosity also still dominates the landscape of central Berlin, having survived both wartime bombing and passing thoughts of potential demolition under communist rule.

Throughout the imperial period, the court and aristocracy continued to enjoy cultural as well as political power, even if observers were aware of the limitations of an increasingly anachronistic system. Marie von Bunsen's memoirs of the 'world in which [she] lived' provide insights into a curious combination: upper-class leisure, pleasure, and concern with displays of social status on the one hand; and yet awareness of restrictions and a desire for greater freedom, including education for women, on the other. She eagerly participated in and was fascinated by the niceties of etiquette at court, with its careful choreography of symbolic hierarchies, yet also went to listen to Bismarck's speeches in the Reichstag, studied hard under the pioneering women's educationalist Helene Lange, and chafed at the lack of opportunities for intelligent women to progress further.[21] In his diary, Count Harry Kessler gave a vivid description of being 'presented' at the Emperor's court in 1895: 'A glittering spectacle: the long flight of rooms, hung with brocade in the muted candlelight, filled with a throng of colorful gold-and-silver-embroidered uniforms, eagerly and busily shoving past the rigid giants of the Garde du Corps who stood entry at doors; the "gossip column" in the Swiss Hall, through which the women with their diadems and white veils passed smiling and greeting, amid the malicious gossip of the colorful crowd on both sides mingling with the bustle of their trailing dresses.'[22] Behind the displays of symbolic power and rituals of social one-upmanship, however, lay real power, as Kessler observed: 'You find in society almost exclusively conventional masks making petty movements for the sake of petty advantages and petty misdeeds'; but, he continued, 'you must not forget that the three or four hundred diplomats, officers, large landowners, financiers, etc. who compose the so-called society of a country have the fate of eighty percent of the population of this country in their hands, and that often only a slight movement of one of these individuals, occupying a very advantageous position at the lever, weighs more than the exertions of many millions who must expend their force in less advantageous positions'. Kessler – who probably even overestimated the numbers of people holding the real levers of power – was not sanguine about the implications: 'if the spectacle of such random power brokers gives you pause, so you may consider what those who are supposedly elected by the people to rule actually end up doing'.[23]

Despite competing with the nobility in terms of wealth, the growing industrial bourgeoisie did not displace it in terms of status; a general deference towards those with titles as well as the officer class remained evident. Yet there were challenges, both cultural and in terms of the changing character of the city itself. The pomp of the Imperial court and the Emperor's preferred artists and architects were countered by the emergence of modernist tendencies in art. The so-called 'Berlin Secession' of 1898 developed out of cultural conflicts and splits in the 1890s, and would contribute to artistic movements that were later more closely associated with the Weimar period.

With the continuing development of industry and commerce, contemporaries such as Philippi and Kessler had noted the rise of the 'new rich'. Commercialisation was everywhere evident. Major department stores were opened, most notably the emporia of Tietz, Wertheim, and KaDeWe. These offered potential customers an all-encompassing experience; swept into palm-filled lobbies, up elegant staircases, invited to explore alcoves and try on clothes in the search for the latest fashions or acquired elegance. Whole areas were transformed by these developments. Wertheim established its first Berlin branch in Kreuzberg in 1885, and soon had branches in more central areas. Tietz, founded in 1900 by Oscar Tietz and named after his uncle and original backer, Hermann Tietz, changed the character of Leipziger Strasse from its previously elevated residential status into a commercial throughfare. The opening of KaDeWe (short for *Kaufhaus des Westens*, 'Shopping store of the West') in 1907, and the adjacent underground station, built in 1902 and extended in 1912, transformed Tauentzienstrasse and Wittenbergplatz from quiet residential streets into a centre for shopping as a pastime. Notably, many such stores were founded by Jewish families, and would later, under the Nazi government, be forcibly expropriated and taken into 'Aryan' ownership, sometimes also having their names changed in the process (Tietz became, and remains, 'Hertie').

Meanwhile, Berlin's café society was no longer quite so exclusive, or based around the few well-known establishments of the earlier nineteenth century; yet certain areas were still predominantly the preserve of the well-to-do. Kerr commented that by five or six in the afternoon, it was almost impossible to get a seat at Café Josty, where even the 'particularly elegant and well-heeled' men in top hats and black suits were outshone by the dazzling appearances of their female companions, 'whether brunette or blond, chatting loudly or phlegmatically sucking their iced coffee out of a straw'. Kerr enjoyed watching 'how they sit there and talk and laugh and nibble – or stare vacantly and nourish false ideas and from time to time cast a sideways glance at Potsdamer Platz, where elegant walkers saunter along and turn into the aristocratic Bellevue Straße'.[24]

The long-held notion that 'city air liberates' (*Stadtluft macht frei*) appeared to be evidenced by the growing Berlin Jewish community, benefitting from at least legal emancipation. The majestic New Synagogue in Oranienburger Straße, inaugurated in 1866, provided physical evidence of confidence in the future. Berlin's Jewish cemeteries similarly illustrated the sheer size and long existence of the Jewish community: the Hamburger Straße cemetery had been in use from 1672 to 1827, when it was replaced by the cemetery near Senefelder Platz; from 1880 this was augmented by the extensive cemetery in Weißensee, Europe's largest Jewish cemetery still in use.

The picture was complex. Despite formal equality in civil and citizenship rights, Jews in Imperial Berlin still faced discrimination in many professions, with obstacles to promotion in the civil service, the judiciary, universities, and the army. They also largely relied on their own welfare institutions, including hospitals and old people's homes. At the same time there was increasing integration and assimilation. One by-product of Bismarck's 'battle for culture' (*Kulturkampf*, intended to assert the power of the state over Catholics) was the legalisation of intermarriage between religious confessions, and increasing numbers of Berlin's Jews were marrying

Christians. Many also converted to Christianity, whether for reasons of conviction or convenience. There were also distinct subcultures. More affluent Berlin Jews lived in the western suburbs, particularly the 'Bavarian Quarter', and were nigh indistinguishable from other bourgeois Berliners. Immigrant Jews fleeing pogroms and poverty in eastern Europe, derisively termed *Ostjuden* (eastern Jews), clustered in the *Scheunenviertel* (barns quarter), just outside the old city centre, close to Hackesche Markt. And there was growing antisemitism – a term popularised by a German journalist, Wilhelm Marr, and given increasing credence by the court preacher, Adolf Stöcker, as well as by right-wing intellectuals including the prominent historian and politician Heinrich von Treitschke, who spread the phrase later used by the Nazis, *Die Juden sind unser Unglück!* ('The Jews are our misfortune!'). The notion of 'the Jew' would soon be expanded and given 'racial' overtones in antisemitic agitation from the 1880s. 'Race' was simply taken for granted as a reality rather than a social construct at this time.

Belief in 'race' also informed activities on a wider stage. In an era of competing nation states, Imperial Germany too began to fight for 'a place in the sun': from the mid-1880s, confirmed in the Berlin Conference in 1884–85, it began to acquire overseas colonies, including those in southwest Africa and eastern Africa (today's Namibia and Tanzania respectively) that are now the focus of debates on genocide, as well as other territories in Africa and islands in the Pacific. More immediately, colonialism stimulated a growing interest in exotic goods and foodstuffs, and a sense of cultural superiority over 'inferior peoples'. In Berlin, this was reflected in landscapes of everyday life, as in shops selling colonial wares (*Kolonialwarengeschäfte*) such as coffee, sugar, rice, and exotic spices (Figure 5.5). The term for these stores is still occasionally visible in old paint over doorways, and is quietly embedded in the everyday name of a well-known supermarket,

Figure 5.5 'Colonial wares' in a shop window in Köpenick
From the 1880s, Germany became involved in competition for colonies abroad. In 1896, a huge industrial exhibition was held in Treptow Park. 'Colonial wares' became increasingly popular, a heritage still traceable today (including in the name of the Edeka supermarket chain).
Photograph by the author

Edeka, which originated as the 'shopping cooperative of traders of colonial wares in the Hallesches Tor area of Berlin' – the *Einkaufsgenossenschaft der Kolonialwarenhändler im Halleschen Torbezirk zu Berlin*, or E.d.K. (pronounced 'Edeka' in German). Streets were named after colonial explorers or exotic places, today often objects of controversy and campaigns for renaming.

The construction of Germans as superior to 'native' peoples at the time was not only evident in the Great

Industrial Exposition of 1896, but also given more permanent embodiment in the German Colonial Museum, opposite the then Lehrter Bahnhof (now Berlin's Central Station or Hauptbahnhof). Here, the 1910 Baedeker guide tells us (with some grammatical eccentricity), visitors could enjoy 'dioramic views from the German colonies, reproductions of the dwellings and types of the natives, etc.' More specifically, people could look at 'native huts from the Cameroons and Togo; a camp of Hereroes; Chinese tavern' as well as 'Ivory-traders on the Victoria Nyanza; Arab dwelling at Dar-es-Salâm, with a diorama of the harbour; Hindoo shop; street and temple in Kiowchoow, with diorama of the bay; panorama of Blanche Bay in the Bismarck Archipelago; native huts from the Bismarck Archipelago; houses from New Guinea, with a diorama of Stephansort' – and so on.[25]

Imperialism was about more than a sense of cultural superiority, economic exploitation, or interest in 'exotic peoples'. Imperialist competition at the turn of the century played a role in an escalating arms race; it also informed Germany's growing interest in the navy, while little boys were now often dressed in clothes reminiscent of naval uniforms. During the 1904–07 war in south-west Africa, Lieutenant-General Lothar von Trotha countenanced genocide in the form of the outright murder of men while driving women and children into desert conditions where they could not survive. Even if there is no direct line to later genocide under Hitler, it is clear that there was little concern for subjugated populations – apart from exceptional individuals such as the colonialist turned pacifist, Hans Paasche.[26] The growing arms race and competition among European nation states, along with domestic political pressures and rash decisions by the German leadership, ultimately combined to ignite what became known as the Great War.[27]

The Impact of War

Berlin had changed massively in the decades since unification. Karl Scheffler, writing in 1910, bemoaned what he saw as the pervasive 'Americanisation' of Berlin. This colonial city, as he saw it, always something of an exception and an outpost, was now a centre to which people from far and wide, and particularly from the eastern provinces, were flocking to make their fortunes in a new era of commerce and industry.[28] Felix Philippi's memoirs, penned on the eve of the First World War, were drenched with nostalgia as he sought to capture the radical contrasts between the Berlin of his pre-unification childhood and the ways in which it had changed over half a century. In his youth, Philippi tells us, Unter den Linden had been a boulevard 'on which there was a concentration of the rich and elegant of the city'; here, one could see 'genteel native families and beautiful carriages'. But, he continues, 'the upper-class patricians who promenaded for pleasure under the aged and glorious trees' had now 'given way to all manner of dark big city characters' who managed to exploit and swindle 'the inexperienced and pleasure-seeking sons of industrialists from the Rhineland or Silesia'. Philippi now feared that the 'once so beautiful and up-market promenade' of Unter den Linden was being turned into 'a barren American shopping street with garish noisy buildings and brash facades'.[29] Like Philippi, Count Harry Kessler in his diaries recorded the radical generational contrasts in Berlin society: he had 'only seen something similar in certain parvenu circles in New York where the father is a cattle dealer and the daughter a marquise'.[30]

The First World War would shatter the dreams and aspirations of the newly rich, the imperialists and colonisers, those who trumpeted racial superiority and dreamed of world mastery. Perceived in some quarters as a means of bringing the nation together, and healing the rifts between the classes, the war in effect widened the chasm and inaugurated a new series of conflicts, both domestic and international.

In August 1914, crowds thronged the streets around the Reichstag, the Brandenburg Gate, and Unter den Linden, cheering soldiers marching off to the war that would supposedly be 'over by Christmas'. This enthusiasm was far from universal; just three years earlier, many Berliners had turned out to a mass rally in Treptow Park to protest against the threat of war during the Moroccan crisis of 1911. But whether enthusiastic or otherwise in the 'August days' of 1914, when the Emperor declared a sense of national unity, Germans now entered a war that was quite unlike the previous military conflicts that had so affected their history.

Berliners were soon overwhelmed by growing poverty, hunger, and civil strife during a prolonged war characterised by carnage and military stalemate. Already by 1915, there were growing food shortages, and in April 1916 Kessler recorded that doctors in Berlin had 'noticed the physical decline of the lower classes due to malnourishment; bad teeth, hair falling out'. He added: 'In the autumn it could come to unrest.' His 'impression of Berlin as a whole' was that the 'only concern is the economic, not the military situation. The next months will not be easy. There is little to eat.'[31]

Berlin's population was affected not only by hunger but also in other ways. Once again, social and economic distress fostered the growth of antisemitism; accusations circulated that Jews were not pulling their weight in the war effort, and were supposedly even prolonging the war to make profits. An official census was carried out in 1916, designed specifically to 'prove' that Jews were not playing a commensurate role in military efforts; when this in fact showed that Jewish participation was entirely proportionate and German Jews were just as patriotic as other

Germans, the results were suppressed. But the damage was done, and antisemitic rumours spread. From 1917, with the Bolsheviks' attacks on wealthy and aristocratic classes, there was an influx of Russians fleeing post-revolutionary Russia; once in Berlin, they largely kept themselves to themselves. And in the wake of the war, with violent pogroms in eastern Europe, traumatised Jewish refugees arrived seeking shelter in Berlin. Distinctive in appearance, language and customs, these new Jewish immigrants would soon become the target of militant antisemitism, combined with anti-communism in the myth of 'Judeo-Bolshevism' and the supposed 'stab in the back', as right-wingers refused to accept that Germany had really been vanquished on the battlefield.

The most significant consequences of war came with defeat. The sailors' and soldiers' mutinies of late October and early November 1918 brought about the abdication of the Kaiser and the proclamation of a Republic. In the short term, some degree of political order was restored. But this resolved little about the longer term future. While authoritarian elites and conservative nationalists waited in the wings, moderate socialists and the more radical socialists, Spartacists or communists, increasingly disagreed over how best to move forwards from a moribund political system; moderates were willing to engage in compromises with the military and business leaders, preferring gradual political change to any outright social revolution without democratic legitimation. At the same time, it was easy enough for disillusioned right-wingers to mobilise former soldiers and youngsters who had missed out on military service into armed bands, or *Freikorps* units, to pursue their rather different goals by more violent means. Conditions in Berlin came close to a civil war, with barricades and fighting on the streets. Even so, national elections were held in early 1919; and the newly elected parliamentary deputies, fearful of the violence in the capital city, engaged in their deliberations to determine a new constitution for Germany in the quieter town of Weimar. Losing its Empire, its monarchy, and subjected to national humiliation, Germany was radically transformed; and with it, Berlin would soon become a very different kind of city.

6
Greater Berlin
The Weimar Era

Murders of Rosa Luxemburg and Karl Liebknecht, 15 January 1919

On 15 January 1919, the communist leaders Rosa Luxemburg and Karl Liebknecht were arrested and taken to Hotel Eden, a prominent hotel on the Kurfürstendamm near the Kaiser Wilhelm Memorial Church and the Zoological Gardens. Here, despite the fact that revolutionary uprisings had already been successfully quelled, thugs from a *Freikorps* unit took over – with the apparent blessing of the moderate Social Democrat government – and engaged in murderous violence. Karl Liebknecht was hit over the head until half unconscious, when he was bundled into a car. Ostensibly driving towards the prison in Moabit, the car veered off into the leafy avenues of the Tiergarten near a small lake, the Neuer See, where it came to a halt. The dazed Liebknecht was pulled out, asked if he could still walk, and helped along an unlit path by the lake, supported on both sides. Then he was shot dead, allegedly 'while trying to escape'. Rosa Luxemburg was also clubbed over the head as she exited the Hotel Eden and thrown into another car. This halted by the side of the Landwehr canal running along the edge of the Tiergarten. Luxemburg was not awarded the dubious honour of being 'shot while trying to flee'; rather, while still in the car she was killed by a further blow to the head and a final bullet, then her body was simply tossed into the canal, recovered only months later.[1]

There are now easily overlooked memorials to these political leaders close to the places where they were murdered. A few of the others killed in the revolutionary upheavals were given a significant burial in the small cemetery in Friedrichshain alongside the graves of the 1848 revolutionaries known as 'those who had fallen in March' (*Märzgefallene*). These modest memorials to radical traditions before the rise of Nazism and subsequent memorialisation of Holocaust victims are relatively isolated and overshadowed in Berlin's landscape of remembrance today; and they represented a far cry from the statues celebrating German militarism and nationalism in Imperial Germany.

Yet even if the memorialisation is modest, this moment was of fundamental importance in the history not only of Berlin, but of Germany as a whole – and indeed eventually the wider world. With the officially sanctioned murders of Liebknecht and Luxemburg, the split between moderate and radical socialists was sealed; and, moreover, an irreversible step had been taken in willingness to use violence to 'impose order'. Fundamental divisions on the left would, eventually, help to pave the way for the rise of the infinitely more radical and violent right-wing nationalists, ultimately preventing any united opposition to the NSDAP or Nazi party under the leadership of Adolf Hitler.

It is vital however also to be clear: it was not splits on the left alone that explain failures to oppose the rise of Hitler. Other forces – conservative nationalists, the army leadership, significant industrialists, authority figures in a range of institutions, and key individuals – must bear the primary weight of responsibility for the eventual appointment of Hitler. And world historical conditions in an era of economic depression and political instability fostered the rising popular support for his party in the early 1930s.

But this particular incident in mid-January 1919, this linked pair of political assassinations, may serve to symbolise the deeper divisions and political difficulties of a fledgling democracy that was not inevitably 'doomed to fail', as some would have it, but certainly faced immense challenges from the outset.

The city was clearly marked by violent political clashes, and extreme social and economic distress. When we think of 'Weimar Berlin', however, quite other aspects come to mind: the imagined city of speed and light, modernity, artistic experimentation, and sexual freedom. Indeed, the wider history of Weimar Germany is often written through the lens of society and culture in Berlin, however atypical. This was a moment of radical, rapid change, and a place of extremes; and a fragile moment at that. But Weimar Berlin has remained in the cultural imaginary as an era of liberation, in which energies were unleashed that have made a lasting impact on the ways in which we live, relate to each other, perceive and think about the world.

During this moment, events of far wider historical significance were taking place in Berlin; yet at the same time, the city itself – the built environment, the living relations among people – was changing in ways that can easily be overlooked if we concentrate primarily on the dramatic political events and enduring cultural currents for which 'Weimar Berlin' has become so well known. History *in* Berlin, and the history *of* Berlin, form intertangled strands of this extraordinary moment of radical transformation.

• • •

At the end of the war, most Germans simply wanted to return to what they saw as 'normal' lives. But in the turbulent conditions of the time it was far from clear how such a 'return to normality' could be achieved. Many yearned for a return of the old authoritarian order, while others strove to construct something radically new. Conflicting visions, and continuing political instability, proved fertile breeding grounds for revisionism and the growth of radical ethno-nationalism. The NSDAP (National Socialist German Workers' Party, or Nazis), which grew out of an earlier party, the DAP (German Workers' Party) was not the only movement on the right at this time: many ethno-nationalist (*völkisch*) groups refused to accept the defeat of Germany, while militaristic *Freikorps* units, often led by former soldiers and garnering support among men who had been too young to fight in the war, engaged in political assassinations and coup attempts, and fomented violence across the country, particularly on Germany's eastern borderlands. Early challenges, including the short-lived Kapp Putsch of 1920, when the government was temporarily forced to flee the capital, and the cataclysmic inflation of 1923, would be overcome. But despite a period of apparent stabilisation in the mid-1920s, Weimar democracy would ultimately prove unable to withstand the shock of economic depression following the Wall Street Crash of 1929. As unemployment rose and political parties failed to achieve a workable compromise, and with rising violence on the streets, Adolf Hitler and the NSDAP were the eventual winners. President Hindenburg dealt the final death blow to Weimar's fragile democracy by appointing Hitler chancellor in a mixed cabinet in January 1933; thereafter, the self-proclaimed Führer would set about destroying the democratic system that had brought him to power. While this history played out across Germany, many key events happened in Berlin and radically affected the lives of Berliners.

History Happening in Berlin

In late 1918, on 9 November – a repeatedly significant date in twentieth-century Germany – the Emperor abdicated and the authoritarian German Empire collapsed. From a balcony at the

Reichstag, the Social Democrat Philipp Scheidemann proclaimed a democratic Republic – a largely spontaneous declaration, without any constitutional foundations – spurred by hearing that at the other end of Unter den Linden, from a balcony at the Hohenzollern palace, the left-wing Spartacist leader Karl Liebknecht was calling for a Bolshevik revolution. These differing declarations on that November day, among mutinies, strikes, and political violence on the streets, symbolised some of the conflicting political currents attending the birth of Germany's first attempt at democracy.

In November 1918, armistice was not as yet followed by a peace treaty, let alone a stable government. Initially, moderate social democrats and more radical independent socialists formed an uneasy transitional coalition under SPD leader Friedrich Ebert, who was cautious about introducing radical change without a democratically agreed new constitution. While the collapse of the empire entailed immediate political transformation, there was far less by way of fundamental change in the social and economic order. Ebert's government rapidly entered into a series of compromises with army leaders, industrialists, and conservative nationalists. The army was not brought under democratic control; and conservative national elites, notably the judiciary, generally remained biased towards the right. The agreement struck between trade unionist Carl Legien and employers' leader Hugo Stinnes on working conditions, apparently highly progressive in terms of workers' rights at the time, nevertheless embodied the politicisation of industrial relations, ensuring that any economic difficulties would inevitably have massive political implications in terms of an attack on the 'system' as a whole.

The fragile unity among moderates and left-wingers that was hammered out in November 1918 did not last long. The following weeks were marked by continuing political uncertainties and jostling for control. Harry Kessler's diary provides vivid insights into the repeated confrontations between rival factions on the streets, with speeches, scuffles, and crowds, to a backdrop of periodic sounds of gunfire, shots being fired from rooftops by day or in streets at night; yet, as Kessler noted, Berliners often seemed extraordinarily unruffled by it. The traditional Christmas Fair in 1918 'carried on throughout the blood-letting', and children played with their presents under lighted Christmas trees while in 'the Imperial Stables lay the dead, and the wounds freshly inflicted on the Palace and on Germany gaped into the Christmas night'. In early January, while all around there were the sounds of shots firing, Kessler stopped for a meal opposite the station in Potsdamer Platz. As he left the restaurant, 'street vendors with cigarettes, malt goodies, and soap were still crying their wares'; looking into 'the boldly lit Café Vaterland', he noticed that although 'at any moment bullets might whistle through the windows, the band was playing, the tables were full, and the lady in the cigarette-booth smiled as winsomely at her customers as in the sunniest days of peace'. Berlin, in short, was carrying on just as an 'elephant stabbed with a penknife shakes itself and strides on as if nothing has happened'.[2]

The situation was nevertheless escalating. Growing splits between moderate and independent Social Democrats (the MSPD and the USPD) came to a head in January 1919, when government forces suppressed the Spartacist uprising, so named after the Spartacus League of Marxists who eventually broke away from the SPD to form the communist KPD. Although the most prominent casualties at this time were Karl Liebknecht and Rosa Luxemburg, more than 150 people were killed.

The German parliament or constituent assembly, which was elected in January 1919 and convened in Weimar (hence 'Weimar Republic'), designed a democratic constitution for the Republic. This included proportional representation, voting rights for women, and an elected President who had power to rule by emergency decree. The provisions of the Treaty of Versailles were severe and humiliating, provoking intense disquiet, exacerbated when the full reparations bill was finally revealed. The loss of German territories both in Europe and overseas, the demilitarisation of border areas, and restrictions on the size of the armed forces, were a massive blow. Demands for revision of the Treaty of Versailles would be a refrain that persisted across many quarters, contributing eventually to support for Nazism.

In the meantime, political violence continued. In 1920, the short-lived coup led by Wolfgang Kapp and General Walther von Lüttwitz was backed by the considerable might of the Freikorps Brigade led by Hermann Ehrhardt; they succeeded in taking over Berlin, and the elected government had to flee. Within days, a massive General Strike organised by the trade unionist Carl Legien mobilised some twelve million workers across the country, bringing the coup to an end. This appeared, in the short term, to represent a success for democracy; but in the elections that summer the parties that had made up the original Weimar coalition lost votes, and political extremism developed further. In 1922, the short-lived Foreign Minister of the Republic, Walther Rathenau, was assassinated on a street near his Grunewald home by the right-wing group Organisation Consul; this highly visible murder of a prominent politician, who was both Jewish and wrongly suspected of being sympathetic to communists, was but one of hundreds of politically motivated murders. On this occasion, the Reichstag was shocked; a huge state memorial service for Rathenau was organised and well attended; and some of the assassins were brought to court. But during most of the Weimar period, murders by right-wing groups went unpunished, while left-wing offenders were dealt with severely by a conservative judiciary that did little to conceal its own right-wing political sympathies.

Political violence was accompanied by acute economic instability. The demand for punitive reparations, revealed in full detail in 1920, hampered attempts to regenerate the economy; and the effects were exacerbated by the political decision to print money in order to demonstrate the impossibility of payment, fuelling existing inflationary tendencies rooted in the previous means of funding the war effort. By 1923, the exponentially spiralling inflation ran totally out of control, giving rise to extraordinary scenes in which workers had to take their earnings home in wheelbarrows, and a loaf of bread would double in price between morning and evening. This unprecedented inflation destroyed lives and livelihoods for millions while catapulting others into undreamed-of fortunes. It also transformed the character of Berlin society. While those who had depended on savings or fixed pensions, and those whose businesses went bankrupt, were ruined, the 'newly rich' rose to extraordinary wealth and indulged in hedonistic conspicuous consumption with little thought for the future.

Everywhere, too, the personal consequences of the war remained evident: crippled beggars, with missing limbs and disfigured faces, selling cigarettes on the streets; children whose stunted growth betrayed the effects of prolonged hunger; orphans and widows dependent on the state for support; and less visibly, shell-shocked and incapacitated former soldiers shut away in institutions. The war had left 533,000 German women prematurely widowed, and there were 1,192,000 war orphans; in 1920, more than one third of Berliners were below the age of thirty.[3] Illnesses were accompanied by increased mortality, including from the influenza epidemic that ravaged Europe from 1918 to 1920.

The character of Berlin society was changing in other ways too. Russian émigrés escaping the Bolshevik revolution were establishing their own, almost hermetically sealed, Russian communities, as in the western borough of Charlottenburg, often jocularly designated 'Charlottengrad'. For many of them, Berlin remained simply a backdrop, not a place where they aspired to integration. The situation was quite different for the Jewish community. Antisemitism was widespread across Europe after the war, but refracted in distinctive ways in Berlin. Many Jewish families had lived for generations in central or western areas of the city, and individuals often held prominent roles in politics, culture, society, and the economy. Increasing numbers of Jews had converted or intermarried, leading over time to a growing number of children of mixed heritage. Meanwhile, the community of poorer Jews in the Scheunenviertel was now swollen by a massive influx of so-called *Ostjuden*, 'eastern Jews' fleeing the murderous pogroms that erupted in eastern Europe after the war. The journalist and writer Joseph Roth, himself Jewish, described these refugees unsparingly: 'Fear of pogroms has welded them together like a landslip of unhappiness and grime that, slowly gathering volume, has come rolling across Germany from the East.'[4] As Roth went on to point out, the only real threat posed by 'these people' arose precisely because they were not permitted to work, and the authorities seemed incapable of processing their paperwork and allowing them to emigrate or disperse across Germany, leaving them little option but to 'become black marketeers, smugglers, and even common criminals'. They would spend weeks in an overcrowded boarding house smelling 'of dirty laundry, sauerkraut, and masses of people' who lay 'all huddled together [. . .] like luggage on a railway platform', before 'literally dying on the charity of their fellow men', starving to death before they were 'allowed to make themselves scarce'.[5] All Jews, whether long-established residents or impecunious recent immigrants, were now ready targets for right-wing racist propaganda which constructed 'international Jewry' as a threat, whether through 'international finance capital' in the capitalist west, or 'Judeo-Bolshevism' in the now communist east.

In the mid-1920s, Berlin remained politically deeply divided, with liberal, socialist, and radical left-wing movements still in a majority within the metropolis, often dubbed 'Red Berlin', yet unwilling to combine forces against radical right-wing extremism. Intimations of what might lie ahead became increasingly evident when Joseph Goebbels became the Berlin district leader (Gauleiter) for the NSDAP in 1926.

Meanwhile, strenuous efforts were being made to transform the situation of the now nearly four million inhabitants of the expanding city. History was not only being made in Berlin; the city of Berlin was itself being reshaped.

Greater Berlin: Expansion and Transformation

Berlin had already been turning into a metropolis before the war. It was not only the size of the city that was changing, but also what might be called its velocity: the speed at which people could move through it, and the speed at which life itself seemed to be moving, whether in the workplace or during leisure time. The concept of the 'machine age' had been given a new and hideous twist in the four years of war, but acquired more positive, if still contested, notions of 'progress' in the following years.

In 1919, within the existing city limits Berlin had a population of just under two million (1,902,200), living in an area covering 66 square kilometres. In 1920, the outer districts, suburbs, and townships that formed the conurbation of metropolitan Berlin were formally incorporated into what became known as *Groß-Berlin* or Greater Berlin. Berlin now had 3,806,000 inhabitants living in a vastly expanded space of 878 square kilometres. A population that had roughly doubled in numbers now lived in an area that was more than thirteen times the previous size. Boroughs that had long had independent identities of their own, from the medieval fortress town of Spandau in the west to the princely residence city of Köpenick in the southeast, now became part of the metropolis; areas of lakes, waterways, and forests, such as the Grunewald, Wannsee, Müggelsee, or the Tegel Forest, as well as still quite agricultural areas, from Zehlendorf or Lichtenberg to Reinickendorf, became part of the city; closer to the old centre, formerly independent townships such as Charlottenburg and Schöneberg were absorbed into the expanded city. Along with New York and London, Greater Berlin was now one of the largest cities in the world.

With the expansion of the city, the distinctive characters of Berlin's constituent districts were more evident than ever. Comfortable bourgeois lifestyles in the affluent western and southwestern suburbs contrasted markedly with the continuing poverty and social distress of working-class areas such as Kreuzberg, Wedding, Moabit, Prenzlauer Berg, and Neukölln, or pockets such as the so-called 'red island' between the railway tracks heading south, later noted as the birthplace of the actress and singer Marlene Dietrich.

Given the rapid population growth, housing in Berlin continued to be a major problem. The older apartments in the 'rental barracks' had been becoming even more overcrowded and unsanitary. Although the numbers cited by Werner Hegemann in his devastating 1930 critique of what he called the 'greatest rental barracks city in the world' are somewhat confusing, the overall picture he paints is clear. In 1905, he tells us, around half of the then two million inhabitants of Berlin lived in apartments in which each habitable room, defined as one that could be heated – desperately necessary given the bitter Berlin winters – accommodated between three and thirteen people. The situation was possibly even worse: according to other figures, perhaps one and a half million Berliners lived in tiny flats in which any habitable room housed between six and thirteen people. Just under a quarter of a million apartments were substandard in some way: around 34,000 had no kitchen space at all, while 188,000 had a space for cooking but no other indoor facilities. Even in 1925, in the middle of the Weimar Republic, some

70,743 Berliners lived in cramped, dark, unhygienic cellars.[6] Back courtyards were dark and dirty, and frequently the scene of unsavoury transactions and occupations. Widespread extreme poverty, squalor and overcrowding led to major public health issues; and there was general recognition of the urgent need to deal with social housing questions.

Some areas in what had been the outskirts of Berlin, such as Tempelhof, still betrayed evidence of their older rural character, but were predominantly now characterised by what the self-professed flaneur Franz Hessel, noting the character of districts in his walks across Berlin, called 'hideous, hurried construction from the time after 1870, built entirely according to the tastes of the construction companies and contractors', as well as 'new housing blocks without side or back buildings'.[7] The suburbs in Neukölln, which 'had hardly ten thousand residents in the 1870s but now have between two and three hundred thousand', were in Hessel's view even worse. 'The broad streets house many emporiums, cinemas, taverns, steamed-sausage stalls, radio hobby shops, and stately facades conceal the misery of the courtyard apartments'; and in some streets 'the squalor is more visible', as 'work-weary people pour out of over-filled trams in the evening, and myriad sickly children roam about on the street'. Hessel summarised Neukölln – still one of the poorest areas of Berlin – as a 'desolate district'.[8]

While property developers were rapidly throwing up extensive housing estates, major architects, many associated with or influenced by the Bauhaus school, designed modernist buildings that remain internationally significant. The Bauhaus itself, founded in Weimar in 1919 by Walter Gropius and from 1925 to 1932 based in Dessau (from 1928 to 1930 under the directorship of Hannes Meyer, followed by Ludwig Mies van der Rohe), was periodically beset not only by internal differences of opinion but also political constraints and attacks. In 1932, the Bauhaus moved to Berlin, where it operated for ten months before Mies van der Rohe closed it down in 1933 under pressure from the Nazis. But the influence of the school proved to be far broader than its short institutional history might suggest. The legacies of modernist and Bauhaus architectural visions continue to mark the cityscape of Berlin alongside more mundane developments.

The urgent need for new housing was widely recognised. What is extraordinary about Berlin in the 1920s was the involvement of cutting-edge architects in designing social housing that incorporated modernist ideas and emphasised space, light, and air, informed by an energetic concern for the health and well-being of ordinary people. The SPD-led city council played a role in commissioning architect-designed social housing that was still seen as highly attractive a century later, in a couple of cases garnering the accolade of being designated a UNESCO World Heritage Site.

In Siemensstadt in north-western Berlin, for example, a modernist housing estate was designed by internationally renowned architects to accommodate workers in local industries (Figure 6.1), including Siemens with its expansive works along the highway heading west to Spandau. Each part of the new, well-spaced housing estate – with numerous balconies, communal gardens, and quiet roads – exhibited a different design, with the involvement of notable architects including Walter Gropius, Hans Scharoun, Otto Bartning, und Hugo Häring. The design of the estate began, remarkably, with the establishment of an adjacent landscaped park complete with open-air swimming pool and leisure facilities set in woodland. Similarly, on the extensive grounds of the Schloss Britz in southern Berlin, the model Hufeisensiedlung ('horseshoe estate') was designed by the architect Bruno Taut.[9] Here, modern dwellings with indoor toilets and bathrooms, separate bedrooms, balconies, and small gardens,

Figure 6.1 Architect-designed housing in Siemensstadt, 1920s
The Social Democratic (SPD) city government supported new housing estates designed by world-renowned architects. Now designated UNESCO World Heritage sites, estates such as Siemensstadt and the Hufeisensiedlung (in Britz) provided workers with apartments that included indoor kitchens and bathrooms as well as access to fresh air and play spaces, in contrast to the slum conditions of the 'rental barracks' (*Mietskasernen*). Photograph by the author

were arranged in a horseshoe shape surrounding a communal green space with a small lake. Although still heated by the *Kachelofen* (traditional tiled stove), and with simple furnishings in stripped-down Bauhaus style, these colourful apartments provided quite revolutionary living conditions for members of the working classes. There were nevertheless still traditionalists at work here. Across the main road from the Hufeisen estate, more conservative architects designed another part of the settlement (and indeed, Adolf Eichmann later lived in one of these more traditional apartments).

Rapid economic development and related population growth had significant implications for Berlin's transport network. Electrification of the S-Bahn and the U-Bahn, and the development of the motor car, had already transformed the possibilities and speed of urban transport; but now, the sheer volume of traffic created new challenges. There was, as Joseph Roth commented, growing chaos on Berlin's streets; in particular, he thought, the traffic juncture of Potsdamer Platz increasingly 'looks like a suppurating wound'. At the beginning of November 1924 Europe's first automated traffic lights were erected here (Figure 6.2). Roth was not initially impressed: 'One had an expectation, perhaps, of something soaring and magnificent' but, in fact, there merely 'stood a little gray [sic] metal stump of a tower' – which still stands, a remnant and symbol of a bygone age, with no current utilitarian purpose. Everywhere, too, Roth observed, the pace of Berlin's traffic was inhibited by 'slow roadworks'; he knew 'of no other city where the streets are patched as glacially as they are in Berlin'. Worse, he felt, was the atmosphere among too many over-stressed people trying to get somewhere in a hurry: he feared that 'a bus full of rancorous, quarrelsome and aggressive passengers is bound sooner or later to have a collision'. Finally, in Roth's litany of complaints, was the fact that workers on the subway, 'Berlin's most important traffic artery', were going on strike, and both the management and the Ministry of Labour seemed to have fallen into a 'catastrophic torpor' with no likelihood of reaching any settlement.[10]

More positively, Franz Hessel – who chose to walk everywhere in the city – was impressed by the new means of air travel, with the vast expanses of the former military parade grounds in

Figure 6.2 Potsdamer Platz, 1932
Europe's first traffic lights were erected in 1924 at this increasingly busy junction, with a concatenation of trams, cars, bicycles, and pedestrians. Advertising, consumerism, and traffic overwhelm a square formerly renowned for its social venues, and later slashed by the Wall.
Photograph by Waldemar Franz Hermann Titzenthaler; public domain

Tempelhof now transformed into an airport where observers could 'watch the buzzing steel birds glide down onto green expanses and roll onto the tarred runways' before they 'ascend again, circle, and fly off in all directions'.[11]

With the growth of concentrated industrial production, travel to employment some distance from home was essential. Factory work became increasingly mechanised as American 'Fordist' production lines were introduced in an effort to increase productivity. Machines whirred, and people became ever less specialised, mere cogs in a wider machinery of production.

Women were increasingly drawn into the workforce – first during the war, with the absence of men at the front, and then as white collar workers, typists, secretaries, shop assistants, in the changing socioeconomic structure of the 1920s. The newly found independence of young women was widely commented on, as female friends went out shopping together, or visited cafés, dance halls, and cinemas. The new medium of radio was spreading, complementing newspapers and magazines as a source of both news and entertainment. While only the wealthy could now afford to shop in the big department stores, consumerism was everywhere evident, with billboards, advertisement hoardings, and painted signs on the sides of buildings promoting an assortment of wares from chocolate to washing powders or stockings.

The picture of Berlin as an increasingly industrial metropolis, with warehouses, factories, and smokestack chimneys dominating the skyline between the ubiquitous late nineteenth-century red brick churches, schools, and municipal buildings, was nevertheless still punctuated by relics of the pre-industrial era. While older cottages were disappearing under new housing estates, market gardeners and farmers from the outskirts still set up stalls of local fruit and vegetables in street markets reminiscent of a previous era.

More widely, there was enthusiasm for escaping the city and seeking fresh air in the woods and beaches of the many lakesides and waterways around Berlin, whether in Köpenick and the Müggelsee region to the east or the Grunewald forest and the lakes of Krumme Lanke, Schlachtensee, Wannsee, and the Havel to the west. Cycling and hiking allowed even the poorest to enjoy nature in their leisure hours, while the well-to-do indulged in sailing and golfing. Ice-skating on frozen lakes and waterways was common in the freezing winters, and the *Badeanstalten* or public baths that had initially been established for personal cleanliness now became swimming pools, *Schwimmbäder*, for learning to swim and take exercise. Among some, the *Lebensreform* or life reform movements that had grown around the turn of the century developed further, with enthusiasm for simple lifestyles, hiking, nudist bathing, and enjoying the sun.

Refractions of Modernity and Mass Society

The ferment of creativity among those who would later be ousted for their Jewish 'racial' heritage, and those associated with left-wing movements, is now virtually identified with 'Weimar culture', even if developments in the 1920s had long roots in the pre-war decades. Not surprisingly, many leading scientists, creative artists, and intellectuals were based in Berlin, including luminaries such as the Nobel Prize-winning theorist of relativity, Albert Einstein; the playwright Bertolt Brecht and his collaborators Kurt Weill, Hanns Eisler, and the actress Helene Weigel; the pacifist painter and sculptor Käthe Kollwitz, who in 1919 became the first woman to be appointed professor at the Prussian Academy of Arts; and the by now elderly Max Liebermann, who became President of the Berlin Academy of the Arts in 1920 and despite his Jewish heritage was chosen to paint a portrait of President Hindenburg. Yet at the same time, progressive currents were aggressively contested by increasingly strident right-wing voices across the universities as well as in the wider and deeply conservative intellectual environment. Racialised forms of antisemitism were on the rise, and many Germans never accepted the humiliation of defeat in 1918 or the imposition, as they saw it, of the new democracy. While Weimar Berlin gained a reputation for progressive political, cultural, and social movements, the new constellations were inherently fragile.

None of these internationally significant cultural and intellectual developments can be restricted to the history of Berlin; but the rapidly expanding capital city refracted the issues of modern mass society in distinctive ways, stimulating conflicting interpretations and engaged interventions.[12] New cultural currents – whether in painting, writing, or the new medium of film – sought to capture and critique the radically transformed appearance and increased speed of the city, as well as the impact of war, poverty, and the shadier undersides of modern life. Artistic movements such as expressionism and dadaism attempted in diverse ways to 'make sense' of modernity, including machine warfare and mass killing, while the notion of *Neue Sachlichkeit* (new objectivity) can be variously interpreted as an attempt to deal with grief through the suppression of unbearable emotions, or as inner emptiness in a society which emphasised consumer entertainment, and where control of the media implied also control of popular opinion. Silent films such as Fritz Lang's *Metropolis* (1927) or Walter Ruttmann's *Berlin: Symphony of a Metropolis* (*Berlin: Die Sinfonie der Großstadt*) (1927) portrayed the extraordinary pace and complexity of life in a rapidly expanding metropolitan city. In particular, *Symphony of a Metropolis* portrays a day in the life of the big city, starting with views from a train taking commuters into Berlin, highlighting the contrasts between urban and rural life. It portrays 'modernity' not in terms of particular buildings or architecture, but rather speed and motion, with the reduction of people to 'masses' defined by their social roles and economic status, regulating working patterns, eating habits, and leisure pursuits, and subjected to time-frames imposed according to class. We only occasionally catch a glimpse of faces hinting at different individual fates: one person of colour, background unspecified; a despairing woman by the river, very likely about to commit suicide, only able to step out of mass society by choosing to end her own life.

These are the significant films that still engage our attention today. For most Berliners at the time, cinema was less an occasion for social critiques than a place to escape the miseries and stresses of everyday life, and even the weather. Hessel noted that 'Berliners are passionate cinema-goers': apart from a number of 'great picture-palaces around the Memorial Church on Kurfürstendamm, near Potsdamer Platz, [and] in the suburbs', there were also 'the thousand small cinemas whose bright, enticing lights can be seen on dim streets in every district', as well as 'a bevy of matinee cinemas, proper warming shelters for body and soul'. In Hessel's view, Berliners in the cinema were not 'as critical' as they were in everyday life, but rather let themselves 'be overwhelmed by the illusion' in a 'life by proxy for the millions who would like to forget their monotonous routine'.[13] The 1930 'film without actors', *Menschen am Sonntag* (*People on Sunday*, story by Billy Wilder), not only portrayed but was also acted by ordinary workers, bickering about their relationships and whether or not to go to the cinema, eventually taking a day trip to the lakes of Nikolassee and Wannsee before returning to their humdrum weekday working lives.

'Weimar Berlin' became widely noted for aspects of cabaret and night life, and particularly for challenges to traditional sexual mores through open acknowledgement of still criminalised homosexuality, cross-dressing, and explicit performance of transgender identities (Figure 6.3). The lively gay scene around the Nollendorfplatz area in Schöneberg was immortalised in the novels of Christopher Isherwood, while the physician, sexologist, and gay rights activist Magnus Hirschfeld was increasingly concerned about high suicide rates among gay men. As well as appearing personally in a film entitled 'Different from the Others' (*Anders als die Anderen*, 1919), Hirschfeld founded an Institute for Sexology, later closed down by the Nazis. But we have also to remember that elements considered progressive in liberal societies a century later faced immense opposition at the

Figure 6.3 Advertisement for an event at the 'Ladies Club Violetta', Kreuzberg, November 1928
Weimar's gay scene, later suppressed by the Nazis, was particularly vibrant in Berlin, as in the Nollendorf Platz area in Schöneberg popularized in the novels of Christopher Isherwood.
Newspaper clip, Magnus-Hirschfeld Society. Image: United States Holocaust Memorial Museum, 47082; public domain

time. A focus on the so-called 'roaring twenties' may risk obscuring the overwhelming weight of both legal restrictions and conservative social conventions, as well as potentially idealising the grinding poverty which made employment as a sex worker the only option for some individuals.

The fragile allure and real undersides of life in 1920s Berlin are vividly evoked in contemporary novels, particularly those highlighting the experiences of outsiders coming to the city in the hope of a new and more liberated life. In Irmgard Keun's *The Artificial Silk Girl*, for example, the protagonist is a naïve young girl from a provincial town with unrealistic ambitions of becoming a star; she sinks ever lower into poverty and near-starvation before being rescued by a kindly man whose wife has just left him; regaining her strength, she sets out anew, adjusting her expectations of how to make compromises in order to survive. Erich Kästner's *Fabian* is explicitly a 'caricature' of life in Berlin, yet with all seriousness evokes the hopelessness of so many people at the time. The suicide of Fabian's friend Labude serves to critique the morality and manners of the day, while the death of the protagonist himself, Fabian, who cannot actually swim yet dives into deep water to save a child, puts a sudden and unexpected end to a book in which there really seems little hope of altering conditions, even among those with high educational qualifications, critical intellects, and relatively independent means. And Hans Fallada's *Little Man, What Now?* (1932) vividly evokes the despair and struggle for sheer survival of a working-class couple in the early 1930s.

It was the Depression that provided the opportunity for those opposed to the new Republic to foment political ideologies and movements that would deal a death blow to the inherently fragile Weimar democracy.

Political Ferment and the End of Democracy

The Weimar Republic was born in the political crisis following defeat in the war. Once inflation had been brought under control, and as reparations and foreign relations were subject to renegotiation, the political system began to stabilise; but it was not secure. The loss of an authoritarian monarchy was never accepted in many quarters; even President Hindenburg, who following his election in 1925 was constitutionally bound to uphold democracy, was not in principle in favour of parliamentary rule.

The history of Berlin, Germany, and the wider world was dramatically shaped by the Wall Street Crash of October 1929. Following a period of intense speculation in the US, the stock markets foundered; and, most significantly for Germany, American short-term loans that had been granted as part of the Dawes Plan for German economic recovery and reparations payments were now withdrawn. As a consequence, the German economy collapsed – further and faster than other European economies also affected by the Depression.

In the absence of any viable parliamentary coalition, from 1930 Hindenburg ruled by presidential decree; democracy had, in effect already crumbled, with the unpopular Brüning cabinet tolerated in power only because the largest opposition party, the SPD, did not want to risk further elections. The experiences of ordinary workers in Germany were made infinitely worse by the way in which the Brüning government chose to deal with the economic challenges by imposing a policy of austerity.

The consequences were devastating. Unemployment soared; one in three workers were soon out of a job, and in some areas this meant that one in two families were entirely without a breadwinner. Across Germany, rising poverty and unemployment led many, in desperation, into the arms of a party willing to offer a saviour figure, a sense of pride and comradeship, and even a uniform or an occasional hot meal. Parties of both the extreme left and the extreme right – communism and Nazism – benefitted from the collapse of confidence in the parties of the centre ground. The only centrist party that retained its core vote was the Catholic Centre party, but across much of Protestant rural and small-town Germany the Nazis began to advance in support. In the election of 1928 the NSDAP had gained twelve seats in the Reichstag; in 1930 this had risen to 107; and in July 1932, the party gained 230 seats. Hitler refused to accept the Vice-Chancellorship, occasioning disappointment and criticism on the part of many in the party; but within a matter of months, the situation changed dramatically.

Conditions in Berlin were distinctive in several respects. Hitler had been distrustful of this reputedly left-wing stronghold in Prussia; but Joseph Goebbels, appointed Gauleiter of Berlin in 1926, had already been campaigning vigorously to increase support for the Nazi movement. Not only events, speeches and posters, but also the stimulation of political violence was an explicit tool in his campaign. With extraordinary organisational skill, Goebbels ensured the development of a network of Nazi cells across the city, and ignited fights between Nazis and Communists with little thought for the injuries and even deaths that were inevitably incurred. Indeed one such death, that of Horst Wessel (from blood poisoning contracted in hospital where he was being treated for a gunshot wound), provided the basis for a Nazi myth of a martyred hero, and a song, the Horst-Wessel-Lied, that would effectively become the Nazi national anthem once Hitler had taken power. In a masterly way, Goebbels not only organised a surprising rise in the number of Nazi supporters in Berlin but presented the party not as one that was actually causing the violence on the streets, but rather as the only one that could potentially restore law and order if it could deal a death blow to communists – a promise that would be rapidly acted upon following Hitler's appointment as chancellor.

The ineptitude of the ageing and senile President Hindenburg, as well as the miscalculations of prominent politicians, particularly the short-lived Chancellor Franz von Papen in the summer and autumn of 1932, massively exacerbated the political situation. On a flimsy pretext, von Papen dissolved the democratically elected Prussian government and installed Hermann Göring to replace it, giving him control of the Prussian police, and lifted the brief ban on the Nazi SA (*Sturmabteilung*, storm troopers) and SS (*Schutzstaffel*, protection squad). Rightly fearing that the Nazi NSDAP and the communist KPD would band together, with an antidemocratic 'wrecking majority' of far right and far left in the Reichstag, von Papen announced its dissolution and called new elections for the autumn. In the event, with evidence of a slight improvement in the economy, the national vote for the NSDAP declined slightly; but counter-productively, this served only to make Hitler appear less of a threat to the conservative elites. Following a short-lived and unsuccessful attempt by General von Schleicher to form a government in December 1932, von Papen joined others in machinations to persuade Hindenburg that they could tame Hitler and harness his evident popularity to their own ends. The result was Hitler's appointment as Reich Chancellor on 30 January 1933.

7
Nazi Berlin
Performance, Persecution, and Destruction

Ruth Andreas-Friedrich Notes the Deportation of Berlin Jews, 1942

On Wednesday, 2 December 1942, the Berlin-based journalist Ruth Andreas-Friedrich wrote in her diary: 'The Jews are disappearing in throngs. Ghastly rumors are current about the fate of the evacuees – mass shootings and death by starvation, tortures, and gassings. No one could expose himself deliberately to such a risk. Any hide-out is a gift from heaven, salvation in mortal peril.' She, and a few others, did their best to hide Jewish friends; but such helpers were far too few in number, and the risks too great, to make much of a difference for the tens of thousands now subjected to deportation and extermination. Three months later, on Sunday 28 February 1943, Andreas-Friedrich noted: 'Since six o'clock this morning trucks have been driving through Berlin, escorted by armed SS men. They stop at factory gates, in front of private houses; they load in human cargo – men, women, children. Distracted faces are crowded together under the gray canvas covers. Figures of misery, penned in and jostled about like cattle going to the stockyards. More and more new ones arrive, and are thrust into the overcrowded trucks with blows of gun butts. In six weeks Germany is to be "Jew-free".' The following year, on Friday 4 February 1944, Andreas-Friedrich wrote a long, agonised diary entry, including news from further afield: 'Already there is muttering about new deportations of Jews. We hear they have made a clean sweep in overcrowded Auschwitz and Theresienstadt. "Two thousand going out of here every week", a man from the Security Service boasted the other day when he was riding a suburban train with us. Two thousand a week. That makes over a hundred thousand human beings murdered annually by the State in one single camp."[1]

Even if the precise numbers and the details of the killing pits and death camps, away in the east, were not entirely clear, the massively destructive energies of Nazi rule were evident right from the outset – particularly to those who were victims of Nazi persecution. And by wartime, the experience of destruction was coming home to non-Jewish Germans too. On Tuesday 2 March 1943, Andreas-Friedrich gave a graphic description of Berlin after an air raid: 'The city and all the western and southern suburbs are on fire. The air is smoky, sulphur-yellow. Terrified people are stumbling through the streets with bundles, bags, household goods, tripping over fragments and ruins. They can't grasp it that they – they in particular – should have been the ones to suffer so. From cause to effect is a very long road.'[2] Ursula von Kardoff, another Berlin journalist who kept a diary through these years, recorded the scenes following the heavy air raid on Berlin on 3 February 1945, in which around 23,000 people were killed within barely an hour. On emerging from the air raid shelter, von Kardorff thought she would suffocate in the 'yellow, poisonous clouds of smoke'. The Columbus House at the Potsdamer Platz 'was burning like a torch'. Everywhere 'grey, bent-over figures' were stumbling through the smoke bearing their most treasured possessions; 'bombed-out, burdensomely laden creatures, who seemed to come out of nowhere and disappear into nowhere'. The advent of evening over the burning city 'was barely noticeable, since it had already been so dark during the day'.[3]

Hitler's rule radically transformed the character of Berlin and the lives and deaths of Berliners in every respect imaginable – and even beyond our capacity to imagine. The impact remains evident today.

• • •

Adolf Hitler never liked Berlin; and he sought to transform it as capital of the Nazi Third Reich. Hitler hailed from the borders of Austria (his father was a customs official), grew up in Linz, and lived for a while as a failed art student and down-and-out in Vienna, before coming to Germany. Based largely in Munich, he remained distrustful and suspicious of Prussians, and particularly Berliners. Along with Joseph Goebbels, Nazi propaganda minister and Gauleiter of Berlin, Hitler was determined to re-model the city; and his favoured architect, Albert Speer, was tasked with redesigning the physical landscape to turn it into a grandiose capital, to be renamed Germania, giving physical expression to Hitler's megalomaniac ambitions.

Nazi visions were never fully achieved; instead, the impact of Nazi rule was overwhelmingly destructive. The overwhelming majority of Berlin Jews who did not flee abroad in time were ultimately deported to ghettos, slave labour and extermination camps, as were Roma and Sinti; only a tiny minority survived. In the mid-1920s there were around 160,000 Jews in Berlin, roughly 4–5 per cent of the city's overall population but as high as 10–14 per cent in southwestern districts of the city, making it Germany's largest Jewish community by some margin; the next largest community was Frankfurt am Main, with around 26,000 Jews in 1925. Nearly 100,000 people of Jewish descent managed to leave Berlin before the war; the rest were variously deported, most of them to death, with perhaps 1,700 to 2,000 managing to survive in hiding.[4] Non-Jewish Berliners who opposed the Nazi regime, or who did not fit in with the ideals of the *Volksgemeinschaft*, were also subjected to exclusion, repression, and violence, often with fatal consequences. Those Berliners who variously supported, went along with, or had little choice but to accommodate themselves to the Nazi regime, were exposed in wartime to devastating air-raids by the Allies, and in the final days, with the Russian advance and occupation, those still resident in the city experienced an unprecedented wave of destruction, frequently accompanied by the more intimate violence of mass rapes and suicides.

The dozen years of Nazi rule were transformative in just about every respect; indeed devastating. The landscapes of Berlin today, and its multiple scars and conflicting self-representations, cannot be understood without confronting this deep caesura in its history.

The Enactment of Power

Berlin's topography of power changed dramatically under Nazi rule. The enactment of Nazi power started on the day that Hitler was appointed Chancellor, with a celebratory torch-lit parade of the SA entering central Berlin from the Tiergarten, through the Brandenburg Gate, and turning down Wilhelm Straße to the Reich Chancellery. This was well organised, and accompanied by cheering crowds; Goebbels even organised a repeat performance the following evening in order to ensure a good photographic record of the event. Many such organised parades and rallies would follow, very soon totally displacing attempts by opponents of Hitler to make their views heard (Figure 7.1).

Within barely four weeks of assuming power, the Nazis benefitted from an arson attack on the Reichstag. On February 27, 1933, the building was engulfed in flames; a lone figure, a mentally unstable Dutch communist by the name of Marinus van der Lubbe, was apprehended at the scene and later that year convicted

Figure 7.1 SPD demonstration against Hitler and the NSDAP, Lustgarten, 19 February 1933
Supporters of the Social Democratic Party (SPD) demonstrating against Hitler in front of the Berlin Cathedral. Just over a week later, the Reichstag fire gave Hitler a pretext to declare a state of emergency and inaugurate a crackdown on left-wing political opponents.
United States Holocaust Memorial Museum, 45000, courtesy of National Archives and Records Administration, College Park

and sentenced to death. Although no wider conspiracy could be identified – and unconfirmed rumours flew about the Nazis themselves having very likely instigated the fire – Hitler seized the opportunity to crack down on communists and pronounce a state of emergency. Yet even so, in the national election held under deeply constrained conditions less than a week later, on 5 March 1933, the NSDAP still did not gain an overall majority: nationally, the party garnered 43.9 per cent of the vote, while in Berlin barely over one third (34.6 per cent) of the electorate cast their vote for Hitler's party. It took a further masterly public performance, on the so-called 'Day of Potsdam' just over two weeks later, for Hitler to enact a symbolic display of continuity with Frederick the Great and President Hindenburg, against the backdrop of Potsdam's Garrison Church, to placate the traditional conservative right. When the newly elected parliament convened in Berlin's Kroll Opera House, since the charred and gutted Reichstag was now unusable, the centrist parties were willing to support an Enabling Decree according Hitler significant power; despite being subjected to intimidation, Social Democrats were alone in raising voices of protest, while communist deputies had been completely barred from entry.

Equally visible were actions against victims of Nazi persecution on 'racial' grounds. This also affected non-Jewish Berliners – now designated, in Nazi racial terms, as 'Aryan' – in a variety of ways. At the beginning of April 1933 there was a Nazi-organised boycott of Jewish shops and businesses; SA men and Hitler youths stood guarding the entrances and intimidating customers, while plaques on the offices of lawyers or doctors were defaced with signs informing clients that these were Jews. This boycott clearly inconvenienced non-Jews in Berlin, as elsewhere, and some tried to ignore it. Given the relative unpopularity of the boycott, it was soon officially called off. Within a week, however, a new law was passed to exclude people of Jewish descent – including even those with only one Jewish grandparent – from state employment, covering a wide range of professions. There were a few temporary exemptions relating to war service, in consideration of President Hindenburg's sensibilities, later rescinded after his death. While some 'Aryans' privately uttered criticisms, in solidarity with Jewish friends, there was no open opposition. Far from inconveniencing non-Jews, this measure opened up new opportunities and possibilities for promotion. Exclusionary policies and practices continued over the following years until the final disappearance of Jewish Berliners, whether by emigration in the 1930s, or wartime deportations and extermination. Later many non-Jews would be unwilling to acknowledge the extent to which they had been complicit in, or had benefitted from, these developments. Yet these changes inaugurated a massive transformation in the character of Berlin society.

Exclusion of 'non-Aryans' was accompanied by public displays attempting to create a sense of community among *Volksgenossen* or 'national comrades'. The Tempelhof Field was used for a Nazi version of the traditional May Day celebration, with hundreds of thousands of workers in attendance, some enthusiastic, others unwillingly dragooned. The following day, raids on trade union offices rapidly made clear Hitler's intention to quash workers' rights and quell any independent labour movements. On 10 May 1933, on the square outside the State Opera (and in university towns across Germany) Goebbels orchestrated the symbolic burning of books by people reviled by the Nazi regime. Included were not only books by Jewish authors but also, for example, novels by Erich Kästner (who was personally present to witness the burning), Thomas Mann, and others deemed hostile to Nazism, including French, British, and American writers, as well as works from the library of Magnus Hirschfeld's progressive Institute of Sexology. Unlike the widespread complicity of people in benefitting from the exclusion of Jews from businesses and professional positions, the specific incident and location has since made this relatively easy to commemorate, by marking the absence of books in the form of empty bookshelves.

Meanwhile, alongside regular police cells and prisons, many buildings and cellars in Berlin were rapidly repurposed as sites of terror, largely carried out by members of the SA against political opponents. In these improvised sites, often termed 'wild concentration camps', people perceived as threats to the Nazi project were held under brutal conditions, starved, taunted, and maltreated. In the so-called Köpenicker Blutwoche (Blood Week) in June 1933, around 500 left-wing opponents were beaten up, arrested, and imprisoned, and more than ninety were killed. Those who died included a young Social Democrat, Anton Schmaus, who was a carpenter studying to be an architect. A group of SA men had broken into the house where he lived with his parents and siblings; in self-defence he shot two of them. Then, having escaped from the others, he naively went to inform the police. Over the following months, Schmaus was moved from police custody into a police hospital; but he was eventually fatally wounded by the SA. Given the hundreds of deaths of left-wing political resisters occasioned by the 'Köpenick Blood Week' it became a focal point for memorialisation in the communist GDR; highly politicised memorials still bear testimony to these 'martyrs' to the communist cause. Other sites of early terror, such as the former SA prison in Papestraße in western Berlin, have also become memorial sites. But many locations where Nazi thugs beat up those who dared to speak out against the Nazi regime now pass unnoticed. At the time, however, the terror was all around to see.

Few Berliners could have been unaware of the central powers of repression. Over the following years, the apparatus of terror expanded and changed. The SA was increasingly seen as an unruly force and a potential threat to the army. In late June 1934, Hitler orchestrated the 'Night of the Long Knives', effectively beheading the SA by killing key individuals, murdering even his loyal follower and friend, SA leader Ernst Röhm. The SS expanded its powers and began to transform the structures and institutions of repression. The early concentration camp at Oranienburg, on the S-Bahn to the north of Berlin, was transformed into the SS-run concentration camp of Sachsenhausen; this camp illustrates both the range of political prisoners and the exploitation by industrialists of concentration camp inmates for their labour. SS-Reichsführer Heinrich Himmler progressively took control of the police forces as well as the SS, and from September 1939 the Reich Security Head Office (RSHA) enjoyed palatial headquarters alongside the Gestapo in Prinz-Albrecht-Straße, just around the corner from Göring's Air Ministry and the Reich Chancellery. Following heated controversies in the late 1980s, an exhibition and documentation centre, now securely established as the Topography of Terror, was constructed on the bombed-out site of this former terrifying centre of repression.

Policies to construct a supposedly 'racially' pure and homogeneous 'national community' proceeded alongside outright violence, including discriminatory legislation and social policies on a national level. People with allegedly hereditary diseases – which could include anything from epilepsy to alcoholism, or even only the occasional inebriation – were subjected to compulsory sterilisation. 'Racial science' was introduced as a subject to be learned in schools. The 1935 Nuremberg Laws and subsequent regulations removed rights of full citizenship and banned intermarriage between Jews and 'Aryans', and tackled policies regarding the ambiguous status of 'half-Jews' or 'mixed-breeds', of whom, given high rates of intermarriage, there were large numbers in Berlin. In view of rising persecution, Jews from younger generations were disproportionately likely to emigrate, often leaving behind increasingly isolated and elderly parents who were less willing or able to leave their homeland and still hoped they would be able to sit it out. In 1936, Berlin's Roma and Sinti population was forcibly removed to a so-called 'Gypsy camp' in Marzahn, in preparation for Berlin's hosting of the Olympic Games. While some may have welcomed this move to 'clean up' the streets for international visitors, Berliners did not materially benefit from the removal of those stigmatised as gypsies in the way that many did from the exclusion of Jews.

On 9–10 November 1938, what later became known as *Kristallnacht* ('night of broken glass') was a nationwide orgy of organised violence, with arson attacks on synagogues, and the smashing up of Jewish homes and businesses, across the now expanded Greater German Reich, including Austria, which had been annexed earlier that year. The night of violence was followed by mass arrests and incarceration of adult male Jews. In Berlin, the great synagogue in Oranienburger Straße and a smaller one in Prenzlauer Berg surprisingly largely survived this assault, with differing rescue stories attached. But most others, like the synagogue on Fasanenstraße, just off the Ku-Damm, were ruined. Some that were only partially destroyed, such as the synagogue in Schöneberg's Münchener Straße, were later affected by war damage; with the destruction of the area's formerly flourishing Jewish community, the ruins were simply demolished after the war, replaced now by a memorial plaque. In 1938, there were sharply divided reactions among the wider population towards these acts of extreme physical violence against synagogues, Jewish symbols and sacred objects, and against Jews themselves and their property. Some Berliners joined in acts of public humiliation, or seized the opportunity to loot goods scattered on the streets outside Jewish businesses; but others muttered muted criticisms, and a few sought to help victims in private by offering shelter, food, and clothing, even helping individuals trying to avoid arrest. Whatever their initial responses to the violence, many subsequently benefitted from the expropriation of Jewish property through 'aryanisation', a process that was stepped up in the wake of *Kristallnacht*, again radically transforming the character of Berlin's society and economy.

Virtually no-one at this time could plausibly claim they 'knew nothing about it', the refrain repeated so often after the war by those refusing to acknowledge guilt or responsibility for the violence perpetrated against fellow-citizens who did not fit Nazi visions for the future. But the combination of Nazi activism and widespread conformity or passivity brought about a radical change in the character of Berlin society even in the peacetime years. Transformation was evident too in the built environment.

The Capital of the Nazi 'National Community'

The grandiose plans of Hitler's architect Albert Speer are often highlighted when considering the impact of Nazism on Berlin. His model for Germania, as Hitler wanted to rename the city, included a major north–south axis, as well as an east–west axis, with a triumphal arch that would be three times larger than the Arc de Triomphe in Paris, and a massive Hall that would not merely overshadow the Reichstag, but more or less eclipse it entirely. Fortunately for Berlin, these megalomaniac plans were not realised in their full magnitude. A squat, round, heavy concrete tower (*Schwerbelastungskörper*) still bears witness to the plans, now sitting more or less deserted, surrounded by weeds and flimsy fencing in a nondescript patch of ground at a road intersection in Tempelhof (Figure 7.2); it was originally designed to test out the weight that Berlin's swampy sandy soil could bear, in advance of any significant building works on an arch at the projected southern end of the axis. Elsewhere, as was so typical of Nazism, the impact of the project was entirely destructive and most evident in the absences it produced: large areas of housing, mostly in the central Tiergarten area, were demolished and cleared, in preparation for construction work that did not in the end materialise, while many Jews were forced out of their homes to make way for

NAZI BERLIN

Figure 7.2 *Schwerbelastungskörper* (heavy load-exerting body)
One of the few visible remnants of architect Albert Speer's
schemes to realise Hitler's grandiose vision of rebuilding Berlin
as 'Germania', this cylindrical body was designed to test the
weight-bearing capacity of Berlin's swampy, sandy ground
before erecting a huge triumphal arch, planned to be around
three times the size of the Arc de Triomphe in Paris.
Photograph by the author

'Aryans' who had been displaced by plans for demolition and reconstruction. There was also a never fully realised plan to reconstruct the old historic kernel of Berlin around Molkenmarkt as a new administrative centre. In preparation, medieval buildings in the old quarter near the Town Hall were torn down in 1936. But while much of Berlin's older heritage was destroyed or displaced, as with so much else in Nazi plans, the new vision was never achieved. A focus on Speer and Hitler, pictured together leaning over models of the nightmarish city they were planning for the Thousand Year Reich, can distract attention from the many other ways in which the physical fabric of Berlin was transformed during this period.

Most obvious in terms of what was actually constructed, of course, was the huge arena and surrounding rally grounds designed by the Berlin architect Werner March for the 1936 Olympic Games. Specifically taking inspiration from Roman and Greek antiquity, the Olympic Stadium replaced the previous German Stadium and could accommodate as many as 110,000 spectators. It was augmented by the May Field, allowing space for a further quarter of a million people to watch outdoor events such as gymnastics, or to attend rallies such as the May Day demonstrations. The adjacent Langemarck Hall was constructed as a national monument to commemorate young Germans who had 'died a hero's death' in the First World War, named in honour of the large number of students who had been killed in the 1914 Battle of Langemarck. Altogether, the Olympic grounds, which included a swimming pool complex and other sports facilities, were designed less to encourage individual physical prowess than to represent commitment to the national community, glorifying personal sacrifice in honour of a greater cause. Renovated and still in use as a popular sports arena, this area continues to convey a sense of the enormity and oppressive atmosphere of Nazi visions.

Equally obvious were the politically significant building projects that were initiated soon after Hitler came to power. Berlin was still seen with some suspicion by the Nazis as a centre not only of older monarchical, aristocratic, and Prussian traditions, but also of more recent left-wing politics ('Red Berlin'); it was important to stamp a new mark on the seat of government. The Wilhelm Straße, running south from Unter den Linden and accommodating significant governmental buildings, was accordingly redesigned to give spatial expression to the imposition of Nazi power. A grandiose new Reich Chancellery was built for Hitler, complete with a marble hall, with every aspect designed to overwhelm and impress visitors by the might of the charismatic Führer. Across the road from the Reich Chancellery was Joseph Goebbels' Reich Ministry for Public Enlightenment and Propaganda, established in March 1933 in an eighteenth-century palatial mansion that was then extended, as Goebbels' empire grew, and given a distinctively Nazi façade. This embodied the ways in which culture, in Berlin and nationally, was increasingly constrained by censorship, and brought under Nazi control with the political reorientation of film, theatre, the visual arts, journalism, and creative writing. Further down the Wilhelm Straße the extensive hulk of Göring's Air Ministry still looms over the surrounding area, reflecting both his own pomposity and power, and the significance accorded to the air force. The importance of flight was emphasised too in the Tempelhof airport, its entrance further developed in characteristically grandiose Nazi style with the eagles on the outer walls still conveying traces of the former atmosphere, even if the accompanying swastikas have been removed.

Not all of these clearly Nazi buildings have survived. The remains of Hitler's Chancellery were blown up after the war, and some of the marble was re-used in Soviet war memorials. The underground bunker where Hitler finally committed suicide was also subsequently destroyed and filled in. Some ghastly murals conveying a nightmarish sense of SS morals and fantasies were however discovered in an adjacent bunker, for Hitler's support staff and protection squad, the SS-Leibstandarte 'Adolf Hitler', in the course of the demolition of the Berlin Wall in 1990. Following careful excavation and recording of the images, this too was filled in and covered. A nearby bunker next to the Anhalter Bahnhof, in which around 10,000 Berliners crammed themselves in a vain attempt to escape the bombing in the closing months of the war, was however deemed less politically contaminated and has now been devoted to a 'Berlin Story' tourist exhibition. Other buildings were quietly re-purposed. Göring's Air Ministry was redeployed in the GDR as the House of Ministries, garnished with a pro-GDR mural, and in united Berlin became the Finance Ministry, with the mural now countered by a photo-montage referencing the 1953 uprising against communist rule. This small corner in Berlin dramatically juxtaposes multiple historical layers and competing, clashing political ideologies.

Less easily noticed, or less obvious to those not actively seeking out the remnants of Nazi architecture, are numerous traces of Nazi ideology in residential estates and mundane institutional buildings across the city. Around Fehrbelliner Platz and the Hohenzollerndamm, for example, administrative buildings still in use today clearly betray elements of the Nazi architectural vision. The Finance Office in Charlottenburg still sports a characteristic eagle over its front entrance portal, while the swastika at the eagle's feet was never removed but merely covered up by the street number after the war. The huge swimming pool – at that time the largest indoor swimming pool in Europe – built for the Nazi cadet training school and barracks of the SS-Leibstandarte 'Adolf Hitler' in Finckenstein Allee, now adjacent to the Federal Archives in Lichterfelde, has been renovated and remains in use. Buildings for Hitler Youth meetings and activities were constructed in different areas of Berlin, including the Hitler Youth Home designed for a 1937 exhibition by the architect Hanns Dustmann to look like a traditional half-timbered rustic building from an earlier century and then moved to the Volkspark Rehberge, where it still stands. Innumerable other buildings, from post offices or employment centres to diplomatic residences around the Tiergarten and even to the expanded Reichsbank, now the German Foreign Office, visually betray their Nazi origins but generally choose not to draw attention to this aspect of their past.[5]

New housing projects ranged in style from the traditional, harking back to an imagined 'homeland' (*Heimat*), with hints of kitsch, or reminiscent of Grimms' Fairly Tales, to the monumentalist and the functional.[6] Curiously, given the political reputation of the modernist Bauhaus School – closed down under Hitler, with prominent exponents fleeing the country – individual Bauhaus architects continued working at this time, lending their stylistic preferences even to works serving the Nazi cause. Also notable are the continuities in personnel and styles between Nazi architecture and what was to come after the war in the two states that replaced the Third Reich. But much of the built environment constructed during the Third Reich was distinctive, specifically designed to create an atmosphere and facilitate a way of life that was imbued with Nazi ideology.

A particularly striking illustration of the ways in which Nazi ideology informed architectural practice is the *SS-Kameradschaftssiedlung* (SS comradeship settlement) in the woods by the lake of Krumme Lanke in southwestern Berlin, now more neutrally known as the *Waldsiedlung* (woodland community) Krumme Lanke (Figure 7.3). This estate was based on a project conceived in 1936 by the SS Race and Settlement Office, and explicitly supported by Himmler in order to promote a sense of comradeship as well as providing a healthy environment for SS families in Berlin.[7] Housing was designed in an old-fashioned, semi-rural *Heimat* style redolent of southern Germany, with steeply pitched red-tiled roofs. There were differently sized homes according to status: larger, stand-alone houses for the higher ranks, and smaller terraced homes or apartments for

Figure 7.3 *SS-Kameradschaftssiedlung* (SS comradeship settlement), Krumme Lanke
This estate, in a picturesque lakeside location, was designed to promote well-being and camaraderie among those working in Himmler's SS Race and Settlement Office. The traditional architectural style represented an idyllic *Heimat* (homeland); despite street name changes, it still conveys a distinctively Nazified atmosphere.
Photograph by the author

lower levels in the SS hierarchy. Buildings were situated irregularly on roads winding and curving through the wooded landscape, with bounteous gardens – but no fences between plots, in order to encourage the sense of community. Conveniently situated close to a main highway into the city centre, the estate also had easy access to the nearby lakeside with its idyllic bathing beaches, as well as extensive woodland paths along streams and around other lakes through the Grunewald. Residents of this estate included SS-Officer and Director of the SS Hygiene Institute, Joachim Mrugowsky, who was responsible for carrying out deadly experiments on inmates of concentration camps; found guilty in the 'Doctors' Trial' after the war, he was executed in 1948. Nazis who worked for the three main offices of the SS in Berlin could hardly have enjoyed better living conditions; many street names were subsequently changed, but how today's residents of this unmarked but still clearly Nazi settlement feel about the murky political past of their accommodation is another question.

Less idyllic and less widely noticed, but equally imbued with Nazi ideology, is the estate built for Berlin's ever-growing working population around Grazer Damm in Schöneberg, which was the largest communal housing project in Berlin under Nazi rule. Speer had in fact planned a massive construction programme for more than 650,000 new flats in Berlin, and this estate was designed as a huge settlement at the southern end of his projected north–south axis. Unlike the architect-designed estates of the 1920s in the Hufeisensiedlung (horse shoe estate) in Britz, or in Siemensstadt, the Grazer Damm estate was from the start built with an eye to cutting costs, and did not include the balconies that are prevalent in German apartment blocks. But it did feature an unusually wide boulevard avenue – not in order to give residents enhanced access to light and air, or for their enjoyment during leisure time, but because even when construction was started in peacetime the likelihood of air warfare was borne in mind, with the width of the street affecting potential fireball effects of bombing. It was, in short, explicitly designed for a working population in wartime. It was also garnished with Nazi symbols, including a figure of a Hitler Youth that still adorns one of the communal doorways, embodying the ideology of youthful commitment to the cause (Figure 7.4).

Figure 7.4 Hitler youth relief on housing estate, Grazer Damm
Even everyday housing for workers was designed with
ideological intent; here, a member of the Nazi youth
organization, the Hitler Jugend (HJ), still stands in front of a flag
in a determined pose above a doorway on a housing estate.
Photograph by the author

Elsewhere in Berlin, Nazi housing projects included smaller and single family homes. For people included in the Nazi 'national community', the individualist pursuit of better living conditions, including private housing, was in the peacetime years facilitated by and perfectly compatible with the Nazi collective vision and aims.[8] Meanwhile, city streets and public spaces were pervaded by Nazi sounds and symbols, with loudspeakers transmitting Nazi speeches, ubiquitous collections for Nazi charities such as the 'Winter Relief Fund' (WHW), people in uniform bearing swastika armbands, and compulsory displays of swastika flags on specific occasions. From 1935 onwards, Jews were forbidden to display such flags, in this way often drawing unwelcome attention to their places of residence. People were also affected by 'block wardens' keeping an eye on residents, or neighbours watching who went in or out and reporting on anything deemed untoward. As Jews, socialists, and other non-Nazis variously left or were forced to move out of their homes, the character of residential areas began to change.

The 'Aryanisation' of Jewish property took off during the 1930s. Well-known department stores, often founded or owned by Jews, were taken over by 'Aryans', as were innumerable smaller Jewish shops and businesses that had managed to stay afloat for a while after the boycott of April 1933. Particularly after *Kristallnacht* in November 1938, Jews were squeezed out of the economy almost completely; many had already lost their positions, and most of those who remained were now forced to sell up at knock-down prices. In the wake of mass arrests and incarceration in the winter of 1938–39, some Jews managed to get out: those who were lucky enough to gain a visa on highly restricted immigration quotas, and had the necessary resources as well as sponsors abroad. Jewish Berliners who remained were predominantly elderly, socially isolated, and increasingly impoverished. Even before the deportations to the east that started in late 1941, virtually no Berliner could have been unaware of the discrimination and exclusion of Jews and the related transformation of Berlin society; even schoolchildren noticed the disappearance of their former Jewish classmates.

After the start of the war, in 1940 Robert Ley, head of the German Labour Front (DAF), was given responsibility for social housing. At this point, much attention was devoted to planning for reconstruction after the war, which was not expected to last long. Curiously, many of the plans developed at this time were put into effect under quite different political conditions in the 1950s, lending a surprising degree of continuity to early post-war styles. But undoubtedly the greatest impact of Nazism on the physical and social fabric of Berlin was brought about by the aggressive and genocidal war unleashed by Hitler.

Destruction: Berlin at War

Wartime experiences in Berlin varied with age, gender, politics, and – existentially – whether or not an individual was doomed to exclusion, deportation or death, or by contrast relatively privileged as a member of the Nazi 'national community'.

From 1939, Germans were directly affected by the misnamed 'euthanasia' programme to murder people with mental and physical disabilities, now deemed a drain on national resources; this was named 'T4' after the Berlin address, Tiergartenstraße 4, from which it was orchestrated. But for the first two years of the war, from 1939 to the summer of 1941, life for healthy 'Aryan' Berliners was little changed. Relatively easy German military victories, from the rapid defeat of Poland in the 'Blitzkrieg' or 'lightning war' of September 1939, through the 'Sitzkrieg' (stagnant war) of the winter of 1939–40, to the speedy defeat of western Europe, including France in the early summer of 1940, gave many Germans a feeling of invincibility. Patriotic sentiments and faith in the Führer were at a peak, even if attempts at defeating Britain were proving more difficult. Ordinary soldiers enjoyed a kind of military tourism, entering foreign countries as conquerors, writing home about their impressions and exploits, and sending some of the spoils of victory. The living standard of many Germans, including Berliners, was enhanced by receipt of luxury items such as wine, chocolates, and silk stockings, as well as meat and dairy products from abroad; increasingly, as Jewish properties were expropriated, other items such as household goods, furniture, and desirable articles of clothing including fur coats, came into circulation at knock-down prices. Millions of Germans were beneficiaries in one way or another of the persecution of the Jews of Europe, whether or not they were aware of it.

With the invasion of the Soviet Union in June 1941 the war began to affect Berlin in more radical ways. Increasing numbers of men were called up in the Russian campaign, as the German army was bogged down first by mud and then by the plummeting temperatures and snow of the Russian winter, for which they were ill-prepared; and hundreds of thousands of lives were lost, most notably in the disastrous battle for Stalingrad in 1943. With men away at the front, women were increasingly drawn into the labour force at home. In addition, growing numbers of foreign forced labourers (*Zwangsarbeiter*) were drafted in as an easily exploitable workforce. More than 400,000 people from more than twenty different nationalities were brought from abroad to work in Berlin. They were held under constrained conditions and on poor rations in more than 3,000 make-shift camps and barracks; Siemens alone employed more than 15,000 forced labourers, held in ninety-three camps. Most camps for forced labourers were simply reused or demolished after the war, but some barracks at one of the largest camps, in Schöneweide, have been preserved and host an exhibition portraying the plight and fates of former inmates (Figure 7.5).[9]

Things were infinitely worse for Berliners of Jewish descent. In September 1941, Berliners who had been categorised by the Nazis as Jews were forced to wear the Yellow Star, and emigration was forbidden. From October 1941 deportations 'to the east' began. Already at the end of November 1941 transports ended in death for many, including those Berlin Jews who arrived in Riga, in Latvia, only to be shot immediately in the forests of Rumbula. Others

Figure 7.5 Forced labour barracks, Schöneweide
During the war, with men away at the front, millions of foreign labourers were brought in to work in the Reich. More than 400,000 worked in Berlin alone, where they were held in around 3,000 makeshift camps and barracks, as in Schöneweide, which now houses an exhibition.
Photograph by the author

were deported to Kaunas (Kovno) in Lithuania, and Minsk in Belarus, or sent to the ghetto of Litzmannstadt (Łódź) in the annexed Warthegau area of defeated Poland; older Jews were often sent to Theresienstadt in the Protectorate of Bohemia and Moravia in defeated Czechoslovakia. Those considered capable of work were engaged in forced labour across the city until the spring of 1943; Jews who still remained in Berlin at this point were rounded up in what became known as the 'Factory Action', when they were taken to collection points for what the Nazis euphemistically described as 'evacuation' or deportation to the east.

The details and scope of what the Nazis termed the 'Final Solution of the Jewish Question', now more widely known as the Holocaust or Shoah, were coordinated in January 1942 at a meeting held in a spacious lakeside villa formerly owned by a Jewish family, picturesquely situated on the Wannsee lakeshore. Not only the obvious figures from the SS, Heydrich and Eichmann, but also representatives of government ministries and civilian administration were involved, spreading the web of 'knowledge' and responsibility for the mass extermination programme among wider circles. The location itself illustrates the expropriation of Jewish properties, including substantial villas previously owned by well-to-do German Jews. And the short time frame – just under nine years after Hitler's appointment – along with the enormity of the murderous agenda discussed in the meeting pose very starkly the fundamental question of how this could have come about.

Thousands of Jewish Berliners had lived in areas such as the Bavarian Quarter; even if 'Aryan' neighbours did not watch deportations with their own eyes, newly vacant apartments drew the attention of those eager to move in; or the arrival of new neighbours, sufficiently high in Nazi hierarchies to have taken over desirable accommodation, provided ample evidence of the scale of deportations. Reactions of ordinary Berliners to the very evident and visible persecution of Jews varied across a full range: from approval, willingness to participate and profit, through feelings of sympathy with victims, or a sense of shock and frustrated impotence, to more active attempts to extend help, or engage in rescue and resistance activities. One of the few public acts of protest related to the deportation of men in 'mixed marriages', when in late February and early March 1943 women demonstrated openly in

Rosenstraße. By definition far less visibly, between 1,500 and perhaps as many as 2,000 Berlin Jews managed to survive the war by 'going underground' – a higher number than survived in hiding anywhere else in the Reich. Berliners who helped Jews to hide included some individuals who were committed to this on political and moral grounds, such as the journalist Ruth Andreas-Friedrich. But the stories of survivors such as Marie Jalowicz Simon also illustrate how other Berliners – including in Simon's case even an old Nazi – may have inadvertently assisted Jews who had assumed a false identity.[10] The trade in forged documents was rife, but inadequate funds for a high quality forgery could result in almost certain unmasking and arrest.

Among Berliners who were not themselves subject to persecution, the atmosphere began to change, particularly when air-raids by the British RAF became more frequent in the winter of 1943–44, and once the Americans began bombing Berlin from the summer of 1944. Bombing continued over succeeding months, with massive attacks in early February 1945. Berliners repeatedly had to rush to overcrowded air-raid shelters, cellars, and underground stations when sirens sounded, and tried to accustom themselves as best they could to the perpetual anxiety, loss of sleep, and disruption to the rhythms of life, while many children were sent away to comparative safety in country areas. During the dreadful bombings of February 1945, nearly 4,000 people were killed and thousands more injured, while nearly half a million Berliners found their homes destroyed. By the end of March 1945, much of central Berlin was reduced to rubble and around one third of homes were no longer fit for human habitation.

Berlin's already militarised architecture was massively augmented during the war by the building of flak towers, bunkers, and air-raid shelters. Large towers with lookout points on the roof were constructed in 1940–42 in the Humboldthain and

Friedrichshain parks, and in the Zoological Garden. These were supposed to have places for around 8,000 civilians, but at times as many as 30,000 people managed to squash into the one at the Zoo. By August 1943, there were also 413 bunkers designed to accommodate 200,000 people, which only amounted to about five per cent of Berlin's population at the time but nevertheless helped to convey a sense of security. In total, there were some 207 bombing attacks on Berlin during the war, and more than one third of homes were rendered uninhabitable, either heavily damaged or fully destroyed. In 1945, 360 large bunkers remained in Berlin; most were blown up and the materials used for rebuilding, but the looming grey hulks of a couple are still extraordinarily present, one cutting through a post-war apartment block in Pallas Straße in Schöneberg, the other transformed into a private art gallery in Mitte. The remains of the massive flak tower in the Humboldthain park were simply covered with rubble, the ground landscaped and replanted, and a little hill created with winding paths to stunning views from the top.[11]

Civilians who remained in their homes and cellars found little protection, as much of central Berlin was reduced to ruins and rubble. But the war waged by the Allies was far from the only violence they had to fear at this time. On 20 July 1944, Hitler narrowly survived an attempt to blow him up in his East Prussian Wolf's Lair Headquarters. Those most closely involved in the plot were executed immediately; others were humiliated in a parody of justice, being screamed at by Judge Roland Freisler in the People's Court, before being given death sentences. This began an orgy of organised political violence over the following months, as some 2,891 individuals were brutally executed in Plötzensee Prison for alleged political offences; some were beheaded by guillotine, others hanged using meat hooks. In the closing weeks of the war, as the Russians closed in on Berlin and the final battle for control of its streets grew ever fiercer – with a shaking and clearly ill Hitler still holding out the hope of 'ultimate victory' or *Endsieg* through the secret 'wonder weapon' – anyone suspected even of being a deserter, or uttering defeatist sentiments, let alone being politically active, risked summary execution by shooting or being hanged from a lamp post.

The slogan 'enjoy the war, for the peace will be frightful' kept many going, and fear of Bolshevism was a powerful motive even if faith in the Führer was crumbling. From September 1944, old men and young boys were being called up into the *Volkssturm* militia, equipped with ill-fitting uniforms and sent out on suicidal missions to defend the streets, while women were also trained in the use of weapons. Whole classes of schoolchildren were called up to serve as anti-aircraft auxiliaries, keeping watch from the flak towers while thousands cowered inside.

As Soviet forces encircled and entered Berlin, Hitler finally committed suicide on 30 April 1945. The German leadership formally capitulated on 8 May 1945 in Karlshorst, in south-eastern Berlin. The city lay in ruins, devastated both by the effects of bombing and having been forced to continue fighting to the last. Surviving Berliners eked out a living among ruins, searching for food and fuel, and fearing rape or robbery by Soviet troops. In the face of bombings and bereavement, of physical violence and fear, of total uncertainty about the future, many preferred to take their own lives. It has been estimated that Red Army soldiers raped between 20,000 and 100,000 women in Berlin alone, and that around 10,000 of these women died afterwards, many by suicide. In April 1945 alone, some 3,881 people killed themselves in Berlin; by the end of the year 7,057 suicides had been officially reported for the city, certainly an underestimate of the true total of numbers of people who had preferred to put an end to their misery than go on trying to live through what became known as the 'Zero Hour' or *Stunde Null*.[12]

8
Double Visions (1)
Divided Berlin from the War to the Wall

Berliners Experience Defeat and the End of War, 1945

The defeat of Nazi Germany in 1945 was a moment of massive transformation, reshaping not only the political and physical parameters of the city's very existence, and the symbolic significance of the city, but also the personal lives of Berliners – in multiple and often mutually contradictory ways. As far as the occupying authorities were concerned, a top priority was simply to ensure that services to the city were restored and people could survive. But very soon, the emerging Cold War between the new western and Soviet superpowers displaced the war against Nazism; and divided Berlin became a central battleground in divided Europe.

Nazism and war had devastated Berlin almost beyond recognition. Vast areas of the city were reduced to ruins, with gaunt and windowless walls teetering uncertainly along the sides of rubble-heaped streets. Even relatively intact buildings were deeply pockmarked from the final days of fighting. The city's population had shrunk to little over a quarter of its pre-war level of 4.3 million; large numbers had been killed in battle, with horrific casualties in the closing months of the war, including the boys and men aged from sixteen to sixty who had been thrown into the *Volkssturm* ('people's troops') from September 1944. It was predominantly women, children, and the elderly who were now emerging from cellars, living in skeletal remnants of houses without walls or windows, and scrabbling around in the ruins for food, clothing, and possessions. When the city's population rose again to around two million, around half the pre-war level, many of the additional numbers were refugees and expellees from lost territories in eastern Europe, putting an extra strain on resources. Capacity to withstand calamities varied significantly with age, gender, social class, and particularly material resources and personal connections – as well as, among those without other means of survival, willingness to engage in pursuits such as prostitution or the black market.

Virtually all Berliners experienced acute hunger and fear about the future, as well as concern about missing loved ones. Disease, dislocation, and suicidal despair were widespread. Water, food and electricity supplies were disrupted, and civilian transport links were more or less non-existent. Those who tried to get around the rubble-strewn streets by bicycle faced not only potholes and punctures but also the risk of having this precious possession ripped away from them by Russian soldiers, along with their watches. Contemporary letters and diaries reveal that it was almost impossible to make a journey by bicycle without being attacked; even bicycle parts would be stolen while their owners were sleeping.

Although exact figures are impossible to calculate, given unwillingness to talk about it, perhaps one third of Berlin women were raped, even on multiple occasions; some committed suicide in the aftermath; and most lived in terror. Rapes by Red Army soldiers are captured vividly in contemporary diaries. The journalist Margret Boveri, for example, cycled across Berlin to pick up some of her possessions that had remained with friends in Dahlem. On arrival she at first did not recognise the 'old woman' who greeted her: with bloodshot eyes, black marks across her face, a 'hole' in her forehead, and just a few stumps of her teeth remaining 'like an ancient peasant woman'; suddenly Boveri realised with a shock that this was her friend Elsbeth, who had been

DOUBLE VISIONS (1)

seriously maltreated by Russian soldiers. Elsbeth recounted not only her own experiences but also how they had found their neighbours – 'Frau Giese and her four charming daughters and a Frau von Sydow and her daughters' – hanging in the cellar, with a Russian lying on the floor, snoring, between their corpses. Boveri had last seen the four daughters, aged from eight to fourteen, on an Easter Egg hunt, 'so happy and full of the joys of life'.[1]

Accounts of rape, while passed from one acquaintance to another and often recorded in diaries, were often suppressed in public because of the trauma and associated shame; more widely publicised were the images of supposedly strong 'rubble women' passing buckets of debris along human chains in an effort to clear the ruins. Forced by the occupying authorities into this heavy manual labour, many of these women were probably more resentful than enthusiastic about being effectively press-ganged into the physical reconstruction of their city. Yet the photographs have come to stand for a moment of 'building up again'.

Less frequently discussed in accounts of post-war Berlin are the ways in which many also had to face up to the consequences of their past involvement in Nazism. Denazification files held in the Berlin district archive (Landesarchiv), for example, provide fascinating insights into attempts to justify past Nazi affiliations and wartime activities. Walter K., a former member of both the SS and the NSDAP, claimed that he 'had not been able to believe the reports of atrocities that slowly trickled through', adding that 'indeed millions of Germans had passively watched and remained silent'. He also claimed, rather typically, that he had personally helped some Jews, and had provided one Jewish friend with food and shelter. The denazification commission in Treptow, a Soviet-controlled district in eastern Berlin, turned down Walter K.'s application on the grounds that it was self-contradictory: on the one hand, he had neither known nor believed anything about the persecution of Jews; yet on the other, he had allegedly taken the considerable risk of helping them. David K. too had his application rejected, despite his claim to have helped two young Russian girls in 1944 who were homesick – presumably forced labourers working in Berlin against their will – and had, so he said, provided a leather rucksack for a friend of 'mixed descent' whose Jewish cousin was trying to flee.[2] Neither of these applicants were denazified or given work permits at this time. More generally, stories circulated about how, for example, parents advised a son who had been involved in Nazi organisations to flee to the west, where they thought (rightly) that he would have a better chance of sliding through denazification without penalty; and how refugees and expellees from lost eastern provinces also had an easier time getting through denazification because they could claim all their papers had been burnt in the fighting in their lost homelands.[3] Meanwhile, memoirs by survivors of Jewish heritage or socialist inclinations often reveal prevailing hostility among a wider population that had become thoroughly imbued with antisemitism.[4]

It is only too easy to portray the post-war period as one of international high politics, repeatedly punctuated by extraordinarily dramatic moments, while 'ordinary Berliners' suffered or remained stoic in face of world historical events: the Soviet blockade and the western airlift that kept West Berliners warm, fed, and clothed through the winter of 1948–49; the political division of Germany and Berlin in 1949; the 1953 uprising against communist rule in East Berlin; and the continuing exodus of people from East Germany through Berlin, culminating in the 1961 erection of a Wall dividing the city into quite contrasting halves. These are the key moments on which current myths of Berlin are constructed: symbolic outpost of western freedom and democracy, survival under communist rule, divided city. Yet the turmoil and the uncertainties of the era were echoed, refracted, and experienced differently according to personal circumstances. The communist 'veterans' reports' penned at a later date in East Berlin, for example, give uplifting stories of how, often following a period as a prisoner of war, they had eventually seen the error of their former ways and had become convinced communists. These accounts by people from humble backgrounds, who felt they had been given new chances in life, provide quite different perspectives from those of post-war letters, diaries, or denazification files: they often claim the Russians were friendly to children, portray the 1953 uprising in terms of the official line about western *agents provocateurs*, and defend the construction of the Wall as ensuring a better future for the German Democratic Republic (GDR; *Deutsche Demokratische Republik, DDR*).[5]

Both the historical accounts and the conflicting memories of this transformative moment are deeply imprinted by the wider political and ideological divisions of the Cold War; Berlin was its broiling epicentre.

• • •

Occupation and Division

At the 1943 Yalta conference, it had been agreed that a defeated Germany would be administered by the Allies, and that Berlin would similarly be divided into different zones under Allied administration – initially the US, Britain and the USSR, but with France subsequently included and territory carved out of the western zones. Soviet forces initially controlled the city, having fought the final battle for Berlin and having occupied it before the western Allies could join them. With their initial advantage, the Soviets took as much out of the city as they could: valuable machinery, equipment, and goods including looted art treasures were transported back to the Soviet Union as 'reparations'. Living amidst the ruins, and plagued by a lack of reliable news channels, rumours flew; few Berliners knew what was happening on the international stage, although the signs of Russian takeover were widespread. There was widespread uncertainty as to what might be the best course of action to take, on a personal level.[6]

Once the western Allies arrived, the city was divided into the separate zones. Meeting in Potsdam from 17 July to 2 August 1945, the Americans, British, and Soviets initially agreed on broad abstract principles: denazification, demilitarisation, democratisation. They soon discovered that these principles meant something quite different in practice for the Soviets than for the western powers (Figure 8.1). Nor were the re-drawn borders in eastern Europe fully agreed, with the Soviet Union taking over the Baltic states and eastern Poland, while Poland was compensated by further territory in the west. The so-called 'Oder-Neisse' boundary was interpreted differently according to whether it was the western or eastern branch of the Neisse river that was held to be relevant; and since the Soviets had already taken the territory, the more westerly branch of the river became the de facto border of post-war Poland, remaining a point of contention until German reunification some 45 years later. Two years after the end of the war, the Allies also dissolved the state of Prussia, of which Berlin had so long been capital. The political status of the city was, in this way, radically transformed.

Tensions between the wartime Allies rapidly grew, and joint administration from Berlin's Red Town Hall eventually broke down. While the Soviets retained control over the central and eastern districts of the city, the western sectors were administered from Schöneberg Town Hall by the Americans, British, and French. The communists in the eastern sectors, under Walter Ulbricht, preferred to install puppet 'democrats' as nominally in charge while a communist deputy held the real power; but democracy in the Soviet sector was increasingly a sham. As tensions

DOUBLE VISIONS (1)

Figure 8.1 American and Soviet soldiers in front of a portrait of Stalin, 1945
American and Soviet soldiers were clearly still sufficiently friendly as joint administrators of Berlin under four-power control to pose together at this time. But the super-sized portrait of Stalin clearly indicates Soviet domination of central Berlin – only relinquished 45 years later.
United States Holocaust Memorial Museum, 26310.
Provenance: Aviva Kempner

between communists and social democrats grew, it became increasingly clear that the population preferred the re-founded SPD over the KPD; so in April 1946 the communists forced a merger between the two parties to produce the Socialist Unity Party (SED). Backed by Soviet power, the SED would effectively rule East Germany (from 1949 the German Democratic Republic, GDR) until 1989, initially under the control of Ulbricht and from

1971 under Erich Honecker. In western Berlin, the SPD refused to agree a merger with communists. In open competition with other newly founded political parties, the conservative Christian Democratic Union (CDU) and the liberal Free Democratic Party (FDP), as well as the KPD, the Social Democrats gained an overwhelming majority. The veteran socialist politician Ernst Reuter (who had emigrated in 1935 following a spell in a concentration camp) became democratically elected Mayor in West Berlin.

With growing international tensions, American policy priorities increasingly switched from dealing with former Nazis to concern about the advance of communism. Following the change of direction signalled in a speech by US Secretary of State George Marshall in 1947, in April 1948 US President Truman announced an economic recovery plan for Europe. The idea of the Marshall Plan was to inject both significant material support and technical knowhow into the shattered economies of post-war Europe in order to stave off the threat of growing communist movements. Aid was (intentionally) offered on terms that were unacceptable to the communist-controlled eastern zone; but West Germany would eventually benefit hugely from this financial support, playing a significant role in what became known as the 'economic miracle'. In the first couple of years after defeat, the black market was rife, and desired goods such as cigarettes and stockings became a common means of exchange; a currency reform was urgently required to introduce the Marshall Plan. In 1948, the old Reichsmark was replaced by the new Deutschmark – a currency also offered to the Soviet zone, which the communists rejected. The situation in divided Berlin now became acute.

At first, the Soviets attempted to block all land and water routes into West Berlin, in order to starve it out of existence. But despite attempts at interference, they were not able to block air routes. With the Americans determined to keep the city going at

DOUBLE VISIONS (1)

virtually any price, an allied airlift was organised to drop tonnes of supplies into the western zones; this even required the rapid construction of a new airport, Tegel, on a military training base, to assist the western powers by complementing the Tempelhof airfield. With flights dropping cargoes not only of essential supplies, but also little parachutes with packets of sweets and raisins to children waiting excitedly below, West Berlin was transformed into a symbol of freedom and democracy, the last outpost of the west amidst a sea of communism. Yet for Berliners, the future was uncertain; in view of the difficulties of everyday life, the reports of repression, arrests, and imprisonment in the Soviet sector, or painful memories of friends who had met violent deaths, even committed democrats and anti-Nazis such as the journalist Ruth Andreas-Friedrich daily wondered whether to stay or to leave.[7] It was a frantically difficult and uncertain time for Berliners in both east and west, as rumours flew and no one knew what the Allies might do next, or how international tensions would play out.

In May 1949, the Soviets realised that their attempt to blockade Berlin had been unsuccessful, and abandoned the policy; and the western powers no longer needed to keep the city alive through the airlift. The western zones of Germany had already come together as an economic unit – first the American and British in 'Bizonia', subsequently joined by the French – and in May 1949 the Federal Republic of Germany (FRG) was formally established with a 'provisional' constitution, or Basic Law, with its capital in the provincial Rhineland town of Bonn in the far west of Germany. In October 1949, the communists followed suit, establishing the German Democratic Republic (GDR) in the Soviet zone of occupation.

Technically, Berlin remained under four power control, and for two decades the west even refused to recognise the GDR which it continued to call 'the zone'; in practice, the communists eventually restyled their part of the city as 'Berlin, Capital of the

GDR'. But this was a very different kind of capital city from the Berlin of Imperial, Weimar, or Nazi Germany.

While West Berlin was still a city in ruins, following the 1948 currency reform there were signs of economic recovery, with American aid giving a massive boost to the West German economy more generally. Moreover, the conditions for political organisation and cultural expression were markedly more liberal than in the GDR. From the moment the communists took over in the eastern sectors of the city, it was apparent that there were severe constraints on freedom of speech and association. Life was increasingly uncomfortable for anyone who wanted, in Rosa Luxemburg's words, the freedom to 'think differently'. Even so, some individuals who had been in exile during the Third Reich, including prominent writers such as Bertolt Brecht and Anna Seghers, chose to return to East Berlin, still harbouring hopes that a better society could be developed there than in the west, where they saw the continuity of structures and the retention of former Nazis in high places. Victor Klemperer, a Professor of Philology who had for years survived Nazi persecution through the support of his non-Jewish wife, Eva, and then escaped deportation only by the chance coincidence of the bombing of Dresden, also chose to remain in the GDR. Although he was deeply critical of the communist east, and repeatedly recorded incidents of anti-semitism, he felt that the continuing presence of Nazis and prevalence of national socialist sentiments in the west offered even less chance of renewal and the creation of a better society: it was, for Klemperer, a matter of a choice between two evils.[8]

Relatively stringent denazification in the Soviet zone had entailed not only political turnover but also meant that large numbers of professionals, such as teachers, at least initially lost their jobs while reliable communists, preferably of working-class or peasant origins, were installed in their place. A notable exception to radical turnover was the medical profession, where technical expertise in surgery and specialised treatment of the sick was initially prioritised over political credentials in a period when illness was rife and disabilities widespread, including the long-term impact of war wounds.

Radical socioeconomic reforms under communist rule, starting during the occupation period and continuing in the GDR, entailed the forced dispossession of landowners and redistribution of land, first in non-viable small plots to individuals who often lacked both the tools and the expertise to farm profitably on their own, and subsequently followed by sequential waves of collectivisation into different types of agricultural cooperative (*Landwirtschaftliche Produktionsgenossenschaft*, LPG). The first major wave of collectivisation was in 1952–53, adversely affecting food supplies to the cities, including Berlin, precipitating a rise in the numbers of people seeking to flee to find a better life in the west. At this time also the long land border between the Federal Republic and the GDR began to be more tightly controlled, denuded of vegetation and with tracks along which tanks could roll, and now with a five-kilometre forced exclusion zone and enhanced border security rendering flight across this border far more difficult. But people still moved across the sectors within Berlin, with many Berliners working on one side but living in another, or visiting friends and family, or even simply crossing the border for a little bit of shopping (desired goods in the western sectors, cheaper items, and 'bargains' in the east). The second major wave of agricultural collectivisation, in 1960–61, and consequent food shortages and increase in numbers of flights west, would play a role in the final tightening up of this remaining escape route by the building of the Wall.

The early expropriation of significant industrialists and capitalists, particularly those with a Nazi past, was followed by increasing pressure on members of the bourgeoisie and independent owners of small business. Major production was taken over in the so-called 'People's Own Enterprises' (*Volkseigene Betriebe*, VEBs), or factories allegedly 'owned' by the people but effectively run by the state. Central planning of the economy introduced difficulties in production and supplies. This was further exacerbated by the fact that East Germany was cut off from its former economic links with western areas of Germany and forcibly incorporated into the less economically developed eastern bloc. Far from receiving outside assistance in recovery – as in the case of American aid to West Germany – eastern Germany had not only been bled by early reparations to the Soviet Union but was also now having to contribute to the regeneration of less economically developed regions in the Soviet bloc.

Many people initially simply remained or returned to where they had families and homes, assuming current conditions were provisional, temporary, and uncertain about the future. During the 1950s, many Berliners still crossed the inner-Berlin border daily, some commuting between work, home, family, and leisure activities. Some facilities still operated on a city-wide basis, such as the S-Bahn transport network, which was run by East Berlin, while the U-Bahn was controlled by the west. But increasingly, each half of the city was becoming a self-contained community. Even before formal division, it had already become evident that the city was splitting in half. Tegel Airport first complemented (and eventually took over from) Tempelhof airport to serve visitors to West Berlin; East Berlin's air traffic, meanwhile, focused on the re-purposed Schönefeld airport to the southeast of the city, originally constructed in 1934 for the Henschel aircraft production works which from 1936 supplied planes to the Luftwaffe. Transport links, whether by land, water or air, were beginning to be severed and subjected to political control. Moreover, West Berlin began to prioritise the motorcar as the most flexible means of transport for

DOUBLE VISIONS (1)

an individualistic, supposedly liberal lifestyle. While new roads were built, including highspeed city freeways, and the U-Bahn was extended, the tram network in the western half of the city was progressively dismantled. The last tram in the western sectors was closed in 1967. Even a third of a century after reunification in 1990, the public transport map of the city still betrays the contours of Cold War division, with the intricate network of tram lines in eastern Berlin barely augmented by a couple of extensions into the western part of the city. Any tourist can in this way easily guess when he or she has crossed the former border, even where there are no other visible traces of the Wall.

In the East, the imposition of communist rule rapidly effected fundamental changes. Despite the existence, formally, of distinct political parties and mass organisations with pre-allotted numbers of seats to represent separate interests in the 'People's Parliament' (*Volkskammer*), the GDR was effectively a one-party dictatorship under the rule of the SED and its Politburo. The SED always held the reins of power, using the so-called 'bloc parties' to harness particular groups and interests: the Christian Democratic Union (CDU) for the religiously committed, the Liberal Democratic Party (LDPD) for the middle classes, the German Peasants' Party (DBD) for farming communities, and even a National Democratic Party (NDPD) to appeal to conservative nationalists. These, alongside significant mass organisations – notably the trade union organisation, the FDGB (League of Free German Trade Unions), and the organisations for youth, the FDJ (Free German Youth), and women, the DFD (Democratic Women's League) – were designed to channel and shape the views of people who might not be attracted to communist ideology but were willing to engage in some way.

The GDR was, moreover, a police state, with a growing presence of the state secret police or Stasi (*Staatssicherheitspolizei*).

Formally founded at the beginning of 1950, this grew rapidly over the following years, and fear of surveillance became a constant feature of life for many East Germans.

East Berliners were clearly constrained – by the transformations in property ownership, by the discrimination against members of the bourgeoisie (including children of professionals being blocked from university places), and by the constraints on freedom of speech and association. It remained, moreover, visibly a more drab and ruined landscape, where residents faced continuing material shortages of one sort or another. Yet in the 1950s, Berliners had little notion of how long division might last. It still appeared to many that current conditions were temporary, provisional, and many continued to hope for imminent change. In 1952, Stalin made overtures towards proposing a neutral, united Germany – likely designed more for propaganda purposes than as a serious suggestion with any chance of success. But whatever Stalin's intentions might have been, West German Chancellor Konrad Adenauer, desperately keen on integration into western alliances and willing to jettison eastern Germany in the process, chose to reject Stalin's approaches with little serious consideration.

Popular unrest in the GDR was most dramatically expressed in the uprising of 17 June 1953. In face of growing economic difficulties and the consequences of agricultural collectivisation, the communists had been taking further measures, including the enhanced fortification of the inner-German border, in 1952 augmented by a five-kilometre exclusion zone designed to prevent unreliable spirits from getting too close. Somewhat against the spirit of the 'workers' and peasants' state', Ulbricht now also sought to increase the productivity of workers without any additional pay. Following the death of Stalin in March 1953, there were potential changes in Soviet policies, and Ulbricht was summoned to Moscow in an attempt to ensure that what were seen as excessively hard-line policies in the GDR were retracted. But on his return to the GDR Ulbricht sent out mixed messages, making some concessions to consumers while still retaining increased work norms for ordinary workers, precipitating significant discontent.

On 16 June, labourers on the prestigious building project in East Berlin's Stalinallee downed tools and marched to the GDR House of Ministries (formerly Göring's Air Ministry, now the Federal Ministry of Finance) to protest against the new policies; one seized a loudspeaker and called for a general strike the following day, a call that was relayed further by reporters for RIAS, the Radio in the American Sector, broadcasting from their office in Schöneberg. The news spread rapidly, and the following day strikes took places in cities and towns across the GDR. The uprising was rapidly suppressed by Soviet tanks rolling into the streets of central Berlin, occasioning possibly more than fifty deaths in the capital as well as unknown numbers of casualties and arrests in other parts of the GDR. Lacking in leadership, and in face of massively superior Soviet might, the strikers soon backed down and the protests fizzled out. While expressing disapproval, West German chancellor Konrad Adenauer passively looked on, as did the western Allies, and a major international crisis was averted – but at the expense of abandoning any chance of democratisation in the east, or early reunification of the divided state.

This first popular uprising in the communist bloc was a significant turning point, From now on, East Germans knew what they would have to face by way of repression by force, with the unpopular communist regime backed up by Soviet tanks. They also knew that the West would not risk sparking another war by intervening on behalf of the East German people. From the official communist perspective, of course, the capitalist West was the supposed instigator of the uprising through the alleged use of *agents provocateurs*. From a western perspective, by contrast, East

Germans were cast as innocent victims of communist oppression rather than as former Nazi enemies, while West Berlin now became a symbol of democracy to be defended at nearly all costs. The tracks were set for scripts that would roll out for another three and half decades, and are easily repeated in history books. Yet it was not such a simple choice, as contemporaries were aware. Klemperer, for example, who had freely chosen to engage in literary and political activities in East Berlin, was witness to the June 1953 uprising and the tales of 'Westrowdys having streamed in through the Brandenburg Gate'. During the following years he was repeatedly frustrated at constraints, clichés, and political repression, but nevertheless still held the East to be the 'lesser of two evils'.[9]

Building Two New Berlins

Already in the 1950s, the appearance of the war-damaged city was changing significantly. Rebuilding housing from the ruins was a top priority on both sides. In the first couple of decades after the war there were striking similarities, as architects with the same sorts of pre-war training and often inspired by common influences, such as the Bauhaus, continued to practise on both sides of the city; some indeed worked on new schemes in the east only to be attracted over to participate in rebuilding the west. The impact of ideological divergence and political competition was of course evident in some highly visible areas. Designed by the architect Hermann Henselmann, the Stalinallee in East Berlin was intended to be a prestige project to showcase imposing building styles and palatial apartments for ordinary people in the new 'Workers' and Peasants' State'. It was also broad enough to accommodate mass parades or military manoeuvres. In West Berlin, the 1957 International Architectural Exhibition Interbau presented a modernist alternative in imaginative designs for the Hansa

DOUBLE VISIONS (1)

Viertel in the Tiergarten, with Bauhaus styles much in evidence, and emphasis on individualism, variety, and freedom. A whole new quarter was constructed in the heavily bomb-damaged area, where remaining ruins were demolished to make way for a new church, educational facilities, a library, restaurants, and shops, alongside well-spaced apartment blocks in an area with plenty of greenery in between buildings. This was meant to showcase the new, forward-looking society of the west, with an exhibition on 'The City of Tomorrow', in contrast to the pompous yet drab facades in the East; and to contrast the ideological imperatives of individualism in the west, collectivism in the east.

Yet on both sides, economic considerations began to prevail over aesthetic or political aspirations. Grandiose GDR architectural ambitions were soon abandoned in favour of cheaper mass housing estates, particularly from the 1960s with the introduction of prefabricated concrete techniques. In West Berlin too housing needs were increasingly met by the rapid erection of functional concrete blocks, generally better maintained than in the east but aesthetically equally wanting. Moreover, while most West Berliners still lived in substandard housing amid the ruins, developers generally thought it cheaper and easier to demolish rather than renovate the large nineteenth-century housing blocks that could still have been salvaged; motorised transport arteries and massive concrete housing estates were prioritised over the preservation of older housing. Only decades later would this be seen as a form of cultural vandalism in the western side of the city. In East Berlin too, a similar shift in emphasis towards renovation – although without adequate material means to effect in practice – was evident by the 1980s. But in the meantime, on both sides of the divided city bomb-damaged housing was often simply demolished and replaced by the functional if ugly concrete structures so typical of the era. And indeed, many people who now for the first time experienced the luxuries of indoor toilets, bathrooms, and cooking facilities were delighted by these developments.

Some outward similarities notwithstanding, and despite continuing uncertainties about the future, it was nevertheless becoming increasingly clear that life would be very different in the contrasting sectors of Berlin.

West Berlin was effectively a political island, marooned within the wider sea of the GDR, and separated from both its immediate Brandenburg surroundings and from more distant western German hinterlands. The economy was insecure, and often faltering – not least because much of West Berlin's industry had been stripped out by the Soviets at the end of the war, and the city had not yet reoriented itself towards the service sector, let alone developed the wealth of creative industries that would proliferate in the reunited city half a century later. Even so, with massive subsidies from the Federal German government, the material conditions of life for West Berliners were palpably improving; and the city was run under democratic auspices. The past was never entirely absent, but often submerged under new layers, literally as well as figuratively (Figure 8.2).

Increasingly, the two sides of Berlin were developing distinct identities, somewhat like conjoined twins; intimately bound together yet trying to grow separately in often painful ways. Over time, there would be repeated doublings, as new art galleries, libraries, and concert halls were established, particularly in the western part of the city. East Berlin had the advantage of including the historic city centre, with its cultural and architectural heritage around the former royal palace or Schloss, the Museum Island, the Protestant and Catholic Cathedrals, the university, the state library, and the central boulevard of Unter den Linden leading to the Brandenburg Gate – where the communist sector came to an abrupt end. It ended too at the previously lively

DOUBLE VISIONS (1)

Figure 8.2 Layers of history: An old wartime bunker beneath a post-war West Berlin apartment block
A wartime bunker remains underneath a post-war apartment block straddling a road in Schöneberg, close to a school dating back to Imperial Germany. The name changes of the school – from Kaiserin Augusta through to Sophie Scholl – also symbolise changing values over time.
Photograph by the author

Potsdamer Platz, which was now turning into a deserted wasteland. The challenge for the communist regime was to imprint its own mark on historical legacies that it rejected on ideological grounds. One major early casualty was the Hohenzollern palace, the Schloss, which, with the exception of a balcony preserved for its alleged political significance, was in September 1950 dynamited and destroyed rather than preserved and renovated; this would occasion major public controversies after reunification.

West Berlin, by contrast, was largely lacking in similarly significant buildings, apart from the ruins of the already destroyed

Reichstag – which at that time had no parliamentary function, since the seat of West German government had been established in Bonn. But West Berlin was already beginning to replace what had been lost. The Free University of Berlin (FU) was founded in December 1948 in Dahlem, in the American sector of West Berlin, in protest against the political constraints experienced in the recently reopened old university on Unter den Linden, now renamed the Humboldt University, in the communist east. Other scientific and technical institutions in West Berlin were further developed, including the Technical University (TU). More broadly, the sense of a city centre was reoriented to the area around the Kurfürstendamm, and the nearby Zoological Gardens transport intersection became effectively West Berlin's central station. The Kaiser Wilhelm Memorial Church, which had suffered significant war damage, was preserved in its ruined state as a symbolic war memorial, rather than repaired and renovated, while new consumer-oriented shopping centres were developed all around (Figure 8.3). The German Opera in Bismarckstraße began to replace the loss of the eighteenth-century Opera House on Unter den Linden; and following the building of the Wall, with the apparent permanence of division, West Berlin's cultural landscape would be further renewed with the assistance of renowned architects, particularly in the bombed out square around the charming old church, the Matthäikirche (built 1846), west of Potsdamer Platz.

Culturally, too, the two sides of the city were diverging. In the east, the Free German Youth organisation (FDJ), founded already in 1946, was designed to socialise young East Germans into a socialist outlook, following a dozen years of Nazi indoctrination. From the mid-1950s, with growing fear of war between the two superpowers and the creation of NATO and the Warsaw Pact, both sides introduced conscription. Despite

DOUBLE VISIONS (1)

Figure 8.3 Kaiser-Wilhelm-Gedächtniskirche (Kaiser William Memorial Church) and Kurfürstendamm, January 1947
The war-damaged ruins of the church have been preserved as a 'warning memorial' (*Mahnmal*), with a new site for religious services alongside. The Kurfürstendamm was soon rebuilt and augmented by a commercial centre near the Bahnhof Zoo, West Berlin's main station.
United States Holocaust Memorial Museum, 67788, courtesy of Robert L. Kaplan

being politically controlled and increasingly subjected to paramilitary training, young East Berliners who were willing to conform nevertheless enjoyed communal activities and camps, including in East Berlin's Wuhlheide park and leisure grounds. Other young East Germans, particularly those from Christian backgrounds who preferred to receive confirmation in church rather than participating in the secular *Jugendweihe* ceremony, found themselves disadvantaged at school and admission to university. Similar difficulties arose if young adults tried to avoid conscription, although negotiations eventually led to the introduction in 1962 of alternative military service as 'construction soldiers' (*Bausoldaten*). In West Berlin, youth culture was far freer. Enthusiasm for western jazz music, Rock and Roll, and new stars such as Elvis Presley, were shared across both sides of the city, but far more easily accessible in the West. The growing youth culture – from the 1960s typified by androgynous clothing, jeans, and long hair for both sexes – was nevertheless frowned at by conservative older generations in the West, even if it was not politically constrained as in the East. Oddly, older Berliners in both East and West shared a suspicion of Americanisation, even if in the west the Americans were protectors and benefactors while in the east they were ideological arch-enemies.

Cementing Division

Growing discontent with an economically constrained and politically repressive system under communist rule meant that many East Germans – and not only Berliners – were continuing to use crossing points that were still open within Berlin, in order to escape via West Berlin to West Germany. By the later 1950s, hopes of reunification were evidently off the agenda. Yet the question of Berlin remained anomalous: not only a thorn in the side for the communists, but also a loophole allowing the continuing drain of talented, skilled workers to the west, posing serious challenges to economic planning and productivity.

By the end of the decade it was clear that some resolution was essential; and Soviet leader Nikita Khrushchev's proposed solution was to oust the western Allies from Berlin and incorporate it entirely within the Soviet bloc. A showdown with newly

DOUBLE VISIONS (1)

elected US President John F. Kennedy was unsuccessful, and deadlock persisted, with mounting fears from 1958 onwards that the Berlin crisis could precipitate the outbreak of a third world war. Ultimately, however, the communists arrived at a different solution. Ulbricht's explicit disavowal on 15 June 1961 – 'no one has the intention of erecting a Wall' – should have alerted people to what was secretly being contemplated.

The unfolding of rolls of barbed wire in order to encircle and close off the perimeter around West Berlin, starting on the morning of 13 August 1961, proved a horrific shock. Berliners stood and stared in disbelief; friends and family gestured and waved as the barbed wire was first unrolled between them and later concrete blocks were cemented to make a higher, more impenetrable barrier. Crowds gathered as a few individuals took the risk of jumping from upper storey windows of East Berlin buildings directly on the border, hoping to land unharmed in blankets held out for them by helpers below on West Berlin streets. Others waved tearfully at family and friends on the other side. One young East German border guard, the nineteen-year-old Hans Konrad Schumann, spent several hours on duty witnessing painful scenes of separation and emotional anguish, as well as being taunted by protestors chanting slogans in favour of freedom. Towards the end of his shift, Schumann suddenly took the decision to jump the wire himself. He alerted a western passer-by who called a police van in support, and jettisoned his gun as he leapt the fence. Although his escape was widely publicised in the west as a symbol of the human desire for freedom, and he built a new life for himself in Bavaria, Schumann remained deeply scarred by the trauma of abandoning home and family in Saxony. Following the fall of the Wall and German reunification, Schumann committed suicide.

There are no doubt many ways in which this story could be interpreted; but one thing was clear: the erection of the Wall in 1961 sealed both the division of Berlin and the division between West and East Germany. It had devastating human consequences: for those who sought unsuccessfully to escape and were shot, or were caught and imprisoned; for the families, friends, and communities who were now separated; and for members of the wider population who saw their fatherland torn apart in the battle between ideologies and superpowers, many of whom now lived in fear. Particularly in the East there was a sense of having been abandoned, living under considerably worse conditions – economically, politically, socially – than their former compatriots in the West, who seemed to be turning away from them and enjoying material success and political democracy with little thought for their plight.

The situation initially remained uncertain. As previously noted, US President John F. Kennedy visited Berlin on 26 June 1963, giving psychological support to Berliners and famously confirming his solidarity by pronouncing that he too was a Berliner ('Ich bin ein Berliner' – a grammatically incorrect construction which in effect suggested a donut, known as a 'Berliner' in German, causing some mirth despite the seriousness of the sentiment). But apart from Kennedy's rhetorical insistence on support for freedom and democracy, there was no desire to risk reigniting tensions by intervening in practice. In effect, from the later 1960s the attention of the Cold War superpowers was directed elsewhere (particularly Vietnam), and Berlin ceased to be a flashpoint in Europe.

Cementing the division of Berlin was symbolic of divisions throughout Europe and the wider world; but there were also distinctive aspects of the ways in which each side of the city developed in the years that followed. Division was devastating; but it also made all the difference to the history of Berlin – for at least a generation, and with reverberations well beyond.

9

Double Visions (2)

Divided Berlin from the Wall to Reunification

Luxemburg-Liebknecht Demonstration, January 1988

In January 1988, on the occasion of the official anniversary parade through East Berlin commemorating the murdered communist leaders Rosa Luxemburg and Karl Liebknecht, a few demonstrators were arrested before they could unfurl their banner. They were planning to march bearing a slogan that had not been officially approved; yet it was a quotation from Rosa Luxemburg herself, heroine of the communist movement, pronouncing that 'Freedom is always the freedom of those who think differently', backed up by an appeal to an article of the GDR constitution confirming the rights of citizens to express their opinions 'freely and openly'. Despite the banner's impeccable ideological credentials and appropriateness for the occasion, this was not a slogan that the ruling SED could stomach. The bearers of the banner were imprisoned; later, some prominent protesters were exiled to the west in a swap organised by human rights lawyers and church activists.

One of those deported west against her will was Vera Wollenberger (subsequently reverting to her maiden name of Lengsfeld), the daughter of an officer in the East German State Security Service, the Stasi, and for many years herself a member of the SED. In curiously twisting experiences over a number of years, Vera Lengsfeld had been deeply influenced by her husband, Knud

Wollenberger, with whom she had two sons. Knud had encouraged her to begin to think more independently. During the course of the 1980s, she became more involved in the Protestant church, which from 1978 onwards held a unique status in the GDR as an officially tolerated institution in which small groups could meet to discuss matters of concern, including peace initiatives, human rights, and environmentalism. Vera became active in a number of groups, including the Pankow Peace Group founded in 1981 by Ruth Misselwitz and others, the Environmental Library hosted from 1986 in Berlin's Zion Church in Prenzlauer Berg, which monitored pollution and environmental decline, and the 'Church from Below' which organised an unofficial network of events and discussions across the GDR. In all of these activities, Vera's resolve and growing radicalism had been fostered and supported by her husband, Knud.[1]

And yet: unknown to Vera at the time, Knud was himself a Stasi informer. He collected the leaflets produced by the dissident groups in which Vera was involved, promising he would store them in a safe place for fear their own apartment might be ransacked – and promptly handed them over to the Stasi. He encouraged Vera into ever more radical positions, in the hope this would facilitate the exposure of a whole group of dissidents. And ultimately: it was Knud who precipitated the arrest and imprisonment of the unofficial banner-bearers in January 1988, risking the well-being of his wife and even his own two sons in the process. At the time she was living in involuntary exile as a theology student in Cambridge in the summer of 1988, Vera still did not know that it was her own husband who had manipulated her throughout their marriage and who had ultimately betrayed her. This she only discovered, with deep shock, in 1992 when the Stasi archives were opened.

The incident was not only of major significance for Vera Lengsfeld and her family, but also for the far wider for the history of Berlin. It symbolises the moment when the ageing communist leadership under SED leader Erich Honecker and Stasi chief Erich Mielke, rattled by the rising tide of dissent, were prepared to use open force against those who wanted the freedom to think differently. For years they had sought to contain dissent by more subtle means of surveillance, individual intimidation and repression; but, following a raid on the Environmental Library in Berlin's Zion Church just a few weeks earlier, in late November 1987, that had attracted international attention, communist leaders were now prepared to engage in visible repression. At the same time, the incident illustrates how, with ever more evident economic decline and widespread fear about the potential military consequences of superpower tensions during the 1980s, ordinary people were becoming increasingly willing to take the significant risks of engaging in open protests.

It was not the dramatic gesture of the former actor turned politician, US President Ronald Reagan, standing in front of the Brandenburg Gate on a fleeting visit to Berlin on 12 June 1987 and proclaiming 'Mr Gorbachev, tear down this wall', that was the defining moment precipitating the end of the city's division – much as he and others liked to portray it as such. Rather, it was the courage of those who wanted the 'freedom to think differently' and who were prepared to test the limits – first within and increasingly beyond the protective umbrella of the Protestant Churches – that began to rattle the foundations of SED rule. This alone would not have toppled the regime; but, combined with growing recognition even among East German leaders that Soviet leader Mikhail Gorbachev was no longer prepared to sustain the eastern bloc by military force, and in a context of political changes in neighbouring countries providing routes for mass escape to the west, the courage of a dissident minority would ultimately contribute to the implosion of communist rule in the GDR. There were many further steps along the way, and many of the outcomes were entirely unintended, and certainly very far from the visions of a reformed and democratic socialism that many protestors had hoped for. Yet ultimately, the course of events set in train in the later 1980s would lead to the end of the division of Berlin.

In the years before these dramatic events, the divided city and its population, Berliners in East and West, were changing. Reunification would only confirm the depth of the transformations on either side of the city that occurred during the twenty-eight years of division.

• • •

Diverging Societies

The Berlin Wall created a tearing gash across the city; but this deep gash was one that, like a wound, would begin to develop scar tissue over time, as personal ties loosened and the two sides diverged in terms of lifestyles as well as economic and political systems. In the more affluent West, where residents were not so politically constrained, the Wall could over time become easier to ignore; but its anomalous status, an always imperilled island of capitalist democracy stranded in the surrounding communist state, and the difficulties of road or rail transit to West Germany through the GDR, meant that national division could never be ignored, as it often was in the main body of the Federal Republic to the west. The artificiality of West Berlin remained evident in a myriad of ways. Meanwhile, whatever the pain involved, the Wall did in fact ensure a more predictable labour supply in the East, ending the drain of key workers to the West. The stabilisation of the East German economy, in turn, allowed the possibility of experimentation with some decentralisation of economic planning and decision-making in the GDR, alongside a cautious liberalisation in cultural and youth policies.

DOUBLE VISIONS (2)

By the 1960s, quite different societies were developing in the two halves of Berlin. The West Berlin population was initially characterised by a curious combination of elderly war widows and single women, given the disproportionate numbers of men who had died in the war, alongside young men evading military service, since the western Allies upheld the special legal status of West Berlin and it was not considered an integral part of the FRG. Until 1961, refugees from lost eastern territories as well as from the GDR had been a source of cheap and mobile labour, many moving on further to West Germany, but this came to an end in August 1961. From the early 1960s, the West German government began to recruit 'guest workers' (*Gastarbeiter*) from Mediterranean countries, initially particularly from Italy but increasingly from Turkey. They were disproportionately employed in menial, low-paid jobs, such that ethnicity readily mapped onto the class structure. A new immigrant population of Turkish 'guest workers' began to make their homes in poorer areas of West Berlin, such as Kreuzberg, Neukölln, and Wedding. Their isolation was compounded by few official attempts to facilitate language acquisition or social integration, on the mistaken assumption that they would soon return 'home' rather than settling and having families.

The West Berlin economy had suffered a significant loss in manufacturing capacity as well as governmental functions following defeat and division. Despite all efforts, it still did not flourish. Generous government subsidies were continually needed, not only to keep this beleaguered western outpost afloat but also, symbolically, to serve as a poster for capitalism within easy view of the East. The area around West Berlin's affluent Kurfürstendamm and the preserved ruins of the Kaiser Wilhelm Memorial Church, leading up to the rather seedier streets around the central station, Bahnhof Zoo, came to epitomise West Berlin's combination of commercial glitter and constant reminders of war and division. The name of the famous department store opened in 1907, KaDeWe – 'Shopping Store of the West' – now seemed even more apposite as a wider symbol of western capitalism. The virulently anti-communist press baron Axel Springer provocatively placed his high-rise newspaper headquarters right on the inner-Berlin border, hard up against the Wall, making a statement that could be clearly seen from the eastern side. Meanwhile considerable investment was devoted to heightening West Berlin's cultural profile, with architect-designed buildings such as Hans Scharoun's Philharmonie, which opened in 1963, close to the New National Gallery, designed by Ludwig Mies van der Rohe and built in the late 1960s, and the new State Library and other cultural institutions, including the Musical Instrument Museum in what became known as the Cultural Forum around Matthäikirchplatz, close to Potsdamer Platz. The bombed out Potsdamer Platz itself was at the heart of the Cold War, entirely divided by the Wall, with no trace of its former identity as a lively intersection of both traffic and social encounters.

Despite subsidies and support, West Berlin society in the 1960s and 1970s was anything but stable, with growing political conflicts and generational clashes complicated by wider Cold War tensions. On 2 June 1967, a West Berlin policeman, Karl-Heinz Kurras, shot dead Benno Ohnesorg, one of the students demonstrating on the occasion of a visit to Berlin by the Shah of Iran. It was revealed only decades later that Kurras was also an informer for the East German Stasi, and did not seem to have been acting in self-defence, as claimed by the police at the time. This incident, the full details of which remain opaque, in some respects typifies the intricacies of interactions between East and West, and the difficulties in getting at the truth, given the post-unification destruction of many Stasi files. In Berlin it certainly had a significant impact beyond the tragic death of an unarmed young student out

DOUBLE VISIONS (2)

on his first – and last – demonstration, shaping what was to come in the context of wider protests in 1968. This was the high point of student unrest across the world: hippies preaching 'flower power' and 'make love not war' in Berkeley and San Francisco, California; battles on the streets of Paris, where workers and students joined in common demonstrations; demands and hopes for 'socialism with a human face' in Dubček's Prague, Czechoslovakia, brutally suppressed by Soviet tanks; and even, in East Berlin and elsewhere in the GDR, occasional attempts to express solidarity with the Czechs, rapidly nipped in the bud by the Stasi through removal of unofficial slogans and graffiti as well as pre-emptive arrests of potential protestors.

There was a lengthy social, political, and cultural aftermath of this incident, both in West Berlin and in the Federal Republic more widely. Student demonstrations were held in the city's public spaces and on university campuses, often marked by intense intellectual debates; members of housing cooperatives squatted in derelict premises and trialled alternative lifestyles and sexual mores; and there were vocal challenges to the bourgeois parental generation, accused of unacknowledged complicity in Nazism. Among a radical if tiny minority, there was growing willingness to use violence in order precisely to provoke repression and hence 'reveal' the supposedly 'fascist' nature of the state. In the 1970s, the group known as the Red Army Faction (*Rote Armee Fraktion*, RAF) became increasingly extreme across Germany, prepared to engage in terrorism and murder. Their actions did indeed precipitate government legislation that effectively restricted freedom to engage in protests for fear of personal and career implications, in what was termed a '*Berufsverbot*', or ban on appointment in state-funded professions. Even if the wave of left-wing terrorism eventually petered out, despite secret East German support for members of what became known as the

Baader-Meinhof gang (after the names of two of its leaders), the wider generational confrontation with the Nazi past massively affected West German society and culture for many years thereafter.

The partly generational shift towards social critique and grassroots activism also had more practical implications for landscapes of past and present in West Berlin. Citizens' action groups, for example, opposed controversial building projects such as the regeneration of part of Kreuzberg around Kottbusser Tor. Here, city planners and private entrepreneurs concerned for profit prioritised demolition and replacement rather than regeneration of the older, if substandard and war-damaged, apartment blocks or 'rental barracks' for which Berlin had become renowned. Young socialists, known as *JuSos*, successfully joined forces with local residents to oppose at least part of the planned redevelopment, although elsewhere much of it went ahead.[2] Grassroots activists and 'barefoot historians' energetically engaged in digging up aspects of the city's Nazi past, not only through research, but often more literally, to the discomfort of conservatives who wanted to 'put a line under the past', as they repeatedly said. In the late 1980s, the cellars of the former headquarters of Himmler's Reich Security Head Office (RSHA) were uncovered on derelict land on Prinz-Albrecht-Straße, at that time still hard up against the Berlin Wall and being temporarily used for learner drivers to practise. Determination to challenge authorities led, eventually, to the reclamation of this site from the property developers and its preservation for purposes of memorialisation and public education about the past. The site now houses the Topography of Terror.

In East Berlin from the 1960s, living conditions began to improve. The self-proclaimed 'Berlin, Capital of the GDR' was supposedly an internationally visible showcase for communism, in mirror image to West Berlin's symbolic function for capitalism. Official subsidies and material privileges made life here somewhat easier than it was in the stagnant provincial towns and villages across the GDR. Moreover, for a couple of years in the early to mid-1960s, there were controlled experiments with a degree of liberalisation, particularly in relation to youth culture, as well as economic reforms.

For the expanding numbers of workers and communist functionaries in East Berlin who were prepared to go along with the new regime, there were some modest improvements in living conditions, even if nothing on the scale of West Germany. Privileged functionaries enjoyed far better living conditions and provisions than ordinary East Berliners. Members of the political elite moved from their initial base in the north Berlin suburb of Pankow to Wandlitz, an exclusive enclave in woodland north of Berlin often dubbed 'Volvograd' in view of the western Volvo cars in which the communist big-wigs were chauffeured to and from their political work in Berlin. Here, the GDR's leaders were able to live in a relatively pampered environment, make hunting forays in the surrounding countryside (continuing the traditions of Göring), and receiving the best medical treatment the GDR could afford in the nearby clinic at Buch, an off-shoot of the Charité Hospital.[3]

Everywhere in the GDR, there was an emphasis on working together collectively for the common good and a better future. Employment was guaranteed, and rents were cheap. Communal childcare facilities allowed young mothers to remain in or re-enter the workforce, where they were desperately needed in view of the labour shortages consequent on war and flight. 'Handelsorganisation' (HO) shops provided subsidised foodstuffs, even if the choices were limited; and specialised shops known as Intershops and Delikat stores provided more luxurious goods, if at higher prices or for foreign currency. Facilities were provided for the activities of organisations such as the Young Pioneers and Free German Youth for children and young people, while the paramilitary Society for Sport and Technology enjoyed better facilities than those open to members of the ordinary public. There was certainly no real social equality, even if there was a safety net for the working classes. Meanwhile, members of the former bourgeoisie continued to find themselves actively discriminated against, as private ownership was progressively squeezed out of the economy. Church membership dwindled, and independent thinkers and critics of the regime were silenced.

Recognition of the GDR by West Germany came under Chancellor Willy Brandt. Brandt had served as Governing Mayor of West Berlin from 1957 to 1966, when he became FRG Foreign Minister in the Grand Coalition, and subsequently Chancellor of the Federal Republic in 1969. With his front-line Berlin experience, Brandt was only too well aware of the human pain brought about by division. Brandt's press colleague and close political associate, Egon Bahr, had been advocating rapprochement through 'small steps' for several years, and Brandt was determined to bring this about. A committed socialist who had been forced to flee during the Third Reich, and active in resistance to Nazism from abroad, Brandt was critiqued by German nationalists as a traitor to his fatherland; he only narrowly achieved parliamentary agreement to the highly controversial policies known in the West as *Ostpolitik*. Ways of bringing about a degree of rapprochement were also being considered in the GDR, even before Erich Honecker formally took over from Walter Ulbricht as SED leader in 1971. A series of treaties – in 1970 between West Germany and Moscow, and then with Poland, but most importantly in 1972 the Basic Treaty between West and East Germany – resulted in de facto acceptance by West Germany of the post-war borders in eastern Europe, and recognition of the GDR as a separate state, no longer to be referred to in the west as 'the Zone'. In 1974, the GDR entered the United Nations as an internationally recognised state. Even so, West Germany did not officially view the border with East Germany as comparable to other international borders, and the two states exchanged 'permanent representatives' rather than ambassadors.

Most importantly for everyday life in Berlin, travel restrictions between West and East were somewhat eased, and Berliners now faced slightly fewer restrictions on making contacts across the Wall. This was of course asymmetrical, with westerners able to get visas to visit the East far more readily than the other way round. Only East Germans of pensionable age wanting to travel were seen as a minimal loss – even as good riddance, being no longer a drain on state pensions, health services, and welfare provisions – if they chose to defect while on a visit to the west. Telephone wires were reconnected, and those privileged few who had access to a telephone were able to talk again across the border. This did not, however, necessarily make life any less restricted – indeed, in many ways East Berliners were subjected to greater surveillance, with the rapid growth of the Stasi in the 1970s and 1980s.

The increased flow of visitors across the border after recognition meant, from the perspective of the communist authorities, a greater danger of ideological contamination from the West. A highly visible response was to take on some of the apparent colours (although not the liberal substance) of western culture. Honecker rapidly proclaimed that there should be 'no taboos' under socialism, and his policies emphasised improvements for individual lives in the here and now rather than working hard for a better future as a community.

The modernity of 'actually existing socialism' was already being visibly expressed in significant new buildings, including the

Figure 9.1 Landscapes of power in East Berlin: Unter den Linden, 1981
This view shows the then still new and prestigious television tower, as well as the Palace of the Republic, housing the People's Parliament, now demolished and replaced by the Humboldt Forum.
Photograph by the author

Fernsehturm (television tower; Figure 9.1) which was constructed from 1965 and opened in 1969 at Berlin's central Alexanderplatz, being the highest building at the time in Europe. Solidarity with progressive currents and oppressed peoples around the world, including Vietnam, Chile, and Palestine, was emphasised in the Tenth World Festival of Youth and Students hosted in East Berlin in 1973, in which young people participated with apparent enthusiasm. The Palast der Republik (Palace of the Republic, popularly dubbed the 'ballast of the Republic'), which housed not only the East German parliament (*Volkskammer*) – essentially a rubber-stamping body – but also three restaurants, a bowling alley, social facilities

DOUBLE VISIONS (2)

and a dance floor, was built from 1973 to 1976 on the site formerly occupied by the Hohenzollern Palace or Schloss, the war-damaged remnants of which had been demolished rather than renovated by the communists after the war. Shops and restaurants in the central area of Berlin along Unter den Linden towards Alexanderplatz, often the only part that western visitors would see, were provisioned with books, fashionable items, and foodstuffs that were virtually impossible to obtain outside the capital city. The new emphases were even subtly reflected in the changing character of films, which began to appear less obviously ideological in terms of building a better future, but focused rather on individual happiness at a personal level (as in, for example, the 1973 film *The Legend of Paul and Paula*).

While areas of older housing in some parts of central Berlin were left to crumble and became ever more dilapidated, as in Prenzlauer Berg, the promise of improvements in living standards was given renewed energy and considerable substance, as housing for the masses continued to be a major priority. Costly prestige architectural projects such as Stalinallee (belatedly renamed Karl-Marx-Allee in 1961, in the wake of the destalinisation proclaimed by Khrushchev in 1956) were abandoned, and from the later 1950s onwards, rather cheaper modernist styles of architecture were adopted. Particularly from the 1960s, apartment blocks were rapidly constructed using prefabricated concrete slabs; large open spaces between high rise buildings first allowed cranes to swing in every direction while constructing a cluster of apartment blocks, and were then repurposed for playgrounds and communal facilities. The ambition in East Berlin was not only to provide modern housing with indoor sanitation – greatly desired – but also to design estates that would foster a sense of community and a new kind of society.

In some areas, such as the Leipziger Straße – such an upmarket address in the nineteenth century, where sewage had been collected from the better houses by cart at night – the war-damaged older houses were demolished and replaced by a complex of relatively prestigious new tower blocks, with retail outlets on the lower floors. Given the centrality of the location, these apartments were often reserved for significant members of East German society; moreover, they provided a socialist showcase and visible counterpoint to the ideologically resonant Axel Springer building on the other side of the Wall. But elsewhere, there was a genuine impetus to provide better housing for the masses.

The vision of the desired new society was most evident in the extensive development in the north-eastern suburb of Marzahn, the largest East German housing estate – or, rather, complex of estates. The East German architect Wolf-Rüdiger Eisentraut, who had participated in the team that designed the prestigious Palace of the Republic, played a major role in designing a series of residential centres across a vast area. The former fields and market gardens that had so long marked this area of Greater Berlin, supplying city dwellers with fresh fruit and vegetables, now entirely disappeared. The tower blocks and smaller apartment buildings were connected not only by trams and buses, but also by pedestrian walkways; a branch of the S-Bahn and several tram lines also facilitated rapid transit to places of work. The estates were clustered around neighbourhood centres featuring shops, restaurants, children's playgrounds, health and social facilities, event halls, and a cinema. But the visionary design for the area included, extraordinarily, preservation of the former village centre of 'Old Marzahn', a long cobbled street retaining something of its nineteenth-century character, with a village green, the old school building, a church, and a pub. Many East Berliners were only too keen to exchange apartments in the dilapidated, crumbling housing

DOUBLE VISIONS (2)

blocks without indoor sanitation for a place in Marzahn. After reunification, many of the social facilities and neighbourhood centres were demolished; and Eisentraut retooled his designer skills to make imaginative use of discarded prefabricated slabs for the construction of low-rise apartment blocks and individual houses.

Interestingly, both because of the widespread desire for modern housing with indoor bathrooms and toilets, and because of a general levelling of incomes and class differences for those who were not part of the elite, these estates housed a greater social mix than would later be the case: professors and plumbers, dentists and dustbin collectors, bureaucrats and bricklayers, often lived side by side in the new estates. At the same time, many East Berliners found fresh air and leisure in their allotment gardens, or in parks such as Friedrichshain or Wuhlheide, or by going swimming, camping, and walking around nearby lakes such as the Müggelsee.

Far less visible, and infinitely more insidious, was the exponential growth of surveillance by the Stasi and its growing army of 'unofficial informers' (IMs), as well as the constant refinements made to the physical apparatus of control along the full stretch of the Wall surrounding Berlin. Similarly, less attention was drawn to the growth of political privilege, or to the real power of the Politburo, which was far more important than the Parliament. The top political elite of the ruling SED met to make the real decisions about policy, along with Stasi chief Erich Mielke, in the building originally built by the Nazis as an extension of the Reichsbank, and which is now occupied by the Foreign Office of the Federal Republic of Germany. Infinitely more evident, and frighteningly so, were the increasingly sophisticated fortifications along the Berlin Wall, with watchtowers, mined strips, patrolling tanks, dogs, and armed guards. The possibility of crossing the border at selected transit points according to category, including by road at Checkpoint Charlie or S-Bahn at Friedrichstraße, was complemented by growing western awareness of communist oppression. Through novels by John Le Carré and many others, Berlin became seen as the capital of spying and intrigue, enhanced by highly visible exchanges of prominent individuals at the Glienicke Bridge between Potsdam and West Berlin.

Divided Approaches to a Common Past

Diverging approaches to a common past were also changing the face of Berlin, right from the moment of defeat and the construction of ideologically opposed regimes. This was particularly evident from the outset in East Berlin. Memorials to Ernst Thälmann, the former leader of the German Communist Party (KPD) who had stood against Hitler and Hindenburg in the presidential elections in 1932, and who, following more than eleven years of imprisonment in solitary confinement was executed in Buchenwald concentration camp in 1944, were ubiquitous. Streets, squares, youth groups, schools, and other institutions were renamed not only after Thälmann but also other communist heroes. A massive statue of Marx and Engels faced the Palace of the Republic, a huge statue of Lenin graced a square in front of an apartment block, while an enormous bust of Ernst Thälmann sat in the square named after him. The heroism of the Soviet 'liberators' from Nazi oppression was given recognition not only in the Soviet tank memorial just on the West Berlin side of the border, close to the Reichstag, but also, on a monumental scale, in Treptower Park alongside the Spree in East Berlin – on precisely the space that had housed the by now largely forgotten Great Industrial Exposition of 1896, with its problematic colonialist overtones. Here, the gigantic statue of a Red Army soldier clutching a rescued child in his arms trod on a crushed and broken swastika, and towered over a field surrounded by sarcophagi bearing inscriptions taken from Stalin, marking the graves of soldiers who had died in the battle for Berlin. Free German Youth groups were regularly brought to this arena, but many East Berliners also came here for pleasure, to walk in the surrounding park grounds. Further out, a striking memorial to the communists and socialists murdered in the 'Köpenick Blood Week' of June 1933 ensured that heroic resistance among members of the wider population was also celebrated (Figure 9.2). It was impossible to escape the lessons of recent history in East Berlin.

Figure 9.2 East Berlin memorial to the 'Köpenick blood week' This memorial celebrates the heroism of communists murdered by Nazi thugs in the 'Köpenick blood week' of June 1933. Left-wing anti-fascists were prominently memorialised in East Berlin, but far less present in the western memorial landscape. Photograph by the author

The further distant past was also brought into active service in attempted legitimation of the communist present. The cemetery in the Friedrichshain park, holding the graves of those 'fallen in March' (*Märzgefallene*) in the upheavals of 1848 had been augmented by the graves of left-wing revolutionaries killed in the revolutionary winter of 1918–19, and plaques were erected to honour others who had died in the communist fight for freedom. Although a statue of Frederick the Great was left standing in the middle of the park, near the 'rubble mountain' made out of the ruins of war-damaged Berlin, there was also a memorial to Polish soldiers who had assisted the Russians in the fight against fascism. This whole area constituted a curious time capsule, and it is impossible to know whether ordinary East Berliners made much of the multiple layers of symbolism and memorialisation in its grounds. It was one of the earliest parks to be laid out, in the early nineteenth century, for the enjoyment of local people, and was adorned at its western entrance by a sumptuous waterfall surrounded by characters take from the Grimms' fairy tales, perhaps promoting reflections on early nineteenth-century nationalism among visitors even under communism. Meanwhile, a café, pond or small lake, trees, paths, and playgrounds probably meant that few local residents or visitors paused to contemplate the significance of the graveyard or other memorials to communist heroes.

More explicit attempts at harnessing history for the present were mounted in the centre of East Berlin. Exhibitions in the German Historical Museum in the eighteenth-century Zeughaus stressed the historical inevitability of the 'workers' and peasants' state', the GDR, as the penultimate stage of history on the way to a glorious communist future. In the later 1970s and 1980s, there was a broadening of historical focus and a re-envisioning of the whole of German history, with the GDR now appropriating even the dubious

DOUBLE VISIONS (2)

heritage of Prussia and harnessing it to the communist cause; even if the restoration of Sanssouci itself was slow, Frederick the Great's statue was brought back and re-erected on Unter den Linden. The celebrations of the Luther anniversary in 1983 and, even more, the 750th anniversary of Berlin itself in 1987, occasioned massive efforts to rival and surpass West Berlin's efforts to mark these milestones. The Nikolaiviertel in East Berlin, earlier a casualty of Nazi modernisation efforts as well as wartime and post-war destruction, was rebuilt as an attempted tourist attraction. While heroisation remained the dominant mode of memorialisation, here too there were changes in the later 1980s. In the Sachsenhausen concentration camp exhibition, Jewish victims received some official recognition alongside the more active communists who were praised as 'anti-fascist resistance fighters'. It took a demonstration by East German women in 1987 to assert unofficial recognition of lesbian victims in Ravensbrück concentration camp. Somewhat surprisingly, the former Nazi camp for gypsies in Marzahn received a small memorial in the late 1980s, again as a result of an individual initiative.

West Berlin chose rather different heroes and victims. Not left-wing opponents of Hitler but rather Stauffenberg and other predominantly conservative nationalists who had participated in the belated 1944 July Plot were commemorated in the Memorial Site to German Resistance (*Gedenkstätte Deutscher Widerstand*). It also took a while even for resistance movements such as the White Rose associated with Hans and Sophie Scholl to be acknowledged, and even longer for the left-wing *Rote Kapelle* (Red Orchestra) to be granted attention and space. There was initially strong opposition to establishing exhibitions at 'perpetrator sites' such as the villa of the Wannsee Conference and, when it was accidentally unearthed in the late 1980s, the site of the former Gestapo and RSHA headquarters in Prinz-Albrecht-Straße, which

Figure 9.3 Topography of Terror, on the site of Heinrich Himmler's Reich Security Head Office (RSHA)
The Topography of Terror is hard up against the remains of the Wall. Behind, on the right, can be seen what was Göring's Nazi Air Ministry, then the communist House of Ministries, and now the Federal Republic's Ministry of Finance. To the left is the Martin Gropius Bau, and in the middle distance the building housing Berlin City Council, formerly the Prussian Parliament until 1934.
Photograph by the author

did eventually become the Topography of Terror (Figure 9.3). Yet despite some push-back under West German Chancellor Helmut Kohl, a left-liberal approach to historical commemoration began to predominate in West Berlin, and exhibitions such as 'Berlin–Berlin', on the occasion of the 750th anniversary, were marked by critical engagement and historical detail of a wholly different scope and quality from the East Berlin counterparts. It was, however, only after unification in 1990 that efforts to display the darker sides of German responsibility and guilt, as well as express very public remorse, would truly begin to dominate the cityscape of the once again unified capital.

The End of Two Berlins

The economic and environmental decline of the GDR became ever more visible following the oil crises and growing Cold War confrontations from 1979 onwards. Alternative scenes were emerging in East Berlin among peace campaigners, human rights activists, and environmentalists, particularly in the environs of the Protestant Churches and among writers and artists living in increasingly dilapidated old apartment buildings in the Prenzlauer Berg district. Initiatives for reform already in the early 1980s were given a massive boost after 1985 by changes in the USSR under its new leader, Mikhail Gorbachev, with his slogans of 'openness' and 'restructuring'. For once, the GDR political leadership was unwilling to act on the official slogan that 'to learn from the Soviet Union is to learn to be victorious', and the ageing leadership around Honecker resisted reforms, seeking rather to crack down on dissent. This became particularly evident in Berlin from late 1987 onwards, with the Stasi raid on the unofficial Environmental Library based in the Zionskirche, and the arrests and enforced exile of dissidents carrying unofficial banners at the annual Luxemburg-Liebknecht demonstration in January 1988. Growing unrest within the GDR was influenced also by movements for reform elsewhere, including the Solidarność (Solidarity) movement in neighbouring Poland.

Changes across the eastern bloc combined to produce the triple crises of the summer and autumn of 1989: there was a stream of refugees seeking ways out to the west, often through the ever more porous border between Hungary and Austria; there was growing confidence among those who came out to demonstrate on Monday evenings in Leipzig, chanting 'We are staying here!' and 'We are the people!'; and the ruling communist party's own authority began to disintegrate, as even SED functionaries of a new generation began to doubt Honecker's capacity to deal with the situation. On 7 October 1989, Erich Honecker and Mikhail Gorbachev together celebrated the 40th anniversary of the GDR, with a full military parade through the centre of East Berlin; but Gorbachev took the opportunity to make it clear that Honecker's time was up; and on 9 October, the Leipzig demonstration was allowed to go ahead without the planned crackdown by the Stasi and the use of troops.

From then on, disintegration of communist rule was rapid. Within less than two weeks Honecker was replaced by the younger Egon Krenz, in the hope that presenting a new face might stem the tide of dissent, particularly after Krenz returned from a trip to Moscow in which he had been given clear instructions to engage in reforms. On 4 November 1989, a massive public demonstration in East Berlin took place, with prominent speakers including civil rights activists such as Jens Reich, and writers such as Christa Wolf, Christoph Hein, and Stefan Heym, addressing a crowd of over half a million people at the Alexanderplatz. But it was too late to engage in calls for a reformed socialism within a still existing GDR, or to think that altering the personnel at the top of the SED would make any substantial difference.

On 9 November 1989, at a press conference announcing changes to the visa requirements and travel restrictions, a weary government spokesperson, Günter Schabowski, slipped up over the intended timetable and, in response to a question, inadvertently suggested the changes would be valid with immediate effect. Seeing the slightly misreported news on western television, thousands of East Berliners rushed to the Wall. Taken aback and completely unprepared for the throng that now faced them,

DOUBLE VISIONS (2)

border guards at the checkpoint at Bornholmer Straße were eventually instructed to let them through rather than risk multiple casualties. People stormed across the bridge, to be greeted ecstatically by West Berliners, and a night of celebrating what became known as the fall of the Wall began.

The night of 9–10 November 1989 was a major historical moment, captured in images of East Berliners streaming westwards past baffled border guards, and people from both sides climbing onto the Wall, dancing and drinking, celebrating this almost inconceivable event. This moment also marked the beginning of the ultimate demise of the GDR. Once the borders had been breached, the East German communist regime began to collapse. Despite political concessions and apparent reforms in the still existing GDR, there was a continuing exodus of East Germans to the west where they had automatic entitlement to citizenship, putting a growing strain also on West German economy and society. It was increasingly clear to both sides that this haemorrhaging could not continue for long; but in the event, the speed of events was startling. Helmut Kohl's initial 'ten point plan', announced on 28 November 1989 and envisaging closer cooperation with a view to union within ten years, was taken over by events within a matter of months.

By the winter of 1989–90, it was clear that Gorbachev's Soviet Union was no longer prepared to uphold communism in its former satellite states by force. In March 1990, the first free elections in the GDR took place, brought forwards because of the continuing economic and social crises. A conservative-led coalition won, in part by having tarred the re-constituted SPD with the taint of communism, and more importantly by having promised an economically unviable one-to-one currency exchange. When put into practice in July 1990, this policy not only brought the highly desired western Deutschmark to the GDR but also ensured rapidly rising unemployment and social distress. By August, the East German economy was effectively collapsing, as factories were unable to pay workers their wages in Deutschmarks and closed down in face of western competition. As four-power talks between the former wartime Allies proceeded apace, the quickest constitutional solution to rapid reunification was adopted: the reconstitution of regional states (*Länder*) in eastern Germany, which could then request accession to an enlarged Federal Republic of Germany under western auspices.

The collapse of communism precipitated the end of the GDR. On 3 October 1990 – within less than a year since the fall of the Wall, and just a few days before what would have been its 41st anniversary – East Germans automatically became citizens of a reunited Germany. This was not a complete 're-unification' in the sense of a complete return to Germany's pre-war borders, since former provinces beyond the post-war border with Poland were not reclaimed; but it certainly marked an end to the period of dramatic Cold War division of Germany, and with it the division of the city of Berlin.

10
Re-connection
United Berlin since 1990

The Unification of Germany, 3 October 1990

On 3 October 1990 the Unification Treaty came into effect, as the newly constituted federal states (*Länder*) of eastern Germany were incorporated into an enlarged Federal Republic of Germany under Article 23 of the West German Basic Law. This key historical moment was designated the 'Day of German Unity', a public holiday to be observed annually. Nationally, there were massive public celebrations and ceremonies, designed to be both joyful and solemn in tone; at midnight, fireworks exploded across the Berlin night sky, marking not only the demise of the GDR, but also a radically new beginning for the city and the nation. This was a moment that, unimaginably, would turn Berlin once again into a cosmopolitan metropolis, capital city of a reunited country in a dramatically altered wider European and international environment.

Reunification had a fundamental impact on Berlin in just about every respect: topographically, in terms of borders, buildings, and infrastructure; socially, in terms of the economy, communities, culture and lifestyles; and also in the sphere of the imaginary, of self-representations and reflections, and selective preservation of traces of an always controversial past. This moment inaugurated less a reshaping than an almost total transformation of the city – which nevertheless also served to illuminate so many aspects of Berlin's history, even while obliterating or obscuring others, embodying both the vibrancy and the uncertainties of a multifaceted present.

Yet at the time, many viewed this moment with ambivalence. Unification, and the consequent transition to western structures and processes, brought the most significant immediate changes to the lives of East Germans. The personal implications of unification varied significantly with class, gender, and generation, as people with differing levels of resources and aspirations adjusted to new conditions. Some felt unadulterated joy at new freedoms and opportunities; many others, however, registered fear and uncertainty about what the future would bring, along with a loss of a sense of agency that they had won so recently, during the revolutionary upheavals. As one woman confided in her diary on 3 October 1990: 'A country is erased, just like that, struck out, finished, over, full stop. Now we are Germans. Citizens by accession, relocated, annexed; without name or face. Helpless – well yes, that goes for me.' She continued: 'At the beginning – a year ago – we did it ourselves, we discussed halfway through the night, in the family, with friends. Then the "speakers" arrived, all of them best quality imports. And the people [*Volk*], that had wanted to be one and wanted to become itself, was silent, listened, let itself be lulled. Gently and peacefully let everything be taken out of its hands, just as peacefully as it had earlier taken things up.'[1]

The sense of a loss of agency, of not knowing the new rules – whether formal or unwritten, informal – pervaded the atmosphere among East Germans, whose habits and patterns of life had been fundamentally broken in nearly every respect. In the first two years after reunification, the birth rate in eastern Germany plummeted down to half its previous level – a dramatic fall only paralleled in times of war, and a startling measure of the widespread sense of apprehension about the future. There was also enhanced awareness of what they had previously valued in their lives. As another diary writer presciently put it on 3 October 1990, the 'mentalities and feelings, the solidarity with one another, the being-there-for-each-other, will be progressively lost'.[2] This too would be a sentiment repeatedly expressed over the following years. All historical transitions, and particularly one as dramatic – if also extraordinarily peaceful – as this one, are challenging for those who live through them.

During the period of division, the city itself had been torn apart. As the borders began to open, East Germans had rapidly changed their slogan from 'we are the people' to 'we are one people'; but with reunification it became clear just how far the two sides had in fact diverged. Initial exhilaration as easterners and westerners ('*Ossis*' and '*Wessis*') were able to meet up in person, families and friends were able to hug and talk, soon gave way to the realisation that over the decades of division social customs, practices, and ways of thinking had changed. Two different kinds of society had formed that would not be as easily reconnected as the severed transport links between the eastern and western parts of the city. Even as physical traces of the Wall were erased, segregated patterns of friendship and marriage still for years reflected a continuing 'wall in people's heads'. It was initially far from clear that, in former Federal Chancellor Willy Brandt's phrase, 'what belongs together will grow together'. Yet over time, as new issues arose, the distinctions between 'easterners' and 'westerners', which seemed so striking at the time, began to fade.

A third of a century later, the divided Berlin of the Cold War era was becoming virtually unimaginable. Only older Berliners now had personal experiences of the period of division; and memories remained divided. Most traces of the Wall itself had disappeared, and the city's demographic profile had radically changed, with both the passage of generations and a continuing influx of immigrants. Opening up to the wider world affected who, indeed, actually were Berliners: no longer the war widows, draft dodgers, or radical students in the west, the communist functionaries and subdued workers in the eastern sector, but rather a wide range of newcomers: from the professionals who staffed the relocated government offices, cultural institutions, and regenerated or new organisations, through globally mobile individuals seeking new horizons along with cheap housing and cafés with internet connections, to poverty-stricken immigrants and refugees from war-torn regions of the world. In the early twenty-first century, the city was being actively reshaped as a place of diversity and cultural productivity. And a quarter of a century after reunification, the profile of the city was further significantly affected by major new waves of immigrants and refugees, following the confident announcement by Angela Merkel – the first female, and East German, Chancellor of the Federal Republic of Germany – that *'wir schaffen das'* ('we can do it'). These too were key moments shaping the multi-ethnic, multicultural Berlin of the twenty-first century – all made possible by the momentous collapse of communist rule and the unification of Germany that followed.

• • •

Cityscapes of Transformation

The end of the Cold War fundamentally altered the character of Berlin. The American and Soviet forces whose presence had been so significant over the decades of division gradually made their exits. The last troops were seen off in September 1994, with more fanfare and expressions of gratitude towards the western forces than those in the east, where patrolling tanks along transit routes and around the heavily guarded borders had been an ominous reminder of Soviet might. And Berlin once again became capital of a united Germany. Following much debate, on 20 June 1991 the German parliament narrowly voted (by 338 to 320) to move the seat of government of the Federal Republic from Bonn to Berlin. This decision was strongly contested. A speech by the then Bundestag president, Wolfgang Schäuble, was a tipping point before the final vote. Schäuble argued that it was not simply a pragmatic matter of weighing up the astronomical costs involved in moving, or the foreseeable impact on jobs and housing markets; rather, he argued, what was at stake was nothing less than 'the future of Germany'. Berlin, he claimed, was a 'symbol for unity and freedom, for democracy and constitutional statehood for all of Germany'; and indeed, Berlin now represented a far wider yearning for peace and unity across the whole of Europe.[3]

The decision to move the seat of government to Berlin instigated a massive building programme to construct a modern government quarter near the Reichstag. A new Chancellery was designed, alongside a fleet of office blocks on the banks of the Spree to accommodate the influx of civil servants and administrators. The Reichstag was itself revamped and repurposed for a return to active use as the seat of the German parliament, the Bundestag (although the building itself retains the anachronistic name). For two weeks in the summer of 1995 it was symbolically 'wrapped', in a flamboyant artistic act by Christo and Jeanne-Claude that reportedly attracted some five million visitors. In 1999 the Reichstag was finally reopened for parliamentary business, complete with a new transparent dome designed by British architect Norman Foster to symbolise the supposed transparency of Germany's democracy, open to visitors seeking both rooftop views over Berlin and glimpses of parliamentarians carrying out the work of democracy below (Figure 10.1).

With the initially rapid restructuring, westerners deemed to have superior experience and qualifications took up many significant positions. This massive transformation also entailed conflicting interpretations and narratives about past and present. In the 1990s, the German parliament held a series of hearings in two highly controversial Parliamentary Commissions of Inquiry, seeking to

Figure 10.1 Reichstag dome: Transparent democracy?
The dome was designed by Norman Foster to replace the burnt-out shell of the former ruins when the building once again became the seat of the German parliament in the 1990s. Visitors can not only gain breathtaking views of Berlin all around but can also look down at members of parliament conducting their business below.
Photograph by the author

gain a more comprehensive understanding of the East German dictatorship. Older arguments about totalitarianism, and comparisons between dictatorships of the right and the left were resurrected. And with the opening of the Stasi archives, a wave of revelations led to public scandals, as well as traumatic breakdowns of relationships among those who felt their trust had been betrayed. The former dissident and later MP, Vera Lengsfeld, discovering the role of her husband Knud Wollenberger in manipulating and betraying her, promptly divorced him and reverted to her maiden name; she was but one of the more prominent early figures in a wave of exposures and rising mutual suspicion.

In many quarters, the notion of the 'peaceful revolution' was appropriated as a founding myth to legitimise the new unified state. There was nevertheless a slow shift away from castigating the GDR towards remembering victims, and critically celebrating GDR opposition figures. Any apparent empathy with those who had supported or complied with the demands of the communist regime remained a subject of continuing controversy.

While these debates became less heated over time, they had an impact on the physical reshaping of Berlin. The first major change, the significance of which can hardly be overstated, was of course the tearing down of the hated Wall. Enthusiastic hacking for souvenirs soon gave way to removal of landmines, fences, and watchtowers, as well as the concrete slabs that had formed the outer perimeter of this explosive gash surrounding West Berlin. The belated realisation that some parts should be preserved for public education and commemoration purposes, even while seeking to eradicate all traces of division, proved controversial.

A line of coloured bricks and metal plates set in the ground was inserted to trace the former course of the Wall over some of its length. But there was wider disagreement about whether the former death strip should be obliterated by rebuilding, or transformed into life-affirming cycle pathways or parks open for the enjoyment of all. In central areas, with real estate values soaring, commercial and entrepreneurial interests generally came to the fore. The visions relating to leisure were partially realised in some places, such as the Mauerpark (Wall Park) running south from near the Bornholmer Straße border crossing towards the new memorial park at Bernauer Straße, or cycle routes in outer areas. But elsewhere, sites in previously unattractive locations which had been too close to the Wall for comfort were simply redesignated for building. Housing sprang up in areas that had previously been part of the no-man's-land by the Wall, leaving little trace of where it had been, except perhaps the occasional old spotlight lamp post or overgrown former tank tracks.

The visible remnants of the Wall remained objects of continuing controversy.[4] In Bernauer Straße, a significant segment was retained, following hefty debates between engaged citizens, local, regional, and eventually also national politicians. Key memory activists included Pastor Manfred Fischer and representatives of the parish whose church within the border strip had been blown up by the East German authorities. Eventually this location became a concentrated site of memory, landscaped to give some impression of the former depth of the Wall, and with exhibitions, events, and periodic commemoration ceremonies. A slightly reduced segment – even so, still 1.3 kilometres long – of the 'East Side Gallery' of artwork close to the Ostbahnhof survived the predations of real estate developers who prioritised construction of profitable apartment buildings by the waterside over preservation of what they saw as merely graffiti on remnants of the Wall. There were also privately-funded ventures exhibiting the Wall, as both tourist attraction and politicised site of remembrance, at the iconic former Allied crossing point of Checkpoint Charlie. From 1962 onwards, two Cold Warrior memory entrepreneurs, Rainer and Alexandra Hildebrandt, had run a museum there, celebrating daring escapes using false bottoms in cars, forged identity papers, underwater swimming, or flight over the border in hot air balloons. Following reunification, controversial new open-air exhibits included a temporary field of crosses symbolising those who had lost their lives at the Wall, and the location remained a spot for tourist selfies. Elsewhere, generally only isolated pieces of Wall served as passing reminders, stimulating reflection rather than conveying an impression of the sheer extent of the Wall.

The less visible means of repression in the GDR were selectively displayed to visitors in two locations a little off the beaten tourist tracks. The former headquarters of the Stasi, in a forbidding complex of buildings between Normannenstraße and Magdalenenstraße, was repurposed to portray the dark control centre of surveillance and secret means of coercion. Stasi chief Erich Mielke's office, with its large desk and old-fashioned telephones, alongside rooms furnished in the uniform beige style with drooping pot plants so typical of the GDR, might now appear almost pathetically out-of-date, even inappropriately harmless, despite the accompanying exhibition portraying the apparatus of repression. A greater sense of physical terror was presented in the former Stasi prison at Hohenschönhausen, where previous inmates spoke of their own experiences of incarceration while giving guided tours of prison cells and describing the methods of torture used during the early Stalinist period of the GDR.

Even if few visitors braved the S-Bahn and tram journeys required to get to these authentic physical sites of memory, the Stasi loomed very large in the cultural imagination. And, as ever, uncertainties about interpretations of Berlin's past were thematised in creative representations. The West German film-maker, Florian Henckel von Donnersmarck, produced a somewhat a-historical glimpse of Stasi surveillance and the oppression of the East Berlin cultural intelligentsia in his box-office success, *The Lives of Others* (2006). Other films adopted a more humorous, ironic approach. In some respects both Wolfgang Becker's satire, *Goodbye Lenin!* (2003), and Leander Haussmann's comedy, *Sonnenallee* (1999), perhaps precisely because of their wilful rejection of realism conveyed a more complex and yet in many respects authentic image of conflicting experiences of life in East Berlin. Museums seeking to portray a comprehensive view of everyday life in the GDR veered between emphasising coercion and control, or private contentment despite repression and deprivations. Achieving a balance between sensationalising and trivialising was never easy, while aiming to inform and engage visitors of all ages and backgrounds.

Any portrayal would inevitably provoke controversy. In a period of social upheaval and personal dislocation, many East Berliners experienced a form of 'nostalgia for the east', *Ostalgie*, or longing for a lost sense of security and the idealised warmth of interpersonal relationships under communism, as contrasted with the individualistic, competitive 'elbow society' of the west. Mundanely, capitalism both profited from and fed this 'ostalgia' by selling trinkets symbolising the GDR. East Berlin's surprisingly amiable traffic light figures – *Ampelmännchen* – were among the few markers that West Berlin happily adopted, with purposeful-looking stocky figures wearing walking hats replacing the western stick men on pedestrian traffic lights across the city. Small replicas of these, along with colourful plastic eggcups in the shape of chickens, and paperweights allegedly containing fragments of the Wall, were sold in souvenir shops alongside tee-shirts, mugs, and tote bags with the ubiquitous logos of the Berlin bear and the Brandenburg Gate.

Virtually nothing about the effort to symbolise a new beginning for Berlin was uncontentious. The television tower (*Fernsehturm*), East German symbol of technological progress and still a landmark that could be seen from afar, was left in place. But the controversial decision was taken to demolish the GDR's Palace of the Republic and to rebuild the façade of the former Hohenzollern Palace that had been blown up by the communists. The target itself was arguably misplaced: the Palace of the Republic, seat of the GDR parliament, had also hosted social events and activities, and had not been a real centre of political power. If anywhere, that had been in the Politburo building, now quietly taken over by the German Foreign Office, yet the far greater political significance of that building was barely noted; security considerations were prioritised over historical display. Despite the cost of asbestos removal, the Palace of the Republic could have been sanitised and put to other purposes. Furthermore, erecting a new building that reconstructed the outward appearance of the former royal Palace, at least around three sides, seemed to be harking back to traditions that democratic Germany had renounced. Moreover, even the laudable purpose of housing the Humboldt Forum, a centre supposedly symbolising openness by exhibiting and engaging with world cultures, provoked criticism. While encouragement of public debate and global responsibility was central to Germany's new identity, displaying objects often deriving from colonial ventures was problematic. Opinions were divided between those who enjoyed the resurrection of an old Berlin landscape while acquiring a new cultural venue, and those who felt it was both politically inappropriate and a massive waste of money. At the same time, the location was used to display revolutionary events that had taken place on this site in 1848, 1918, and 1989 (Figure 10.2).

Generally, only relatively harmless relics of the lost society, or those so large or significant as to be irremovable, were preserved. Some major monuments to communist heroes and the Red Army were retained. The Soviet tank memorial in the Tiergarten remained, as did the massive Treptower Park memorial grounds with their oversized statues and extraordinary sarcophagi. The German-Russian Museum in Karlshorst, the historic site where German surrender had been signed on 8 May 1945, still conveyed a tinge of the Soviet version of history, emphasising Soviet heroism and suffering. The housing estate around East Berlin's Thälmann Park was radically transformed, yet the massive bust of Ernst Thälmann himself was kept, even if generally covered in graffiti. Lenin was however toppled from his post outside an apartment

Figure 10.2 Revolutionary demonstrations by Berlin citizens in March 1848 on the site of the former Royal Palace, now occupied by the Humboldt Forum
Memorials to the revolutionary moments of 1848, 1918, and 1989 are displayed on the exterior wall of the Humboldt Forum, including this image of the citizens demonstrating on this spot in March 1848. The interior of the Humboldt Forum also includes a display of archaeological layers, including the uncovered basement walls of the medieval Dominican monastery and the foundations of the Berlin Palace, with shards of pottery and other items found on the site across the centuries, and culminating in objects left by East German workers engaged in demolition of the ruins after the war. This rendering visible of the layering of history is typical of Berlin today. Unknown author; public domain

block. Oversized statues of Marx and Engels still sit in the city centre, facing sagely towards the east, but now with the new Humboldt Forum rather than the Palace of the Republic behind

Figure 10.3 Communist heroes who remain: Marx and Engels
The grave-faced outsize statues remain, but behind them the new Humboldt Forum – three sides replicating the old royal palace – has replaced the East German Palace of the Republic, which had housed the GDR parliament. To the right is the Berlin Dom, or Cathedral, redesigned in Imperial Berlin, beneath which lie the ancestral graves of Hohenzollern rulers. This overlapping, selective (in)visibility of layers of contrasting historical periods is typical of Berlin.
Photograph by the author

them (Figure 10.3). Politically loaded street names proved surprisingly difficult to resolve. It was not always straightforward to revert to older names, since previous eras threw up their own challenges. It was clearly impossible to go back to the Nazi period, but names from earlier periods were not always much easier: discredited militaristic, monarchical, or colonial references were problematic. Prussian generals from the wars of liberation seemed just about acceptable (or sufficiently forgotten as not to rouse hackles). Yet again, Berlin was trying hard to reinvent itself.[5]

Moving Berliners

Berlin had to be reconnected in fundamental ways, and this right from the start. Former transport links were joined up again across the city, and U-Bahn ghost stations reopened, re-connecting east and west. Links to surrounding areas were resuscitated, including the S-Bahn lines from Potsdam and the lakes of the southwest right through to the housing estates of Marzahn and beyond in the former east; from the villas of Wannsee, one of which had hosted the 1942 conference coordinating the Nazi 'Final Solution of the Jewish Question', up to Oranienburg, location of the former Sachsenhausen concentration camp; and from the medieval citadel of Spandau in the west to the Renaissance hunting lodge of Köpenick and the Müggelsee lake in the southeast. Perhaps strangest for those aware of the Cold War spy swaps, immortalised in thrillers and films, is the now mundane crossing over the Glienicke Bridge between Berlin and Potsdam (Figure 10.4), once the site of Cold War terror. Less obviously strange, but nevertheless a shade disconcerting, is the way in which tram lines suddenly terminate at an invisible border where the Wall used to stand, and serve only northern and eastern parts of Berlin.

Over the decades following unification, despite incessant grumbling on the part of Berliners, communication links were continually improved and extended. What had been the nearly deserted Lehrter Bahnhof on the S-Bahn line towards the Friedrichstraße station – a dead end or a tearful transit point, depending on the traveller's visa – acquired wholly new status as Berlin's Central Station or Hauptbahnhof, with high-speed train connections in all directions. A new U-Bahn spur was built to link the government quarters to the Brandenburg Gate, and thence all the way down Unter den Linden to Alexanderplatz, with a new station along the way for Museum Island and the new

RE-CONNECTION

Figure 10.4 Glienicke Bridge between Berlin and Potsdam
It is hard to believe that this was the infamous crossing point over which significant political prisoners were swapped between East and West during the Cold War. The site of innumerable spy thrillers and films, it now is simply a humble bridge over which traffic rumbles.
Photograph by the author

Humboldt Forum on the site of the former Palace. And Berlin was itself re-connected with the wider world, not just with fast rail links across Germany and Europe, but also a new international airport, the Berlin-Brandenburg Airport Willy Brandt (BER). This was finally officially opened on 31 October 2020 after years of delay, complementing the shabby and outdated East German terminal of Schönefeld, and replacing the overstretched Tegel airport of West Berlin as well as the already disused older Tempelhof airport. The long-awaited opening of the new BER airport in the event took place in the quietest possible manner in 2020, during the Coronavirus pandemic. One symbolic flight was timed to land and another to take off, observed by a select handful of high-profile individuals in an otherwise entirely deserted scene.

By the time BER was opened, the character of the city had been radically transformed. Social, economic, and political tensions in eastern Germany had initially been exacerbated by the rapid privatisation and closure of unproductive industries, alongside the loss of guaranteed employment, subsidised housing, and childcare. Housing across Berlin was affected by the growth of private ownership, the renovation and gentrification of formerly run-down older districts, and the end of guaranteed tenancies and cheap rents. And while affluent newcomers felt that they could snap up bargains, less well-off residents viewed with horror the rising rents and house prices.

The wider implications of unification in the physical environment were most immediately evident in East Berlin, although with striking variations across different areas. The district of Mitte once again became a vibrant city centre, as Unter den Linden, the Nikolai quarter, and Hackescher Markt, were renovated, with the area hosting many tourist attractions. Heading north from the centre, the previously dilapidated Prenzlauer Berg was radically transformed, socially as well as physically. In the early 1990s, it was estimated that around 90 per cent of the housing stock required urgent renovation. Many apartment blocks had become effectively uninhabitable during the 1980s, when those who could obtain a place in the new concrete housing estates in Marzahn gladly moved out; often, squatters, artists, and dissidents took their place, and the area gained a reputation as a hotbed of citizens' initiatives and alternative subcultures, with residents ranging from the artist and human rights activist Bärbel Bohley through to the poet and secret Stasi informer Sascha

Anderson. Many residents experienced an incredible atmosphere of renewal and awakening (*Aufbruchsstimmung*) during the 'peaceful revolution' in 1989, only to be disappointed, like Bohley, by post-unification developments and what was seen as a western takeover. Now designated as one of the largest contiguous areas for redevelopment in Europe, in the 1990s Prenzlauer Berg experienced rapid gentrification, accompanied not only by essential renovation of dangerously crumbling buildings, but also by the growth of private ownership and rising rents. While tourism and street life began to flourish, with lively cafes and restaurants, many ordinary Berliners could no longer afford to live there. Other areas of East Berlin, such as Friedrichshain, remained magnets for those seeking alternative lifestyles, but even here the extensive renovation of dilapidated housing, along with gentrification of the social environment, made the area increasingly unaffordable for many. In the northeastern suburb of Marzahn, by contrast, what had in the 1980s been seen as highly desirable and socially mixed apartment blocks, with indoor sanitation and central heating, now began to appear a great deal less attractive, in places even verging on high-rise slums for the socially marginal or temporary shelters for waves of immigrants. The situation was made worse by the post-unification policy of demolishing former GDR social centres and related facilities that had been an architectural feature of the attempt to design close-knit socialist neighbourhoods along the lines of the traditional *Kiez*.

In western Berlin, the influx of property developers, government officials, and countless other professionals had implications for urban topography, property values, and residential profiles in slightly different ways. Potsdamer Platz, which following the devastations of wartime bombing had become a forlorn and empty area against the Wall, was subjected to particularly rapid and radical reconstruction. The expanded and modernised Potsdamer Station, gaining greatly in significance as a transport link for high-speed intercity trains as well as local S-Bahn and U-Bahn lines, was rapidly surrounded by an extended shopping centre reminiscent of any international airport or western city, soon complemented by the Mall of Berlin in neighbouring Leipziger Platz. With the Sony Centre, cinemas, a film museum, restaurants, and commercial outlets, an attempt was made to recreate in modern terms the vibrant atmosphere of the area in early twentieth-century Berlin; but the speed of rebuilding and the thoughtlessness of the architecture seemed to many to undercut any revitalisation on Weimar lines. Meanwhile, in the district of Kreuzberg, formerly hard up against the Wall and home to Turkish 'guest workers' and others in search of cheap housing or alternative lifestyles, older apartment buildings were renovated and property values shot up. Moving somewhat further out to the southeast, the still desperately poor district of Neukölln began to be seen by some as 'edgy' – to use a then-current word – but remained largely run-down, with some locations gaining reputations for drug-dealing hotspots. The more affluent western areas of the city, such as Wilmersdorf or Charlottenburg, previously the centre of West Berlin, began to seem peripheral, even dated; the Cold War glitz of the Kurfürstendamm had faded, and the symbolic profile of the ruined Kaiser Wilhelm Memorial Church no longer evoked such resonance. But the route along the Tauentzienstraße to Wittenbergplatz, with its historic department store, KaDeWe, remained a significant shopping centre. Heading further out towards the southwest, leafy residential areas such as Zehlendorf or Dahlem seemed far less affected by the shifts in the character of central and eastern Berlin.

The transformation of Berlin took place, moreover, in a changing economic and political environment. With the loss of subsidies and support for restructuring in the early 1990s, by the turn of the century the initial 'grand coalition' city government had become increasingly embroiled in financial difficulties. A series of scandals led to its collapse and replacement in 2001 by a 'Red-Red' coalition of the moderate social democrats in the SPD with the more extreme left-wing party, the PDS, a successor party to the hated East German communist SED that later gained further democratic respectability with its renaming as 'The Left' (*Die Linke*). The severe financial situation of the city in the early twenty-first century, and the refusal of the national government to bail it out, led in practice to the new left-wing city government being forced to continue a largely conservative programme of austerity and cuts. Yet at the same time the image of the city changed dramatically. The first openly gay Mayor of Berlin, Klaus Wowereit, who governed the city from 2001 to 2014, devoted considerable attention to marketing Berlin as a place not only of cultural consumption – with its traditional wealth of museums, art galleries, and musical venues of all varieties – but also of new cultural production in an atmosphere of tolerance and diversity.[6] For some, Wowereit's catchy slogan that 'Berlin is poor, but sexy' confirmed the new Berlin as capital of alternative cultural scenes, with a significant impact on demography and tourism.

Berlin society was changing and new issues arising. Younger people without personal memories of Berlin before 1990 could ignore the former lines between east and west far more easily than older generations. Meanwhile, with shifts in cultural attitudes and citizenship laws, long-resident Turkish families and descendants of immigrants were no longer treated as 'guest workers' but rather as Turkish Germans, or Germans 'with a migration background'. And, as throughout the centuries, Berlin's population was continually infused with new blood from far beyond its borders. Particularly from 2015, when the then Chancellor Angela Merkel welcomed large numbers of refugees, Berlin became an increasingly multi-ethnic, multicultural city. New waves of immigration included refugees from conflicts in the Middle East, many of them Muslims. Berlin was home not only to the largest Jewish community in Germany, often coming from Russia or Israel, but also the largest Palestinian diaspora.[7] Following the Russian invasion of Ukraine in February 2022 – which severely challenged Germany's post-war aversion to involvement in military endeavours – Berliners offered housing and help to Ukrainian women and children fleeing the devastation while men remained to defend their country. And many individuals continued to come not primarily because of push factors from former homelands, but rather because of the attractions of Berlin itself. In an increasingly globalised world, with mobile and remote working made possible by the internet and furthered by the Coronavirus pandemic from 2020, people came to Berlin seeking spaces for creativity, productivity, and a relaxed and affordable lifestyle.

Over time, distinctions between Berliners came to be less about living in east or west, cutting the cake in half as it were, but rather about location in what was effectively becoming a donut shape, with distinctions between those affluent enough to live within the S-Bahn Ring, or residing on radial transport routes outside the central areas.

Landscapes of Remorse

Alongside Berlin's many world-renowned museums, musical, cultural, and artistic events, and vibrant nightlife, the tourist trade has actively promoted significant historical sites, whether relating to communism, Nazism, or earlier periods of history. 'Berlin underworlds', reconstructed bunkers, museums of spies, and immersive portrayals of Germany through the ages with all the latest experiential technology, have augmented the long-established national exhibitions of science, natural history, art, and archaeology. And in every district, small municipally-funded museums portray aspects of local history and perpetuate the sense that Berlin is a conglomeration of separate little villages and townships with their own distinctive identities; while often quirky and fascinating, these often subsist well under the radar of any casual visitor to the city. Most notably and unavoidably, however, Berlin has developed an industry around self-representation and memorialisation; and in particular, emphasising its absolute rejection of the Nazi past.

Berlin is perhaps unique among major capital cities in displaying such a level of national shame in public remembrance of the victims of its own previous misdeeds. This, along with the Wall, is arguably one of the most striking features of the city.

Following unification, an entirely new landscape of remembrance sprang up. The expansive and contested Memorial to the Murdered Jews of Europe (*Denkmal für die ermordeten Juden Europas*) was opened in 2005 on the site of the Wall near the Brandenburg Gate. Designed by architect Peter Eisenmann, the 19,000 square metre site of 2,711 concrete slabs is somewhat reminiscent of a massive graveyard; yet many meanings can be read into this maze-like arena, in which it is easy to become disorientated. Below ground, an exhibition portrays the fates of European Jews, with moving individual examples from different countries. This national memorial is dedicated to remembering all the Jews of Europe, while highlighting German responsibility. Right from the outset, the memorial was controversial, criticised variously for overstating national shame or, conversely, being tokenistic and marginalising problems of the present.

The Memorial to the Murdered Jews of Europe was followed over succeeding years by smaller memorials to other persecuted groups. In 2008, the Memorial to the Persecuted Homosexuals under National Socialism was opened, appropriately enough, by Berlin Mayor Wowereit. This was set a little apart in the Tiergarten, surrounded by trees and bushes, and visitors were constrained to 'peep' into a slot affording glimpses of film footage showing same-sex couples. In 2012, a memorial to

Roma and Sinti, or 'gypsies' as the Nazis had called them (*Zigeuner*), was constructed with a reflective pool close to the Reichstag, augmenting the small memorials to this group in Marzahn, East Berlin, the first of which had been established in 1987. Remembrance of victims of compulsory sterilisation and 'euthanasia' was given shape in 2014 on the site of Tiergartenstraße 4, which had been the headquarters of the T4 programme, complete with an informative exhibit. The Nazi Forced Labour Documentation Centre was opened in 2006, in the almost uniquely well-preserved barracks of the former forced labour camp in Berlin-Schöneweide.

Across Berlin, numerous other memorials to victims of Nazi persecution were erected: on platform 17 of Grunewald station, details of transports to destinations in eastern Europe reference the deportation trains; at Anhalter Bahnhof, a large sign indicates how deportations on passenger trains could take place in full view; in Steglitz, a mirror listing names of deported former residents and reflecting the images of onlookers, suggests the complicity of bystanders. These and many other sites, including plaques where synagogues had been burned down, serve to keep the victims of Nazi persecution in mind. Particularly striking is the most decentralised form of memorial: little brass plaques the size of cobblestones, known as *Stolpersteine* ('stumbling stones'), set into pavements across Berlin from the mid-1990s, and increasingly also far beyond (Figure 10.5). Designed by Gunter Demnig, a native Berliner, to memorialise individuals close to their last chosen residence, they bear brief details of the names, dates, places, and ultimate fates of people who were persecuted on grounds of 'race', sexuality, disability, political opposition, or for other reasons, and who had been variously deported, murdered, forced to escape their homeland, driven to suicide, or had simply disappeared, 'fate unknown'. As of

Figure 10.5 Memorials to victims of Nazi persecution: *Stolpersteine* (stumbling stones)
Perhaps the most striking form of memorialisation in Berlin – in a crowded landscape of remembrance that includes the extensive Memorial to the Murdered Jews of Europe, alongside memorials to Roma and Sinti, people persecuted on grounds of homosexuality, and those with mental and physical disabilities – are the ubiquitous small brass *Stolpersteine* (stumbling stones), commemorating individuals, generally at their last chosen place of residence. The group here illustrates a range of fates.
Photograph by the author

May 2023, more than 100,000 *Stolpersteine* had been laid across more than thirty European countries.[8] By the end of 2023, the organisation *Stolpersteine in Berlin* listed details for 9,647 individuals commemorated in this way in the city; the list is clearly incomplete, suggesting that there are well over 10,000 here alone.[9] This symbolic returning of ghosts to their former homes reminds passers-by of just how many people must have been taken away with the full knowledge and indeed often in full sight of their former neighbours.

Perpetrator sites in Berlin are also remarkable. A key location is on the ruins of the Reich Security Head Office (RSHA), where, following predictable controversies, a permanent exhibition was developed in the Topography of Terror. But there was always a risk that 'authentic sites' might become shrines for former Nazis or neo-Nazis. The remains of Hitler's bunker, formerly in the no-man's land of the Wall, had long been unmarked; now the site has an informative placard but nothing more. The ruined remains of a nearby bunker for members of Hitler's SS bodyguard were also covered up, after graphic imagery of the graffiti on its walls had been documented. But the large and still intact bunker close to the Anhalter station, designed by Albert Speer, is open to tourists with an extensive exhibition focusing both on the history of the Third Reich – 'how could it happen?' – and on the post-war period of division. Sites a little further from the centre, such as the former SA basement cells at General-Pape-Straße, or Plötzensee prison, give some indication of Nazi brutality particularly against political opponents right at the beginning of the regime and at the very end of the war. Although such sites convey a sense of terror, there remain difficulties in portraying Nazi perpetrators.

It is in many respects easier to celebrate resistance than to portray perpetration; but the selection of those included is – as with everything in this area – always controversial. The Memorial to German Resistance (Gedenkstätte Deutscher Widerstand) in the Bendler block initially hosted exhibits commemorating the generally conservative-nationalist individuals involved in the 1944 July Plot; but over time it has expanded displays of other types of dissent, resistance, and opposition, including less well-known *Stille Helden* (silent heroes) who helped to hide or rescue Jews. In the Hackesche Höfe, the Blindenwerkstatt or workshop for the blind where Otto Weidt had managed to hide individual Jews also housed a small exhibition to one such 'silent hero'. The former East German resistance memorials to left-wing opponents of Hitler, as in Köpenick, now remain largely unvisited.

It is arguably even more difficult to portray wider complicity. The artistic installation by Renata Stih and Frieder Schnock in the Bavarian Quarter, where Nazi antisemitic proclamations and regulations hanging from lamp posts evoke initial shock and horror among unwitting passers-by, nevertheless goes a long way in emphasising the ubiquity and indeed normalisation of everyday racism during the Third Reich. And the House of the Wannsee Conference, which finally opened as a memorial site in January 1992 following decades of controversy, now not only profiles the key leaders and bureaucrats who participated in the chilling discussions about how best to organise mass extermination, but also uses archival materials, photographs and film footage to open up wider questions about public knowledge and complicity in mass murder across Europe.

Questions of complicity sometimes open up unexpectedly. Second- and third-generation descendants of victims of Nazi persecution increasingly came to see the places their parents and grandparents had unwillingly left, whether by emigration or deportation. Many second-generation returnees sought to reclaim a sense of place and cultural belonging, or to reconstruct a fractured identity; and in exploring family stories, they might uncover unexpected instances of kindness, or betrayal, or turning away when help might have been offered. Some also came to lay claim to former property, revealing much about how it had been taken out of family hands. Issues of restitution or compensation had been both enabled and complicated by shifts in property ownership with the dismantling of the GDR. Even an episode of the hugely popular TV series *Tatort* ('Scene of the Crime') entitled *'Berlin: beste Lage'* saw the fictional Inspector Markovitz dealing with the legacies of shady property deals from 'Aryanisation' in 1938 to the machinations of post-unification speculators.

At the same time, from the 1990s some older Germans began to articulate a sense that they had themselves been victims of the war, and wanted their own suffering as 'war children', even in some cases as 'war grandchildren', to be recognised. There were also demands for remembrance of suffering on the part of refugees and expellees from the lost eastern provinces at the end of the war. Exploring the topic of forced migrations more broadly, the Documentation Centre for Displacement, Expulsion, Reconciliation (*Stiftung Flucht Vertreibung Versöhnung*) was opened in 2021. While vividly portraying the suffering of victims of flight and expulsion, it also reminds visitors of Germany's role in unleashing a genocidal war in Europe; and it seeks to highlight global migrations and expulsions. A cluster of museums in close proximity – not only the Topography of Terror, and the ruins of the Anhalter Bahnhof with its associations of deportation and exile, but also the Jewish Museum Berlin with its exploration of centuries of Jewish residence and traditions in Germany before the Holocaust – serves to highlight the multifaceted, continually emotive character and selective memorialisation of Berlin's society, past and present.

Berlin's extraordinary landscape of remembrance has always been controversial. Beyond the older desire, often voiced by conservatives in the later twentieth century, to 'finally draw a line under the Nazi past', increasingly there have been vocal critiques from quite different quarters of an apparently overwhelming concern with moral responsibility for Jewish victims of persecution while stifling debates about Israeli policies towards Palestine for fear of being labelled antisemitic. These controversies have been cross-cut by related debates over alleged failures to confront the legacies of colonialism and genocides elsewhere. Such imbalance is being rectified, with for example vigorous local campaigns to change the names of streets with colonialist associations. Similarly, the Humboldt Forum highlights precisely the legacies of colonialism, challenging visitors to think about the dubious origins of many objects in its possession and the ways in which restitution or collaboration might be addressed.

And yet: public responses to the brutal impact of the war in Gaza following the Hamas terrorist attack on Israel on 7 October 2023, with a significant rise in both antisemitism and Islamophobia, suggest that no amount of public remorse and memorialisation can provide a clear guide through the conflicting challenges and turmoil of a later present. And the political protests and counter-demonstrations against growing ethnonationalism and far right movements within Germany itself serve as a reminder of the fragility of democracy and the political significance of economic and social distress.

An Ever-Changing Kaleidoscope

It is perhaps a unique characteristic of Berlin that the city itself has become such a physical, visible engagement with both historical legacies and continuing controversies. The doubly dictatorial past could never be entirely absent in Berlin, whether directly addressed and memorialised, or selectively destroyed or forgotten, marking Berlin in ways that are entirely distinctive. Yet at the same time, the character of Berlin's society visibly changed, and with it the imagined connections between the city's current inhabitants and the past.

In the later 1920s and 1930s, the novels of Christopher Isherwood, Irmgard Keun, and Eric Kästner had captured the social experimentation as well as the disorientation, despair, and tenuous search for connections between individuals in a period of extreme economic distress and radical political transformation; Nazi Berlin later provided fodder for widely read portrayals of political crime and corruption, whether in British detective fiction writer Philip Kerr's Bernie Gunther novels, or Volker Kutscher's much heralded *Babylon Berlin* series; and spy stories in the Cold War informed not only John Le Carré's intriguing portrayals, but also countless other works set in Cold War Berlin, with the iconic Checkpoint Charlie crossing point or the Glienicke Bridge over which spy swaps were effected as key locations. But three-quarters of a century after the defeat of Nazism, and nearly a third of a century after the collapse of communism, new notes were being struck. German writers such as Jenny Erpenbeck disturbingly explored the complex entanglements of personal relationships and political developments before and after the fall of the Wall, highlighting distress, betrayal, and disillusion. Meanwhile, the experiences of the multiple layers of immigrants have received increasing attention. Novels by anglophone writers from quite diverse ethnic and national backgrounds, such as Chris Power, Helon Habila, and Hari Kunzru, variously portray characters who had arrived in Berlin in search of a meaningful life, or as a place of refuge, and became entangled with the darker sides of social existence in twenty-first century Berlin. Their works depict multiple forms of disorientation, rooted in the concatenation of conflicting commitments and the difficulties of finding roots or a stable identity in this extraordinary and always multicultural city. Bea Setton's *Berlin* is a particularly introspective variation from a more privileged perspective, portraying a white woman in her mid-twenties who has come, supported by her parents, to learn German, but whose eating disorder and equally self-destructive habit of lying prevent her from settling in the Kreuzberg and Neukölln scenes she inhabits.[10] And a 2023 film, *Der vermessene Mensch* (slightly mistranslated as 'Measures of Men') movingly problematises German colonialism, racial violence, and the complicity of science.

RE-CONNECTION

Contemporary Berlin remains pockmarked by the multiple legacies of Nazism, war, and division, yet is visibly energised by determination to shape a better present and future. As a political and economic powerhouse at the heart of Europe, Berlin contends with wider currents and challenges – whether national, European, or international – in the light of its own distinctive history. As capital of the Federal Republic of Germany, Berlin has played a key role in a wide range of arenas, whether taking a stand on welcoming refugees, contending with European integration in an enlarged EU, battling with Coronavirus, or attempting to combat rising threats of racism, terrorism, and right-wing extremism. Berlin's institutions foster and facilitate engagement with other worlds, from the rich offerings in innumerable museums and exhibitions to a wide range of social activities, forums for political debate, and cultural performances. The city itself offers something of a stage – whether for political demonstrations, for mass cultural and sporting events, for tourism and nightlife, or for presenting itself as history – that is constantly changing its scenery and props. Yet at the same time, with its readily accessible open spaces, forests, and lakes, combined with ease of transport and still relatively affordable housing in comparison with other major national capitals, Berlin remains one of the world's most liveable cities. And for all the perpetual political ructions, the constant grumbling about anything from public transport to private landlords, the internal divisions, caustic repartee, and cultural critiques, united Berlin continues to attract people from far and wide seeking new opportunities and willingly integrating into a distinctive way of life. Energetic processes of re-connection and reflection, combined with new waves of immigration, have inaugurated yet another phase in what is, in some sense, an ever-repeated pattern of Berlin's self-creation across the centuries.

EPILOGUE

Forever Changing, yet Always Berlin

THE oft-repeated critical comment, made in 1910 by Karl Scheffler, that Berlin is 'a city that is condemned to be forever becoming, never to being' – a city in a constant state of flux, never content – has been perpetually played out over the centuries. Berlin's history is characterised by recurrent self-creation, in a pattern of repeated attempts at self-realisation through reflecting on the past while striving towards a different future. Those elements that were valued in later periods became 'traditions'; those aspects that were discarded, rejected, destroyed, were either obliterated or quietly forgotten and absorbed into later cityscapes without too much attention being paid to previous purposes and profiles.

And yet, as the ever-renewed folk song has it: 'Berlin bleibt doch Berlin' – Berlin still remains Berlin, despite all. For all the changes in size, appearance, population, political regime, economic and social structure, borders, and wider context – there is nevertheless some more enduring sense of what it means to be a Berliner. The city has come to stand for a certain spirit, a way of being in the world. This is hard to identify with any precision. It is moreover uncertain whether such a spirit, even if it could be identified – engaging in social interactions with a degree of acerbic wit, cheekiness, assertiveness tempered by humour – can really survive, let alone thrive, under radically changed conditions. In part, indeed, it is because of the ever-changing nature of Berlin, and the unresolved challenges posed

EPILOGUE

for those who have lived through different phases, that it exerts such continuing fascination.

In the words of a song popularised by Marlene Dietrich, who in the 1930s chose to make her home far away from her native Berlin, 'Ich hab' noch einen Koffer in Berlin': 'I still have [emotional] baggage in Berlin'. The 'treasures of times past' in the 'little suitcase' of which she sings inform both a sense of yearning and a reason for repeatedly returning. At the same time, a much beloved old cliché, repeated on innumerable postcards and tourist

Figure 11.1 Tourist boat on the River Spree
One of Berlin's many boats offering sightseeing cruises along the River Spree. This one bears the message, 'Berlin, you are so wonderful!'
Photograph by the author

brochures across the decades, proclaims that 'Berlin ist eine Reise wert' – 'Berlin is worth a visit', sometimes inserting the word 'immer': 'always' worth a visit (Figure 11.1). And the emblematic Berlin bear, in some medieval iterations a shade frightening and realistic, is now a colourful tubby and friendly sign that the new Berlin, and the new Germany, are – or so they hope, and want to signal – all the better for being in a constant state of flux and self-improvement, while remaining always vigilant in the light of the past.

One thing is certain: any attempt to capture the 'essence' of Berlin is predestined to be rapidly outdated, as the city continues to develop and change, and Berliners of widely differing backgrounds and outlooks contest alternative ways forwards in a conflict-ridden world. And this self-awareness, this energetic engagement with both the past and the future, is itself an inherent part of the city's ever ambiguous appeal.

NOTES

Introduction

1 Ruth Köhler and Wolfgang Richter (eds.), *Berliner Leben 1806–1847* (Berlin: Rütten & Loening, 1954), Vorwort (pp. v–vi), p. v.
2 Fontane described the essence of 'das moderne Berlinertum' ('modern Berliner-ness') in terms of a distinctive combination of apparently contradictory characteristics: 'a peculiar something, in which arrogance and self-irony, strength of character and tendency to vacillation, mockery and good nature, but above all criticism and sentimentality, go hand in hand' ('ein eigentümliches Etwas, darin sich Übermut und Selbstironie, Charakter und Schwankendheit, Spottsucht und Gutmütigkeit, vor allem aber Kritik und Sentimentalität die Hand reichen'); Theodor Fontane, 'Die Märker und das Berlinertum. Ein kulturhistorisches Problem', *Aus dem Nachlaß von Theodor Fontane* (Berlin: F. Fontane & Co., 1908) (pp. 295–312), p. 311.
3 Karl Scheffler, *Berlin: Ein Stadtschicksal* (Berlin: Suhrkamp Verlag, 2015; orig. 1910).
4 Heine quoted in Köhler and Richter (eds.), *Berliner Leben 1806–1847*, 'Einleitung' (pp. vii–xvi), p. vii.
5 These are too numerous to list, but see for example: Johann Christoph Müller and Georg Gottfried Küster, *Berlinische Chronik. Altes und Neues Berlin. In fünff Theile verfasset* (Berlin: Bey Johann Peter Schmid), (Erste Abtheilung, 1737; Zweyte Abtheilung, 1752); Friedrich Nicolai, *Beschreibung der Königlichen Residenzstädte Berlin und Potsdam* (1769), (Hildesheim: Georg Olms Verlag, facsimile of original, 1988); Adolph Streckfuß, *Berlin seit 500 Jahren. Vom Fischerdorf zur Weltstadt. Geschichte und Sage* (Berlin: Alexander Jonas, 1864); Henriette Herz, *Erinnerungen in Briefen und Zeugnissen* (Frankfurt am Main: Insel Verlag, 1984); Fanny Lewald, *Meine Lebensgeschichte* (Königstein: Ulrike Helmer Verlag, 1998, orig, 1861/62); Franz Hessel, *Walking in Berlin. A Flaneur in the Capital* (London: Scribe, 2016; transl.

Amanda DeMarco from orig. German 1929); Joseph Roth, *What I Saw. Reports from Berlin, 1920–1933*, transl. with an introduction Michael Hoffmann (London: Granta Books, 2004); Werner Hegemann, *Das steinerne Berlin. Geschichte der grössten Mietskasernenstadt der Welt* (Berlin: Verlag Gutsav Kiepenheuer, 1930).

1 Foundational Moments

1 As Thomas Carlyle put it: 'not from his looks or qualities, but merely from his heraldic cognisance: a Bear on his shield'; Thomas Carlyle, *History of Friedrich II of Prussia, called Frederick the Great* (London: Chapman and Hall, 1869), Part I, Vol. I, ch. IV, 'Albert the Bear' (pp. 58–62), p. 61.
2 Carlyle, *History of Friedrich II of Prussia*, pp. 60, 61, 62.
3 Johann Christoph Müller and Georg Gottfried Küster, *Berlinische Chronik. Altes und Neues Berlin. In fünff Theile verfasset* (Berlin: Bey Johann Peter Schmid), (Erste Abtheilung, 1737), pp. 3, 7.
4 Müller and Küster, *Berlinische Chronik*, p. 3; Friedrich Nicolai, *Beschreibung der Königlichen Residenzstädte Berlin und Potsdam* (1769), reprinted original facsimile (Hildesheim: Georg Olms Verlag, 1988), pp. 1–2; Karl Scheffler, *Berlin: Ein Stadtschicksal* (Berlin: Suhrkamp Verlag, 2015; orig. 1910), p. 25.
5 Portrayed in the *Holzschnitt aus dem "Summarius"*, 1511, reprinted in Julius Schoeps and Bildarchiv Preußischer Kulturbesitz (eds.), *Berlin. Geschichte einer Stadt* (Berlin: be.bra Verlag, 2001), p. 21.

2 Courtly Residence

1 Geoffrey Parker, *The Thirty Years War* (London: Routledge and Kegan Paul, 1984), p. 165.
2 'Brunnen- und Gassenordnung' of 1660, reprinted in Ruth Glatzer (ed.), *Berliner Leben 1648–1806. Erinnerungen und Berichte* (Berlin: Rütten & Loening, 1956), p. 25.
3 Derek McKay, *The Great Elector* (Harlow: Longman, 2001); and Christopher Clark, *Iron Kingdom: The Rise and Downfall of Prussia, 1600–1947* (London: Penguin, 2007).
4 Thomas Carlyle, *History of Friedrich II of Prussia, called Frederick the Great* (London: Chapman and Hall, 1869), Part I, Vol. I, Book III, ch. XVIII, p. 224.

5 Manuela Böhm, 'Kollektives Gedächtnis und Erinnerungsorte der Berliner Hugenotten', in Roland Berbig, Iwan-M. D'Aprile, Helmut Peitsch and Erhand Schütz (eds.). *Berlins 19. Jahrhundert. Ein Metropolen-Kompendium* (Berlin: Akademie Verlag, 2011), pp. 473–90, p. 473.
6 See for example Alexandra Richie, *Faust's Metropolis. A History of Berlin* (London: HarperCollins, 1999), p. 59; she views only three of the four as 'truly outstanding', p. 52.
7 Adolph Streckfuß, *Berlin seit 500 Jahren. Vom Fischerdorf zur Weltstadt. Geschichte und Sage* (Berlin: Alexander Jonas, 1864), Vol. II, Section VI, ch. 2, pp. 167–80; Ruth Glatzer (ed.), *Berliner Leben 1648–1806. Erinnerungen und Berichte* (Berlin: Rütten & Loening, 1956), p. 114.
8 Georg Gottfried Küster (ed.), *Des alten und neuen Berlin*, (Vierte Abtheilung, 1769) (Berlin: zu finden bei dem Auctore, und in Commission im hallischen Buchladen), pp. 363–4.
9 Küster (ed.), *Des alten und neuen Berlin*, pp. 351–64.
10 Müller and Küster, *Berlinische Chronik. Altes und Neues Berlin*, (Zweyte Abtheilung, 1752), p. 1027.
11 Müller and Küster, *Berlinische Chronik. Altes und Neues Berlin*, (Zweyte Abtheilung, 1752), pp. 659, 1029.
12 Population figures at this time are always rough estimates. These figures are taken from Glatzer (ed.), *Berliner Leben*, p. 10.
13 Johann Christoph Müller and Georg Gottfried Küster, *Berlinische Chronik. Altes und Neues Berlin. In fünff Theile verfasset* (Berlin: Bey Johann Peter Schmid), (Erste Abtheilung, 1737), pp. 1, 3, 4.
14 Müller and Küster, *Berlinische Chronik*, p. 1.
15 John Toland, 'A Relation sent from Berlin to the Hague, August 18, N.S. 1702' (1705), reprinted in J. N. Duggan (ed.), *An Account of the Courts of Prussia and Hanover* (Dublin: The Manuscript Publisher, 2013).
16 Toland, *An Account of the Courts of Prussia and Hanover*.

3 Absolutism and Enlightenment

1 See Amos Elon, *The Pity of It All: A Portrait of the German-Jewish Epoch, 1743–1933* (New York: Picador, Henry Holt, 2003), pp. 1–5 and pp. 33–64.
2 Adolph Streckfuß, *Berlin seit 500 Jahren. Vom Fischerdorf zur Weltstadt. Geschichte und Sage* (Berlin: Alexander Jonas, 1864), IV. Band, pp. 78–82.

3 H. M. Scott, *Enlightened Absolutism: Reform and Reformers in Later Eighteenth-Century Europe* (London: Palgrave, 1990).
4 Population figures from Julius Schoeps and Bildarchiv Preußischer Kulturbesitz (eds.), *Berlin. Geschichte einer Stadt* (Berlin: be.bra Verlag, 2001), pp. 31, 35, 54.
5 See, for example, the report of Saxon Minister and Field Marshal Jakob Heinrich Count von Flemming (1667-1728), in Ruth Glatzer (ed.), *Berliner Leben 1648-1806. Erinnerungen und Berichte* (Berlin: Rütten & Loening, 1956), p. 130.
6 Contemporary newspaper reports reprinted in Glatzer (ed.), *Berliner Leben 1648-1806*, pp. 127-8.
7 Figures for 1735 from Schoeps, *Berlin*, p. 33.
8 See particularly Tim Blanning, *Frederick the Great. King of Prussia* (London: Allen Lane, Penguin, 2015).
9 See contemporary sources reprinted in Glatzer (ed.), *Berliner Leben 1648-1806*, pp. 180-5.
10 Friedrich Nicolai, *Beschreibung der Königlichen Residenzstädte Berlin und Potsdam (1769)*, reprinted original facsimile (Hildesheim: Georg Olms Verlag, 1988), population figures from pp. 130-2, quotation from p. 132.
11 See Amos Elon, *The Pity of It All: A Portrait of the German-Jewish Epoch, 1743-1933* (New York: Picador, Henry Holt, 2003), pp. 1-5; 33-64.
12 Blanning, *Frederick the Great*, ch. 6, pp. 138-60.
13 'Über Berlin. Von einem Fremden', *Berlinische Monatsschrift*, 1783, Vol. 2, pp. 462-4. Digitised version from the University of Bielefeld Library, available at https://ds.ub.uni-bielefeld.de/viewer/image/2239816_002/462/LOG_0065/
14 Friedrich von Cölln, *Wien und Berlin in Parallele* (Amsterdam and Köln, 1808), translated from reprint in Ruth Köhler and Wolfgang Richter (eds.), *Berliner Leben 1806-1847* (Rütten & Loening. 1954), p. 3.
15 Julius Schoeps and Bildarchiv Preußischer Kulturbesitz (eds.), *Berlin. Geschichte einer Stadt* (Berlin: be.bra Verlag, 2001), p. 54.
16 See, for example, the vivid descriptions by Eduard Dürre, *Aufzeichnung, Tagebücher und Briefe* (ed. Ernst Dürre, Leipzig, 1881), reprinted in Köhler and Richter (eds.), *Berliner Leben 1806-1847*, pp. 8-11.
17 See, for example, Alexandra Richie, *Faust's Metropolis. A History of Berlin* (London: HarperCollins, 1999), pp. 97-110.

18 Petra Wilhelmy-Dollinger, *Die Berliner Salons. Mit historisch-literarischen Spaziergängen* (Berlin and New York: Walter de Gruyter, 2000).

4 Emerging Powerhouse

1 Adolph Streckfuß, *Berlin seit 500 Jahren. Vom Fischerdorf zur Weltstadt. Geschichte und Sage* (Berlin: Alexander Jonas, 1864), Vol. IV, p. 429.
2 Moritz Daniel Oppenheim, 'The Return of the Jewish Volunteer from the Wars of Liberation to His Family Still Living According to Old Customs' (1833–34). https://bit.ly/4b7T2AU
3 Report of a French Generalstabsoffizier, to Marschall Davout, on 31 March 1809, reprinted in Köhler and Richter (eds.), *Berliner Leben 1806–1847*, p. 54.
4 Heinrich Heine, *Briefe aus Berlin*, reprinted in Köhler and Richter (eds.), *Berliner Leben 1806–1847*, pp. 110–12.
5 Per Daniel Amadeus Atterbom (1790–1855), *Menschen und Städte, 1817–1819* (Hamburg, n.d), reprinted in Köhler and Richter (eds.), *Berliner Leben 1806–1847*, pp. 116–7.
6 Heinrich Eduard Kochhann, *Tagebücher*, Vol. 1. *Im Vaterhause*, reprinted in Köhler and Richter (eds.), *Berliner Leben 1806–1847*, pp. 4–8.
7 Karl Gutzkow, *Aus der Knabenzeit*, reprinted in Köhler and Richter (eds.), *Berliner Leben 1806–1847*, p. 122.
8 Adolph Streckfuß, *Berlin seit 500 Jahren. Vom Fischerdorf zur Weltstadt. Geschichte und Sage* (Berlin: Alexander Jonas, 1864).
9 Hugo Wauer, *Humoristische Ruckblicke auf Berlins "gute alte" Zeit von 1834 bis 1870* (Berlin 1910), reprinted in Köhler and Richter (eds.), *Berliner Leben 1806–1847*, pp. 125–7.
10 Heinz Reif, 'Das Tiergartenviertel. Geselligkeit und Gesellschaft in Berlins "Neuem Westen" um 1900' in Roland Berbig, Iwan-M. D'Aprile, Helmut Peitsch and Erhand Schütz (eds.), *Berlins 19. Jahrhundert. Ein Metropolen-Kompendium* (Berlin: Akademie Verlag, 2011), pp. 259–83.
11 Petra Wilhelmy-Dollinger, *Die Berliner Salons. Mit historish-literarischen Spaziergängen* (Berlin and New York: Walter de Gruyter, 2000), pp. 1–2.
12 See, for example, the comments made by Rahel von Varnhagen in letters to her husband, reporting on Heinrich Heine's periodic visits to her

salon, reprinted in *Heinrich Heine. Gespräche, Briefe, Tagebücher, Berichte seiner Zeitgenossen*, ed. Hugo Bieber (Berlin, 1926).
13 Fanny Lewald, *Meine Lebensgeschichte* (ed. Ulrike Helmer; Königstein: Ulrike Helmer Verlag, 1998, orig. 1861/62), Vol. 2. *Leidensjahre*, pp. 5; 6–7; 7 ff; 13.
14 Henriette Herz, *Erinnerungen in Briefen und Zeugnissen* (Frankfurt am Main: Insel Verlag, 1984).
15 Deborah Hertz, *How Jews Became Germans: The History of Conversion and Assimilation in Berlin* (New Haven: Yale University Press, 2007); Amos Elon, *The Pity of It All: A Portrait of the German-Jewish Epoch, 1743–1933* (New York: Picador, Henry Holt, 2003).
16 See the wonderfully detailed exploration in Leonard Barkan, *Berlin for Jews* (Chicago: University of Chicago Press, 2016), ch. 1, pp. 13–41.
17 Adolph Streckfuß, *Berlin seit 500 Jahren. Vom Fischerdorf zur Weltstadt. Geschichte und Sage* (Berlin: Alexander Jonas, 1864), Vol. II, pp. 328; 329–30.
18 See the fascinating description of the opening of Potsdam railway line in 1838 by Adolph Streckfuß, *Berlin seit 500 Jahren. Vom Fischerdorf zur Weltstadt. Geschichte und Sage in gekürzter Darstellung und bis in die neueste Zeit fortgeführt*, ed. Leo Fernbach (Berlin: Verlag von Albert Goldschmidt, 1900), pp. 556–7.
19 *Der Publizist*, 10 February 1847, reprinted in Köhler and Richter (eds.), *Berliner Leben 1806–1847*, pp. 375–6.
20 See Axel Körner (ed.), *1848 – A European Revolution? International Ideas and National Memories of 1848* (London: Palgrave Macmillan, 2000).
21 See, for example, the close eye-witness account by Karl Gutzkow, *Unter dem schwarzen Bären. Erlebtes 1811–1848*, ed. Fritz Böttge (Berlin: Verlag der Nation, 1971), pp. 529–52.
22 Fanny Lewald, *A Year of Revolutions. Fanny Lewald's "Recollections of 1848"*, transl., ed. and annotated by Hanna Ballin Lewis (New York: Berghahn, 1997; orig. 1850), April 11, 1848, p. 89.
23 Adolf Streckfuß, *1848. Die März-Revolution in Berlin. Ein Augenzeuge erzählt*, ed. Horst Denkler with Irmgard Denkler (Köln: c.w.leske 1983), pp. 208–9; 212–13.
24 Lewald, *Year of Revolutions*, p. 90.
25 Lewald, *Year of Revolutions*, pp. 114–15.

26 See, for example, Felix Philippi, *Alt Berlin: Erinnerungen aus der Jugendzeit*, ed. and introduced by Marion Krämer (Berlin: Mittler & Sohn, 1950 edn; orig. 1914), pp. 82–90.
27 Philippi, *Alt-Berlin*, pp. 1–12; 60–62; 46–56.
28 On the planning, development and impact of Hobrecht's plans, see Gabi Dolff-Bonekämper, Angela Million and Elke Pahl-Weber (eds.), *Das Hobrechtsche Berlin. Wachstum, Wandel und Wert der Berliner Stadterweiterung* (Berlin: DOM publishers, 2018).
29 Julius Schoeps and Bildarchiv Preußischer Kulturbesitz (eds.), *Berlin. Geschichte einer Stadt* (Berlin: be.bra Verlag, 2001), pp. 60–1.

5 World City

1 A detailed analysis of the event is given by Alexander C. T. Geppert, 'Weltstadt für einen Sommer: Die Berliner Gewerbeausstellung 1896 im europäischen Kontext', Die Geschichte Berlins. https://bit.ly/43LpgiV.
2 Figures from Geppert, 'Weltstadt für einen Sommer'. A lower figure of five million visitors is cited by David Clay Large, *Berlin: A Modern History* (London: Allen Lane, 2001), p. 2, rendering it a 'financial disaster'.
3 Alfred Kerr, 'Von Treptow bis nach Afrika. Die Stadt holt sich die Welt ins Haus. Die Gewerbeausstellung' in *Mein Berlin* (pp. 100–13), 3 May 1896, p. 106.
4 Alfred Kerr, 'Brüder aus Neu-Guinea', in *Mein Berlin*, 10 May 1896, p. 108.
5 Figures from Geppert, 'Weltstadt für einen Sommer'.
6 www.museumsportal-berlin.de/en/exhibitions/zurueckgeschaut-looking-back. Curiously, this colonialist aspect of the exhibition does not even receive a mention in David Clay Large's summary in *Berlin: A Modern History*, pp. 81–2.
7 For a clear summary of the Reich constitution and the Prussian system, see Christopher Clark, *Iron Kingdom. The Rise and Downfall of Prussia, 1600–1947* (London: Penguin, Allen Lane, 2006), pp. 556–62 and ff.
8 An unusually sympathetic portrait is painted by Felix Philippi, *Alt-Berlin. Erinnerungen aus der Jugendzeit* (Berlin: Ernst Siegfried Mittler und Sohn, 1913), ch. 4, pp. 36–45.
9 Harald Bodenschatz, 'Auf dem Weg zur Mietskasernenstadt?', in Roland Berbig, Iwan-M. D'Aprile, Helmut Peitsch and Erhand Schütz

(eds). *Berlins 19. Jahrhundert. Ein Metropolen-Kompendium* (Berlin: Akademie Verlag, 2011), (pp. 297–307), figures from pp. 297–8.

10 Bodenschatz, 'Auf dem Weg zur Mietskasernenstadt?', p. 298.

11 Heinz Reif, 'Das Tiergartenviertel. Geselligkeit und Gesellschaft in Berlins "Neuem Westen" um 1900', in Roland Berbig, Iwan-M. D'Aprile, Helmut Peitsch and Erhand Schütz (eds). *Berlins 19. Jahrhundert. Ein Metropolen-Kompendium* (Berlin: Akademie Verlag, 2011), (pp. 259–83).

12 Kerr, *Mein Berlin*, 'Neuer Luxus, alte Not', pp. 72–3.

13 Barkan, *Berlin for Jews*, ch. 2; and Bodenschatz, 'Auf dem Weg zur Mietskasernenstadt?', pp. 302–4. See also Georg Haberland, *Der Kampf um das Tempelhofer Feld* (Berlin, 1911).

14 Bodenschatz, p. 304.

15 Bodenschatz, pp. 304–7.

16 Albert Kohn (ed.), *Unsere Wohnungs-Enquête im Jahre* [various dates] (Berlin: Ortskrankenkasse für den Gewerbebetrieb der Kaufleute, Handelsleute und Apotheker, 1902–1913, and 1913–1920). See also Gesine Asmus (ed.), *Hinterhof, Keller und Mansarde. Einblicke in Berliner Wohnungselend 1901–1920* (Reinbek: Rowohlt, 1982).

17 See, for example, Kerr, *Mein Berlin*, 'Dora auf dem Eis', pp. 69–71 (28 November 1897); and Philippi, *Alt-Berlin*, pp. 36–8.

18 See, for example, Philippi, *Alt-Berlin*, pp. 46–56.

19 Details of each statue are given in Karl Baedeker, *Berlin and its Environs. Handbook for Travellers* (Leipzig; Karl Baedeker, 1910; 4th edn), pp. 141–3.

20 Alfred Kerr, 'Wo Bismarck ging und Tietz erschien', in *Mein Berlin. Schauplätze einer Metropole*, ed. Günther Rühle (Berlin: Aufbau Verlag, 1999), pp. 93–8, 30 September 1900.

21 Marie von Bunsen, *Die Welt in der ich lebte. Erinnerungen aus glücklichen Jahren 1860–1912* (Leipzig: Koehler & Amelang, 1929).

22 Harry Kessler, *Journey to the Abyss. The Diaries of Count Harry Kessler, 1880–1918*, ed., transl. and introduced by Laird M. Easton (New York: Alfred A. Knopf, 2011), pp. 127–8.

23 Kessler, *Journey to the Abyss*, p. 131.

24 Kerr, *Mein Berlin*, p. 38.

25 Karl Baedeker, *Berlin and its Environs. Handbook for Travellers* (Leipzig; Karl Baedeker, 1910; 4th edn), p. 140.

26 On Paasche, see for example, Mary Fulbrook, *Dissonant Lives: Generations and Violence through the German Dictatorships* (Oxford: Oxford University Press, 2011).
27 For the wider context, see for example, Mark Hewitson, *Germany and the Causes of the First World War* (Oxford: Berg, 2004); and Christopher Clark, *The Sleepwalkers: How Europe Went to War in 1914* (London: Allen Lane, 2012).
28 Karl Scheffler, *Berlin: ein Stadtschicksal* (Berlin: Suhrkamp verlag, 2016; reprint of original of 1910), pp. 123-7.
29 Felix Philippi, *Alt-Berlin. Erinnerungen aus der Jugendzeit* (Berlin: Ernst Siegfried Mittler und Sohn, 1913), p. 57, p. 60.
30 Harry Kessler, *Journey to the Abyss. The Diaries of Count Harry Kessler, 1880-1918*, ed., transl. and introduced by Laird M. Easton (New York: Alfred A. Knopf, 2011), entry of 3 March 1898, p. 201.
31 Kessler, *Journey to the Abyss*, entries of 8 and 17 April 1916, pp. 713, 714.

6 Greater Berlin

1 See, for example, the vivid description of these events given by Emil Julius Gumbel, *Vier Jahre politischer Mord* (1922) reprinted in Ruth Glatzer (ed.), *Berlin zur Weimarer Zeit. Panorama einer Metropole 1919-1933* (Berlin: Siedler Verlag, 2000), pp. 28-9.
2 Harry Kessler, *Berlin in Lights. The Diaries of Count Harry Kessler (1918-1937)*, transl. and ed. Charles Kessler (New York: Grove Press, reprinted with an introduction by Ian Buruma, 1971), pp. 41-2, p. 55, pp. 59-60.
3 Figures from Alexandra Richie, *Faust's Metropolis. A History of Berlin* (London: HarperCollins, 1999), p. 364.
4 Joseph Roth, *What I Saw. Reports from Berlin, 1920-1933*, transl. with an introduction by Michael Hoffmann (London: Granta Books, 2004), p. 37.
5 Roth, *What I Saw*, pp. 37-8.
6 Werner Hegemann, *Das steinerne Berlin. Geschichte der grössten Mietskasernenstadt der Welt* (Berlin: Verlag Gutsav Kiepenheuer, 1930), p. 21.
7 Franz Hessel, *Walking in Berlin. A Flaneur in the Capital* (London: Scribe, 2016; transl. by Amanda DeMarco from orig. German 1929), p. 166.
8 Hessel, *Walking in Berlin*, p. 175.
9 On Schloss Britz, see above, Chapter 5.

10 Roth, *What I Saw*, 'Some Reflections on Traffic', *Frankfurter Zeitung*, 15 November 1924 (pp. 97–103), pp. 97, 101, 103.
11 Hessel, *Walking in Berlin*, p. 165.
12 Compare also, for example, the critical social theories of the Frankfurt School associated with Max Horkheimer and Theodor Adorno, or the growing influence of Freudian psychoanalysis, initially based in Vienna.
13 Hessel, *Walking in Berlin*, p. 169.

7 Nazi Berlin

1 Ruth Andreas-Friedrich, *Berlin Underground 1938–1945*, transl. by Barrows Mussey (New York: Henry Holt and Company, 1947), pp. 83, 90, 116. See also Ursula von Kardorff, *Berliner Aufzeichnungen 1942 bis 1945* (München: Deutsche Taschenbuch Verlag, 1994; ed. Peter Hartl), p. 44, letter of 17 October 1942.
2 Andreas-Friedrich, *Berlin Underground*, p. 91.
3 Von Kardorff, *Berliner Aufzeichnungen*, p. 287, 3 February 1945.
4 For various reasons, the figures are not entirely clear; particularly in Berlin, with high degrees of assimilation, conversion, and intermarriage, not all those people of Jewish descent who were designated by the Nazis as 'racially' Jewish were Jewish by religion.
5 For curious-minded tourists, there are maps of Berlin with guides to 'where was what' in previous eras.
6 See Matthias Donath, *Architektur in Berlin 1933–1945. Ein Stadtführer* (Berlin: Lukas Verlag und Landesdenkmalamt, 2004).
7 Donath, *Architektur in Berlin*, pp. 154–6; Himmler quoted on p. 154.
8 Moritz Föllmer, *Individuality and Modernity in Berlin: Self and Society from Weimar to the Wall* (Cambridge: Cambridge University Press, 2015), ch. 4, 'Redefining legitimate individuality', pp. 105–31.
9 *Berlin 1933–1945* (Berlin: Stiftung Topographie des Terrors, 3rd edn, 2014), p. 148.
10 Andreas-Friedrich, *Berlin Underground*; Marie Jalowicz Simon, *Gone to Ground*, transl. Anthea Bell (London: Profile Books, 2016).
11 Many figures here are from Donath, *Architektur in Berlin 1933–1945*, p. 20, pp. 39–40.
12 Christian Goeschel, *Suicide in Nazi Germany* (Oxford: Oxford University Press, 2009), p. 160.

8 Double Visions (1)

1 Margret Boveri, *Tage des Überlebens. Berlin 1945* (Berlin: Wolf Jobst Sieder, 2004), pp. 114–15. See also, for example, the now well-known memoir by German journalist Marta Hillers, *A Woman in Berlin*, first published anonymously in 1954; or the post-war entries in Ruth Andreas-Friedrich, *Der Schattenmann. Tagebuchaufzeichnungen von Ruth Andreas-Friedrich 1938–1948* (Frankfurt am Main: Suhrkamp, 2000; orig. 1947 and 1984).
2 Landesarchiv Berlin: LAB C Rep 375–01–13, Nr. 3554 A.02, Walter K.; LAB C Rep 375–01–13, Nr. 3554 A.04, David K.
3 See, for example, Karin Dohmen, *Märkisches Tagebuch* (Frankfurt am Main: edition fischer im Rita G. Fischer Verlag, 1981), pp. 47–8.
4 See, for example, Anetta Kahane, *Ich sehe, was du nicht siehst. Meine deutschen Geschichten* (Berlin: Rowohlt, 2004).
5 See for example: LAB E Rep 061–23 Nr 26, Franz S.; LAB E Rep 061–23 Nr 14, Johanna K.
6 See, for example, the vivid accounts in Boveri, *Tage des Überlebens*.
7 Ruth Andreas-Friedrich, *Schauplatz Berlin. Tagebuchzeichnungen 1945–1948* (Berlin: Suhrkamp Verlig, orig. 1947, repr. 2016).
8 Victor Klemperer, *So sitze ich zwischen allen Stühlen. Vol. I. Tagebücher 1945–49* and Vol. II. *Tagebücher 1950–59* (Berlin: Aufbau-Verlag, 1999).
9 Klemperer, *So sitze ich zwischen allen Stühlen* Vol. II, pp. 387, 578.

9 Double visions (2)

1 Vera Wollenberger, *Virus der Heuchler. Innenansicht aus Stasiakten* (Berlin: Espresso/Elef.Press, 1992).
2 Tim Verlaan, 'The Neues Kreuzberger Zentrum: Urban Planners, Property Developers and Fractious Left Politics in West Berlin, 1963–1974', *German History*, Vol. 38, no. 1, pp. 113–32.
3 See further Mary Fulbrook, *The People's State: East German Society from Hitler to Honecker* (London: Yale University Press, 2005).

10 Re-connection

1 German Diary Archive (DTA) Emmendingen, 1350.131, female aged thirty, teacher of sports and German, mother of two children, entry of

1. 3 October 1990. Also quoted in Mary Fulbrook, *Dissonant Lives: Generations and Violence through the German Dictatorships* (Oxford: Oxford University Press, 2017, two-vol. second edition), Vol. II, pp. 209–10.
2. DTA 1350.123, female, aged thirty-five, medical technician for x-ray diagnostics, married, one teenage child, entry of 3 October 1990. Also quoted in Fulbrook, *Dissonant Lives*, vol. II, p. 210.
3. German Bundestag, ed., *Stenographische Berichte* (Stenographic Reports), 12th legislative period, 34th session, 20 June 1991 (Bonn, 1991), pp. 2736–8 and 2746–7. Extracts translated by Thomas Dunlap for 'German History in Documents and Images' available at: https://ghdi.ghi-dc.org/print_document.cfm?document_id=3386 (last accessed 18 October 2022). An initial error in counting the votes led to the figure of 337 in favour creeping into the secondary literature, but the final tally was officially determined to be 338 votes supporting the move.
4. Hope M. Harrison, *After the Berlin Wall: Memory and the Making of the New Germany, 1989 to the Present* (New York: Cambridge University Press, 2019); and discussion at https://bit.ly/3J4j9gj
5. See, for example, Brian Ladd, *The Ghosts of Berlin: Confronting German History in the Urban Landscape* (Chicago: University of Chigaco Press, 1997).
6. Claire Colomb, *Staging the New Berlin. Place Marketing and the Politics of Urban Reinvention Post-1989* (London: Routledge, 2011), ch. 8.
7. Sa'ed Atshan and Katharina Galor, *The Moral Triangle. Germans, Israelis, Palestinians* (Durham, NC: Duke University Press, 2020).
8. https://bit.ly/3VFtMO6
9. www.stolpersteine-berlin.de/en/finding-stolpersteine?page=321.
10. See for example: Jenny Erpenbeck, *Kairos* (transl. Michael Hofmann, Granta, 2023); Chris Power, *A Lonely Man* (London: Faber and Faber, 2021); Helon Habila, *Travellers* (London: Penguin, 2019); Hari Kunzru, *Red Pill* (London: Scribner, 2020); Bea Setton, *Berlin* (London: Penguin Random House, 2022).

INDEX

Academies of Arts and Sciences, 33, 47
Adenauer, Konrad, 174, 175
agricultural collectivisation, 171, 174
agricultural production, Frederick the
    Great's fostering of, 51
air-raids, 158
Albert, Margrave of Brandenburg
    (Albert the Bear), 9–12
  conquers the Wends, 10
  statue, 12
Alexander I, Emperor of Russia,
    honouring of in Berlin, 64
Alexandrowka, Potsdam, 64
Allied bombing campaign, impact on
    Berlin, 158–60
allotment gardens, 94, 199
Alte Halle swimming pool,
    Charlottenburg, 94
Altes Museum, 67
'Americanisation' of Berlin, 105
Andreas-Friedrich, Ruth, 134–5,
    158, 169
Anhalter Bahnhof, 147, 234
  memorial to victims of Nazi
      persecution, 230
antisemitism
  growth of during WWI, 106–7
  late nineteenth-century rise of, 84
  post-WWI growth across
      Europe, 117
  recording of incidents in the
      communist East, 170
  rise in racialised forms of, 126
architecture of Berlin,

architect-designed housing,
    Siemensstadt, 122
Atterbom's comments, 63
'Horseshoe Estate'
    (Hufeisensiedlung), 121
John Toland's reports, 37
'rental barracks' (*Mietskasernen*), 79,
    88, 119, 192
aristocracy, cultural, and political
    power of during the imperial
    period, 98–9
'Aryanisation' of Jewish property, 143,
    153, 234
assassination of Walther Rathenau, 115
assassination plot against Hitler, 159,
    203, 232
Atterbom, Per Daniel Amadeus, 63
austerity, 131, 227
Austria
  annexation (1938), 143
  invasion of Berlin (1757), 45
  Prussia's war with (1866), 79
authority, German proclivity for
    obedience to, 57
Axel Springer building, 198
Ayim, May, 27

Baader-Meinhof gang, 192
Babylon Berlin (Kutscher), 236
Bach, Johann Sebastian, 67
Bahnhof Zoo, 189
Bahr, Egon, 194
barbed wire, encircling of West Berlin
    by, 183

INDEX

Bartning, Otto, 121
Basic Treaty between West and East Germany (1972), 194
Battle of Jena-Auerstedt (1806), 60
Battle of Langemarck (1914), 146
Battle of Stalingrad (1942–43), 155
Bauhaus School of architecture, 120–1, 149, 176, 177
Becker, Wolfgang, 217
Berlin
  750th anniversary, 203–4
  and the post-WWI political transformation of Germany, 112–18
  becomes capital of a reunited Germany (1991), 212
  changing character of Berlin society, 116
  cultural topography transformed by Frederick III/I, 33
  description of the city (1783), 52–3
  divergence between East and West, 188–200
  easing of travel restrictions between West and East, 195
  eighteenth-century status, 36
  ever-changing character, 236–40
  Friedrich von Cölln's 1808 description, 54
  historical representations, 6, 8, 217–18
  increasingly multi-ethnic, multicultural city, 227
  key sites, 6
  landscape, 1
  liveability, 237
  location and climate, 1
  map of (1739), **40**
  map of (c. 1600), **20**
  naming of, 11
  origins, 1, 3, 10–20
  place at the heart of Europe, 237
  political division of Germany and, 164
  positive comments of visitors to, 36
  post-WWI expansion and transformation, 118–26
  scientists, creative artists, and intellectuals based in, 126
  status as imperial capital, 79, 83
  transformation into significant European capital, 40
  See also architecture of Berlin; East Berlin; invasions of Berlin; population of Berlin; post-war Berlin; West Berlin.
Berlin (Setton), 236
Berlin Airlift, 164, 169
'Berlin bleibt doch Berlin' (folk song), 238
'Berlin Indignation' (1447–48), 16
'Berlin Story' tourist exhibition, 148
Berlin: Symphony of a Metropolis (Ruttman), 8, 127
'Berlin underworlds', 228
Berlin Wall
  building of, 164, 171, 183
  demolition, 147
  fall of, 206
  fortifications and security apparatus, 199
  impact on the city, 188
  silent visibility on transport maps, 222
  tearing down of and memorialising, 215, 216
Berlin Zoo, 67
'Berlin-Berlin' exhibition, 204
Berlin-Brandenburg Airport Willy Brandt (BER), 223

INDEX

Berliners
 accent and speech patterns, 5
 characteristics and sense of identity, 4, 238
 new-found power after the events of 1848, 72
Berlinische Boden-Gesellschaft, 89
Berlinische Monatsschrift, 52
Bismarck, Otto, Fürst von, 58
 arrival in Berlin, 76
 'battle for culture', 101
 designs the imperial constitution, 83
 introduction of social welfare policies, 85
Bizonia, 169
Black Death (bubonic plague), 15, 48
boating, popularity of, 94
Bolshevik revolution, 3, 113, 116
books, public burning of, 51, 140
border control, between the Federal Republic and the GDR, 171
Borsig, August, 70
bourgeois house on Unter den Linden, porcelain plate portraying, 77
bourgeoisie
 accommodation for, 52, 66
 communist rule and, 171, 174, 194
 growth of, 49, 75, 83
 status, 99
Boveri, Margret, 162
Brandenburg Gate, 106, 178, 218
 and the 'essence of Berlin', 8
 and the industrial expansion of Berlin, 77
 commissioning of, 53
 designer, 53
 Emperor Napoleon rides through (1806), 57, **58**
 landscape of remembrance and, 229

Quadriga, French seizure and return, 60, 62
 Reagan's proclamation from, 187
 torch-lit parade of the Sturmabteilung through, 137
 transport links, 222
 uprising and, 176
Brandenburg marches, 1
Brandenburg-Africa Company (BAC), 26
Brandt, Willy, 194, 211
Brecht, Bertolt, 126, 170
Bülow, Friedrich Wilhelm von, 63
Bundestag, 213
Bunsen, Marie von, 98
Bürgerwehr (citizens' militia), 72

café society, 100
capital city, Berlin's path to becoming, 17
Carlyle, Thomas, 9, 26
Central Station (*Hauptbahnhof*), 222
Charité Hospital, 47, 61, 65
Charles I, King of England, 24
Charles VI, Holy Roman Emperor, 45
Charlottenburg, 89, 119, 226
 Alte Halle swimming pool and public baths, 94
 'Generalszug', 64
 namesake, 32
 remnants of Nazi architecture, 148
 Russian community, 116
Checkpoint Charlie, 199, 236
Christian church, role in the 'germanisation' of lands east of the river Elbe, 13
'Church from Below', 186
churches, medieval origins, 14
cinema, Berliners' passion for, 127
citizens' revolt (1447–48), 16

255

INDEX

citizens' revolt (1848), 72
city government, reformation during Napoleonic wars, 60
coins, Berlin gains the right to mint, 16
Cold War spy swaps, 222
collectivisation, agricultural, 171, 174
Cölln
   and the origins of Berlin, 5, 10-11, 16
   derivation of the name, 13
   location, 3, 10
Cölln, Friedrich von, 54
Cologne, 13
colonialism
   and a sense of cultural superiority, 102-4
   'colonial wares' in a shop window in Köpenick, 103
   debates over failures to confront legacies of, 235
   depiction in *Der vermessene Mensch*, 236
   Frederick William and, 26
   Great Industrial Exposition and, 200
communism
   American concerns about the advance of, 168
   collapse of, 207
compulsory sterilization and euthanasia, remembrance of victims, 230
concentration camps
   Buchenwald, 200
   conditions in, 141
   Ernst Reuter's imprisonment, 168
   Ernst Thälmann's imprisonment, 200
   experimentation on inmates, 151
   exploitation of inmates, 142
   Ravensbrück, 203
   Sachsenhausen, 141-2, 203, 222

Congress of Vienna (1815), 62
Coronavirus pandemic, 224, 228
court
   domination of Berlin society, 18, 34, 69
   etiquette, 98
   Fanny Lewald's view of, 76
   language of, 50
creative representations of Berlin's past, 217-18
cross-dressing, attitudes towards in Weimar Berlin, 128
cultural and intellectual developments in Berlin, 126-30
cultural topography of Berlin, transformed by Frederick III/I, 33
Customs Union, formation of, 69
Czechoslovakia, student unrest, 191

dadaism, 127
Dahlem, 90, 162, 180, 226
'Dance of Death' mural, Marienkirche (St Mary's Church), 14, **15**
Dawes Plan, 131
'Day of German Unity' 209
demilitarisation, 115, 166
Demnig, Gunter, 230
democracy, birth of Germany's first attempt at, 113
democratic constitution, design of, 114
denazification, 164-5, 166, 170
Denmark, Prussia's war with (1864), 79
department stores, opening of, 100
Depression, 130-1
'Der Freischütz' (Weber), 67
Der vermessene Mensch (Kraume), 236
destalinisation, 197
Dietrich, Marlene, 119, 239

INDEX

Different from the Others (Anders als die Anderen) (1919), 128
diversity of Berlin's population, 2–4
Döblin, Alfred, 8
Dresden, 170
Dustmann, Hanns, 148

East Berlin
　building programme, 195–9
　celebration of the 40th anniversary, 206
　cultural and architectural heritage, 178–9
　exponential growth of surveillance, 199
　impact of the imposition of Communist rule, 173
　landscape of Unter den Linden, 196
　living conditions, 192–4
　Luxemburg-Liebknecht demonstration, 185
　memorial to 'Köpenick blood week', 201
　memorials and statuary, 200–3
　return of exiled individuals to, 170
　Tenth World Festival of Youth and Students (1973), 196
　uprising against Communist rule, 164
East Berliners, leisure pursuits, 199
East German parliament (Volkskammer), 196
'East Side Gallery', 216
Ebert, Friedrich, 113
Edict of Emancipation (1812), 61
Edict of Nantes, revocation, 28
Edict of Potsdam (1685), 28
education
　introduction of universal primary education across Brandenburg-Prussia, 48
　prestigious high schools, 49
Ehrhardt, Hermann, 115
Eichmann, Adolf, 123
Einstein, Albert, 126
Eisenmann, Peter, 229
Eisentraut, Wolf-Rüdiger, 198
Eisler, Hanns, 126
Elbe river, 13
electrification, 84, 123
emblems of Berlin, 11, 53, 240
English Civil War, 24
enlightened absolutism
　Berlin as a centre of, 41
　era of, 39
　policies of, 47
Environmental Library, 186–7
Eosander, Johann Friedrich, 32
Erpenbeck, Jenny, 236
ethnic and cultural diversity, 11
expressionism, 127

Fabian (Kästner), 130
Fallada, Hans, 8, 130
Federal Republic of Germany (FRG), formal establishment, 169
Fichte, Johann Gottlieb, 62
fiction, Berlin in, 235
'Final Solution of the Jewish Question', planning of, 157
fire
　at the Reichstag, 138
　city set on fire by imperial troops, 23
　destruction of houses by, 15, 22
First World War
　evidence of personal consequences, 116
　impact on Berlin and its inhabitants, 105–8
　political contributions to outbreak of, 84–5

INDEX

Fischer, Manfred, 216
Fontane, Theodor, 5, 90
forced labour barracks, Schöneweide, 156
'Forum Friedericianum' 50
Foster, Norman, 97, 213–14
'founding' of Berlin, anniversaries celebrated by contrasting regimes, 10
France
  February Revolution (1848), 71
  Prussia's war against (1870), 79
Francke, August Hermann, 48
Französische Dom (French Cathedral), 29
Französisches Gymnasium (French high school), 49
Frederick I, King of Prussia (Frederick III of Brandenburg), 26
  coronation, 30–1
  death, 35
  enlightenment role, 47
  shaping of Berlin, 30
Frederick II, King in Prussia (Frederick the Great), 27
  administrative reform under, 51
  and transformation of Berlin, 40
  character, 44
  constraints imposed on the Jewish population, 39
  death, 52–3
  deploys Prussian army to invade Silesia, 45
  Napoleon pays his respects to, 57
  population growth under, 42
  restrictions on Jews, 39
  statue, 47
    designer, 46
    left standing in Friedrichshain park, 202
    re-erected in Unter den Linden, 203
  support for production of luxury goods, 51
  support of religious toleration and enlightenment thinking, 50
Frederick 'the Iron Tooth' (Eisenzahn), Elector of Brandenburg, 16–17
Frederick William I, King of Prussia ('the Soldier King'), 30, 35, 40
  accession to the throne, 41
  death of, 45
  expansion of state bureaucracy, 42
  military expansion under, 42–4
  support of Pietist movement, 48
Frederick William II, King of Prussia
  accession to the throne, 53
  most visible legacy, 53
Frederick William III, King of Prussia, 53
Frederick William IV, King of Prussia, 67
  accession to the throne, 71
  assassination attempt on, 71
  declares Prussia a constitutional monarchy, 75
Frederick William, Elector of Brandenburg ('Great Elector'),
  accession to electorship, 23
  death, 29
  first wife, 25
  immigration policies, 27
  interest in waterways and shipbuilding, 26
  involvement in overseas colonialism, 26
  military campaigns, 26
  policies introduced by, 25
  successor, 26

INDEX

Free German Youth (FDJ), 180
Free University of Berlin (FU),
    founding and location,
    180
Freikorps, 107–9, 111, 115
Freisler, Roland, 159
French Colony, privileges awarded
    to, 48
French influence, post-Napoleonic era
    continuation, 69
French Revolution, German view, 59
French troops, quartered in Berlin
    during Napoleonic wars, 60
Friedeberg, Heinrich and
    Bernhardine, 76
Friedrich Wilhelm University, 61
Friedrichshain
    cemetery, 73, 110, 202
    first state-run hospital opened in, 91
    housing, 88
    memorials, 110
    Volkspark, 53
Friedrichstadt Tränenpalast (Palace of
    Tears), 77
Friedrichstraße, 199
Friedrichswerdersche Gymnasium, 49

Gastarbeiter (guest workers), 3, 189
Gaza, public responses to the war
    in, 235
General Strike, 115
'*Generalszug*', 64
gentrification, 224–5
Georg Wilhelm, Elector of
    Brandenburg
    death of, 23
    flees the city, 22
German Colonial Museum, 104
German Democratic Republic
    (GDR), 167
    appropriation of Prussian
        heritage, 202
    celebration of the 40th
        anniversary, 206
    collapse of the communist
        regime, 207
    dismantling, 234
    effective one-party dictatorship
        rule, 173
    enters the UN, 195
    first free elections, 207
    formal establishment, 169
    historical representations of, 217–18
    living conditions, 192–4
    marking the demise of, 209
    'nostalgia for the East', 218
    popular uprising, 175
    radical socioeconomic reforms
        under Communist rule, 171
    recognition of by West
        Germany, 194
    redeployment of Göring's Air
        Ministry, 148
    state secret police, 173, 185
    visible decline, 205
German Historical Museum (*Deutsches
    Historisches Museum*),
    exhibitions, 202
German nationalism, 55, 62
German unification, Berlin on the eve
    of, 76–9
German-Jewish community, 27, 38, 61
Germany
    political division of, 164
    post-WWI political transformation,
        112–18
    post-WWII occupation and division
        of, 165–76
    unification of, *see* unification of
        Germany

INDEX

Glienicke Bridge, 200, 222, **223**, 236
Gneisenau, August von, 62
Goebbels, Joseph
  and the public burning of books, 51, 140
  and the re-modelling of Berlin, 136
  and the torch-lit parade of the *Sturmabteilung*, 137
  appointed Gauleiter of Berlin, 118, 132
  Reich Ministry for Public Enlightenment and Propaganda, 147
Goethe, Johann Wolfgang von, 54
Goodbye Lenin! (Becker), 217
Gorbachev, Mikhail, 187, 205–6
Göring, Hermann, 132
Graues Kloster (evangelical high school), 49
Grazer Damm estate, Schöneberg, 151, **152**
Great Industrial Exposition, Treptower Park (1896), 81, 82, 103, 200
Gröben, Friedrich von der, 26
Gröben-Ufer, renaming, 26
Gropius, Walter, 120–1
Grunewald, 18, 89–90, 118, 151
Grunewald station, memorial, 230
Gutzkow, Karl, 65
'Gypsy camp', Marzahn, 142

Haberland, Georg, 90
Habila, Helon, 236
Hackescher Markt, 224
Hallesches Tor, 103
Hanseatic League
  Berlin joins, 16
  Berlin withdraws from, 18
  Hamburg's membership, 16

Hansemann, David J. L. 66
Hardenberg, Karl August von, 60
Häring, Hugo, 121
Haussmann, Leander, 217
Havel river, 1, 10, 26, 125
Hein, Christoph, 206
Heine, Heinrich, 63
Henckel von Donnersmarck, Florian, 217
Henselmann, Hermann, 176
Herz, Henriette, 55, 68, 76
Hessel, Franz, 120, 128
Heym, Stefan, 206
Himmler, Heinrich, 142, 149
Hindenburg, Paul von
  appoints Hitler as chancellor, 112
  election, 130
Hirschfeld, Magnus, 128, 140
historical periods, selection criteria, 2
Hitler Youth, portrayal on Grazer Damm housing estate, 152
Hitler, Adolf
  appointed Chancellor, 112, 133, 137
  bunker, 232
  July 1944 assassination plot against, 159, 203, 232
  'Night of the Long Knives', 141
  plans for Berlin, 136, 144–6
  responsibility for appointment of, 110
  suicide of, 160
Hitzig, Friedrich, 66
Hobrecht, James, 78, 89
Hoflieferanten (deliverers to the court), 69
Hohenschönhausen, former Stasi prison, 217
Hohenzollern dynasty
  extent, 29
  fifteenth-century advent, 13

INDEX

location of family vault, 98, 221
residence, 17
territory, 30
Hohenzollern Palace, 113
   controversial decision to rebuild the façade, 218
   demolition, 197
   post-war destruction, 179
Holocaust, 7–8, 110, 157, 234
Holocaust Memorial (*Denkmal für die ermordeten Juden Europas*, Memorial to the Murdered Jews of Europe), 229
Holy Roman Empire, 9, 16–17, 25, 31, 62
   abolished by Napoleon, 59
homosexual victims of Nazi persecution, memorial to, 229
homosexuality
   attitudes towards in Weimar Berlin, 128
   lesbian concentration camp victims, unofficial recognition of, 203
Honecker, Erich, 168, 187, 194, 206
Horseshoe Estate (Hufeisensiedlung), 121, **122**
housing
   architect-designed housing, 121, **122**
   citizens' opposition to controversial building projects, 192
   Heimat style, 149
   late nineteenth-century building programme, 88
   post-reunification renovation, 224–6
   post-war developments in East and West Berlin, 176–8
   problems caused by rapid population growth, 119
   social division and, 88–9

Huguenots
   influence on Berlin's architecture, language and customs, 3, 28
   influence on manufacturing, fashions, and everyday habits, 34
   loyalty to the ruler of the day, 48
Humboldt Forum, 32, 219, 222, 235
Humboldt University, 52, 61, 180
Humboldt, Wilhelm von, 61
Humboldthain, 77

immigrant minorities, evident influence on the city, 42
immigration, patterns of, 3
Imperial Germany, foundation of (1871), 83
Imperial Parliament (Reichstag), construction of, 97
industrial relations, post-WWI politicisation, 113
industry
   and expansion of the population, 5, 86
   early influence, 69
   Frederick the Great's fostering of, 51
   growth of
      late nineteenth-century, 76, 84
      post-WWI, 124–5
influenza epidemic, 116
Institute of Sexology, 128, 140
International Architectural Exhibition Interbau, West Berlin, 176
invasions of Berlin
   Austrian, 45
   Russian, 45
   Swedish, 23

INDEX

iron foundry, Moabit, 70
Irrungen Wirrungen (*On Tangled Paths*) (Fontane), 90
Isherwood, Christopher, 8, 128, 235

Jagdschloss, 18, 89
Jahn, Johann Friedrich Ludwig Christoph, 63
Jena-Auerstedt, Battle of (1806), 60
Jewish cemetery, Senefelder Platz, 69
Jewish Museum Berlin, 234
Jewish victims, official recognition, 203
Jews
   attitudes towards during WWI, 106–7
   citizenship rights granted to, 39, 61
   deportation of, 134, 137, 155
   Frederick the Great's attitude towards, 50
   gendered expectations, 69
   German-Jewish community, 27, 38, 61
   given permission to build a new synagogue, 35
   invited in by Frederick William, 27
   Koppenplatz memorial, 65
   legal emancipation, 101
   life for in Imperial Berlin, 101
   Memorial to the Murdered Jews of Europe, 229
   population of in 1920s Berlin, 136
   post-WWI influx, 3, 117
   racialised persecution, 139
   restrictions on, 35, 39, 48, 61, 68
   scapegoating of, 15, 84
   social changes, 69
   survival of in hiding, 158
   targeting by right-wing racist propaganda, 117
   treatment of by the authorities, 117

Joachimsthaler Gymnasium (high school), 49

KaDeWe (*Kaufhaus des Westens*, 'Shopping store of the West'), 100, 190, 226
Kaiser Wilhelm II, *see* Wilhelm II, Emperor of Germany
Kaiser Wilhelm Memorial Church, 109, 180, **181**, 189
Kapp Putsch (1920), 112
Kapp, Wolfgang, 115
Kardorff, Ursula von, 135–6
Kästner, Erich, 130, 140, 235
Katte, Hans Hermann von, 44
Kennedy, John F., 4, 183–4
Kerr, Alfred, 82, 89, 98, 101
Kerr, Philip, 236
Kessler, Harry
   insights into violence in the streets of Berlin, 114
   on cultural and political power in the imperial period, 99
   on wartime public health, 106
Keun, Irmgard, 129, 235
Khrushchev, Nikita, 182, 197
Klemperer, Victor, 170, 176
Knobelsdorff, Georg Wenzeslaus von, 50
Kochhann, Heinrich Eduard, 64
Kohl, Helmut, 204, 207
Kollwitz, Käthe, 126
Königsberg, 22, 25, 30, 68
Königsplatz, 96
Köpenick, 5, 10, 118, 125, 233
Köpenick blood week, 141
   memorial to, **201**
Köpenick hunting lodge, 18, **19**, 222
Koppe, Christian, 65
Koppenplatz, 65

INDEX

Krenz, Egon, 206
Kreuzberg, 27, 119
  Bea Setton and, 236
  commercialisation, 100
  'Generalszug', 64
  naming, 63
  regeneration, 192, 226
  Turkish community, 189
Kristallnacht, 143, 153
Kroll Opera House, 139
Krumme Lanke, 125, 149–50
Kunzru, Hari, 236
Kurfürstendamm (Ku-damm), 89
Kurras, Karl-Heinz, 190
Küster, Georg Gottfried, 13
Kutscher, Volker, 236

'Ladies Club Violetta' advertisement, 129
Lang, Fritz, 8, 127
Lange, Helene, 99
Langemarck Hall, 146
Langemarck, Battle of (1914), 146
Langhans, Carl Gotthard, 53
language
  cultural capital of French manners and, 69
  Huguenot influence, 28, 48
  influence of immigrant minorities, 13, 42
  teaching of, 49
Le Carré, John, 200, 236
Legien, Carl, 113, 115
Lehrter Bahnhof, 222
Leibniz, Gottfried Wilhelm, 33
Leipzig demonstration (1989), 206
Leipziger Platz, 226
Leipziger Strasse, 65, 98, 100, 198
leisure pursuits, 94
  enthusiasm for, 125

Lengsfeld, Vera (Vera Wollenberger), 185–6, 214
Lenné, Peter Joseph, 64, 66
lesbian victims of Ravensbrück concentration camp, 203
Lessing, Gotthold Ephraim, 49
Lewald, Fanny, 68, 73–6
Ley, Robert, 153
Lichtenberg, 119
Liebermann, Max, 126
Liebknecht, Karl, 109, 113, 114, 185
'Linden Club', 73
literary salons, 55, 55, 68, 76
literature, oldest surviving written piece, 15
Little Man, What Now? (Fallada), 130
London, comparison with Berlin, 20, 91
'Long Bridge' (*Lange Brücke*), 16
Louis Philippe, King of the French, 71
Louise Henriette of Orange, 25
Lubbe, Marinus van der, 137
Lunapark leisure facility, 94
Lustgarten, 18, 43, 98
Lüttwitz, Walther von, 115
Luxemburg, Rosa, 109–10, 114, 185
Luxemburg-Liebknecht demonstration (1988), 185, 205
luxury goods, Frederick the Great's support for production of, 51

Magdeburg, 22
Mall of Berlin, 226
Mann, Thomas, 140
map of Berlin (c. 1600), 20
map of Berlin (1739), 40
March, Werner, 146
Maria Theresa, Empress of Austria, 45
Marienkirche (St Mary's Church), 'Dance of Death' mural, 14, 15
Marr, Wilhelm, 102

INDEX

Marshall Plan, 168
Marshall, George, 168
Marzahn, 142, 198–9, 203, 222, 224–5, 230
Matthäikirche, 180
Mauerpark (Wall Park), 216
Memorial to German Resistance (Gedenkstätte Deutscher Widerstand), 203, 232
Memorial to the Murdered Jews of Europe (Holocaust Memorial), 229
memorials
  to politically significant moments, 220
  to Rosa Luxemburg and Karl Liebknecht, 110
  to victims of Nazi persecution, 231
Mendelssohn, Moses, 38, 48
Mendelssohn-Bartholdy, Felix, 67
Merkel, Angela, 212, 227
Metropolis (Lang), 8, 127
Metternich, Clemens Wenzel Lothar, Fürst von, 62, 71
Meyer, Hannes, 120
Mielke, Erich, 187, 199, 217
Mies van der Rohe, Ludwig, 120, 190
militarism, role of in shaping Berlin's topography and society, 42–6, 62–4
militaristic traditions
  impact on physical and symbolic landscapes of Berlin, 95–105
  persistence of, 95
military, 64
military barracks, 52
Misselwitz, Ruth, 186
Mitte, 159, 224
Moabit, 70, 87–8, 109, 119

Monday demonstrations, Leipzig (1989), 206
monuments, post-unification retention, 219
Moroccan crisis (1911), 106
motor industry, development of, 84, 123
Mrugowsky, Joachim, 151
Müggelsee, 18, 90, 118, 125, 199, 222
Mühlendamm, 13
Müller, Johann Christoph, 11, 36
murders
  of Rosa Luxemburg and Karl Liebknecht, 109
  politically motivated, 115
Museum Island, 222
museums
  Altes Museum, 67
  (Dokumentationszentrums Flucht, Vertreibung, Versöhnung), 234
  German Colonial Museum, 104
  German Historical Museum, 202
  Jewish Museum Berlin, 234
  Museum of the Foundation for Flight, Expulsion and Reconciliation (Stiftung Flucht Vertreibung Versöhnung), 234
  municipally-funded, 228
  Musical Instrument Museum, West Berlin, 190
  National Gallery, 67
  Spandau's Citadelle Museum, 97
music, Frederick the Great's enjoyment of, 50

National Gallery, 190
New National Gallery, West Berlin, 190
Napoleon I, Emperor of the French, defeat of (1815), 62

INDEX

enters Berlin (1806), 57, **58**
forms Confederation of the Rhine (1806), 59
Napoleonic wars
French troops quartered in Berlin during, 60
impact on Berlin, 59–62
Nathan der Weise (*Nathan the Wise*), 49
National Socialist German Worker's Party (NSDAP),
election performance, 131, 139
Goebbels' position, 118
prevention of any united opposition to, 110
roots, 112
SPD demonstration against, **138**
NATO, 180
navy, Germany's growing interest, 104
Nazi Forced Labour Documentation Centre, 230
Nazi Germany, 161
Nazi Party, *see* National Socialist German Worker's Party (NSDAP)
Nazi rule
architectural influence, 146–54
transformation of Berlin under, 137–44
Nazism
drivers of support for, 115
impact on Berlin, 161
post-WWI rise in popular support, 131, 133
Nering, Johann Arnold, 32
Neue Wache (Guardhouse), Unter den Linden, 63, **86**
Neukölln, 42, 119–20, 189, 226, 236

New Synagogue, Oranienburger Straße, 101
Nicolai, Friedrich, 12, 48–9
'Night of the Long Knives', 141
Nikolaikirche (Nicolai Church), 13, **14**
Nikolassee, 128
North German Confederation, 79

'Oder-Neisse' boundary, 166
Ohnesorg, Benno, 190
'Old Marzahn', 198
Olympic Games, 142, 146
opera
Kroll Opera House, 139
Opera House, 52, 180
popularity, 67
Royal Opera House, 50
Oppenheim, Moritz, 61
origins of Berlin, 1, 3, 10–20
Ostalgie (nostalgia for the east), 218
Ostjuden (eastern Jews), 102, 117
Ostpolitik, 194
overseas colonies, acquisition of by imperial Germany, 102

Paasche, Hans, 105
Palace of the Republic (Palast der Republik), **196**, 196, 198, 218
Pankow Peace Group, 186
Papen, Franz von, 132
Paris
comparison with Berlin, 20, 91
student unrest, 191
Peace of Westphalia, 21
Peacock Island, 67
People on Sunday (*Menschen am Sonntag*) (Wilder), 128
Philharmonie, 190
Pietist movement, 48

INDEX

Plötzensee Prison, 159, 232
pogroms, 3, 15, 102, 107, 117
Poland
  defeat of, 154
  flight of Jews to, 15
  post-war situation, 166
  Solidarność (Solidarity) movement, 205
Police President, 78
Polish soldiers, memorial to, 202
political parties
  post-reunification, 227
  post-war Germany, 167, 173
political unrest (1848), 71–5
population growth, importance of, 42
population of Berlin
  by the end of Frederick the Great's reign, 42
  changing character, 18
  characteristics in East and West, 189
  decline during Thirty Years War, 24
  distribution of growth, 88
  diversity of, 2–4
  early eighteenth-century, 41
  early nineteenth-century, 54
  effects of growth in militarisation on, 44
  expansion, 41
  exponential growth through immigration, 84
  impact of growth on the shape and character of the city, 78
  increase under the Great Elector and his successors, 36
  late nineteenth-century industrialisation and expansion of, 76
  late sixteenth- and early seventeenth-century, 20
  post-unification growth and the expansion of the metropolis, 85–94
  post-WWI increase, 118
  post-WWII decline, 161
post-war Berlin
  attempted Soviet blockade, 168
  cementing of East/West division, 182–4
  cultural divergence of East and West, 180–2
  housing developments in East and West, 176–8
  rebuilding the war-damaged city, 176–82
  wartime bunker, 179
post-war Germany
  currency reform, 168
  occupation and division, 165–76
  political parties, 167, 173
potatoes, Frederick the Great's promotion of, 51
Potsdam
  'Day of Potsdam', 139
  first railway line between Berlin and, 70
  Glienicke Bridge, 222
  influence of immigrant minorities, 42
  Napoleon visits, 57
  Russian colony, 64
  Sanssouci palace, 50
Potsdam conference, 166
Potsdamer Platz
  Communist era, 178
  division of by the Wall, 190
  Europe's first traffic lights, 124
  expansion and modernisation, 225
  Joseph Roth's observations, 123
  post-war appearance, 190

INDEX

reconstruction, 225
station, 70
transport network and, 70
villa quarter, 66, 76, 89
Power, Chris, 236
Prenzlauer Berg
 synagogue, 143
 transformation after reunification, 224–5
Prenzlauer Berg, dilapidation, 197, 205
Prenzlauer Berg, Environmental Library, 186
Prenzlauer Berg, Wasserturm (water tower), 92
Prenzlauer Berg, Zion Church, 186–7
prisons
 Hohenschönhausen, 217
 Plötzensee, 159, 232
property developers, late nineteenth-century activities, 89–91
Protestant Cathedral (Dom), 98, **221**
Protestant church, status in the GDR, 186
Prussia
 acquisition of territories, 62
 declared a constitutional monarchy, 75
 growing unrest in, 71
 late eighteenth-century status, 46
 military reforms, 61
 Napoleonic wars, impact, 59–62
 three-class voting system, 75, 83
public bathing facilities, 94
public burning of books, 51, 140
public executions, 65
public health, population growth and concerns about, 91–3

Quadriga, 53

Quadriga, French seizure and return, 60, 62

racial science, introduction as school subject, 142
railway network
 beginnings, 70
 electrification, 87, 123
 expansion across Europe, 83
rapprochement, 194
Rathenau, Walther, 115
Rauch, Christian Daniel, 46
Raule, Benjamin, 26
Ravensbrück concentration camp, 203
reading, expansion of in public life, 49, 50
Reagan, Ronald, 187
Red Army Faction (Rote Armee Fraktion, RAF), 191
Red Army soldier, statue, 200
Red Army, experiences of German women of, 162
'Red Berlin', 117, 146
'Red Orchestra' (*Rote Kapelle*), 203
Reformation, adopted by Berlin, 18
refugees
 Angela Merkel's invitation, 212, 227
 from conflicts in the Middle East, 227
 from lost eastern provinces, 162, 164, 189, 234
 Joseph Roth's description, 117
 Ukrainian women and children, 228
Reich Security Head Office (RSHA), 142, 232
 reclamation and preservation of the site, 192, 203
 Topography of Terror exhibition on the site of, **204**
Reich, Jens, 206

INDEX

Reichstag
  arson attack, 137
  construction of, 97
  reopened for parliamentary
    business, 213
  transparent dome, 97, 214
Reinickendorf, 119
religious toleration
  Berlin's unusual degree of, 47
  first step towards, 27
  'Forum Friedericianum' and, 50
  Frederick the Great's support for, 50
  Lessing's plea for, 49
  relationship with economic growth, 41
remembrance
  Berlin's landscape of, 228–35
  complicity and everyday racism, 233
  of suffering on the part of
    Germans, 234
  perpetrator sites, 232
  resistance and dissent, 232
  victims of Nazi persecution, 229–32
'rental barracks' (*Mietskasernen*), 79,
  88, 119, 192
reparations, economic impact, 115
Residenzstadt, establishment of Berlin
  as, 17
reunification
  and the birth rate in eastern
    Germany, 211
  and the continuing 'wall in people's
    heads', 211
  and the move of the capital from
    Bonn to Berlin, 212
  celebrations, 209
  economic and political implications,
    226–7
  environmental implications, 224–6
  events leading up to, 185–8, 205–8
  impact on Berlin, 209–12

'peaceful revolution' myth, 215
  social and cultural implications,
    227–8
  transport networks, 222–4
  Unification Treaty (1990), 209
Reuter, Ernst, 168
revolutionary uprising (1848), 58
Rhineland, migration from, 13
Rixdorf, 42
Röhm, Ernst, 141
Roma, 136, 142
  memorial to, 230
Romanticism, 54
Roth, Joseph, 117, 123
Royal Library, 50
Royal Opera House, 50
royal palace, *see also* Hohenzollern
  Palace
  destruction, 32
  establishment of, 18
  expanded and rebuilt, 32
Royal Porcelain Factory, 51
Royal Station Connection Railway, 87
Russia
  invasion of Berlin, 45
  invasion of Ukraine, 228
Russian émigrés, impact on the
  character of Berlin society, 116
Ruttmann, Walther, 8, 127

Sachs, Nelly, 65
Sachsenhausen concentration
  camp, 222
  exhibition, 203
Sanssouci, Potsdam, 50
  restoration, 203
Schabowski, Günter, 206
Schadow, Johann Gottfried, 53
Scharnhorst, Gerhard von, 61, 63
Scharoun, Hans, 121, 190

INDEX

Schäuble, Wolfgang, 213
Schauspielhaus theatre, 66
Scheffler, Karl, 5, 13, 105, 238
Scheidemann, Philipp, 113
Schinkel, Karl Friedrich, 63, 66, 86
Schlachtensee, 125
Schloss Britz, 90, 121
Schlüter, Andreas, 32-3
Schmaus, Anton, 141
Scholl, Hans and Sophie, 203 see above
Schöneberg, 4, 190, 119, 175
   gay scene, 128
   'Generalszug', 64
   Grazer Damm housing estate, 151
   housing, 90
   synagogue, 143
   wartime bunker, 159, 179
Schöneberg Town Hall, 4, 166
Schumann, Hans Konrad, 183
Schwarzenberg, Adam, Count von, 22
Second Silesian war, 45
Second World War
   damage to Berlin and post-war living conditions, 161
   end of and its aftermath in Berlin, 161-5
   impact on Berlin and its inhabitants, 154-60
   post-war occupation and division of Germany, 165-76
Seghers, Anna, 170
serfdom, abolition of, 61
Setton, Bea, 236
Seven Years' War, 45
sewerage system, development of, 92
Shah of Iran, visit to Berlin, 190
Siegessäule (Victory Column), 96-7
Siemens AG, 121
Siemensstadt, architect-designed housing in, 121, **122**

'Silent Heroes' (*Stille Helden*), 233
Silesia
   wars over, 45
   weavers' revolt, 71
Simon, Marie Jalowicz, 158
Sinti, 136, 142
   memorial to, 230
slave trade, Frederick William's involvement, 26
slum housing, 88, 93
social housing, architect-designed, 121-3
Solidarność (Solidarity) movement, Poland, 205
Sonnenallee (Haussmann), 217
Sophie Charlotte, Queen, consort of Frederick I, King of Prussia, 32
Soviet Union
   Berlin blockade, 164, 169
   German invasion of, 155
   post-war removal of goods and equipment, 165
   takeover of Baltic states and eastern Poland, 166
Soviet war memorial, 82
Spandau, 5, 87, 118, 121, 222
   Albert the Bear and, 10
   fortress and tower, **6**
   museum, 97
   von Schwarzenberg's retreat to, 22
Spartacist uprising, 114
Spartacus League, 114
'Speech to the German nation' (Fichte), 62
Speer, Albert, 96, 136, 144, 232
Spener, Philipp Jakob, 48
Spree river, 1, 3, 10, 47, 64, 92, 213
Springer, Axel, 190
spy swaps, 236

269

INDEX

'SS comradeship settlement' (*SS-Kameradschaftssiedlung*), 149, 150
Stalin, Joseph
  death of, 174
  overtures towards proposing a united Germany, 174
  portrait of, 167
Stalinallee (Karl-Marx-Allee), East Berlin, 176, 197
Stalingrad, Battle of (1942–43), 155
standing army, 24-5
Stasi (*Staatssicherheitspolizei*)
  archives opened, 186, 214
  as constant feature of life, 173
  chief Erich Mielke, 187, 199
  creative representations, 8, 217
  exponential growth of surveillance, 199
  growth of in the 1970s and 1980s, 195
  Hohenschönhausen prison, 217
  place in the cultural imagination, 217
  post-unification destruction of files, 190
  repurposing of former headquarters, 217
State Library, West Berlin, 190
Steglitz memorial, 230
Stein, Karl Freiherr vom, 60
sterilisation, compulsory, 142
Stinnes, Hugo, 113
stock market crash (1873), 84
stock market crash (1929), 112, 131
Stöcker, Adolf, 102
Streckfuß, Adolph, 31, 39, 65, 69, 73
street names recalling Wars of Liberation, 64
Strousberg, Bethel, 83
student unrest (1968), 191

'stumbling stones' (*Stolpersteine*), 230-1
'Sturm und Drang' movement, 54
Swabia, migration from, 13
Sweden, invasion of Berlin, 23

Tatort ('Scene of the Crime'), 234
Taut, Bruno, 121
technological advancement, Berlin's role, 84, 123
Tegel Forest, 119
Television Tower (*Fernsehturm*), East Berlin, **196**
Tenth World Festival of Youth and Students, East Berlin (1973), 196
Terraingesellschaften, 89
textile industry, importance of to Berlin, 54
Thälmann Park, 219
Thälmann, Ernst, 200, 219
The Artificial Silk Girl (Keun), 129
The Legend of Paul and Paula (Carow), 197
The Lives of Others (Henckel von Donnersmarck), 217
The Tempelhof Field, 140
Third Artillery Regiment, 52
Third Reich, exhibition on the history of, 232
Thirty Years War, 22-4
Tiergarten
  avenue from the palace towards, 32
  Hansa Viertel, 176
  leisure pursuits, 94
  memorials, 219, 229
  political rallies in, 74
  redesigned, 66
  role in social life of Berlin, 49, 66, 77, 94
  Speer's plans for, 96

INDEX

'villa quarter', 89
Tietz department store, 100
Tietz, Herman, 100
Tietz, Oscar, 100
Toland, John, 36
Topography of Terror exhibition, 142, 232, 234
   location, 192, 204
tourism
   and promotion of significant historical sites, 228
   implications of reunification for, 224–5
   role of in Berlin's economy, 8
   tourist boat on the River Spree, **239**
trade, Frederick the Great's fostering of, 51
traffic lights, Europe's first, **124**
transgender identities, attitudes towards in Weimar Berlin, 128
transport networks
   implications of economic development and population growth, 123, **124**
   operation of in East and West Berlin, 172–3
   re-connecting east and west, 222–4
transportation, late nineteenth-century development, 87
treaties
   Basic Treaty between West and East Germany (1972), 194
   Peace of Westphalia (1648), 21
   Treaty of Friendship, Cooperation and Mutual Assistance (Warsaw Pact) (1955), 180
   Treaty of Tilsit (1807), 60
   Treaty of Versailles (1919), 114
   Unification Treaty (1990), 209
Treitschke, Heinrich von, 102

Treptow Park, 77, 80, 82, **103**, 106, 200
Trotha, Lothar von, 104
Truman, Harry S., 168
'Turnvater Jahn' ('gymnastics father Jahn'), 63

Ukraine, Russian invasion of, 228
Ulbricht, Walter, 166–7, 174, 183, 194
'Under the Tents', 74
unemployment, post-WWI rise in, 112
UNESCO World Heritage Site, 64, 121
unification of Germany, 209, 212
   architect of, 58
   Berlin on the eve of, 76–9
   economic impact, 83
Unification Treaty (1990), 209
United Nations, GDR's accession, 195
Unter den Linden
   as centre of commerce, 77
   Brandenburg Gate situated on, 53
   East Berlin (1981), **196**
   Frederick the Great's statue re-erected in, 203
   name, 52
   Neue Wache (Guardhouse), 63, **86**
   Philippi's recollection, 105
   portrayal of a mid nineteenth-century bourgeois house on, 77
   post-reunification renovation, 224
   Stalin's portrait, **167**
   statue of Frederick the Great, **47**
   urban planning, post-WWI debate, 91

Varnhagen, Rahel Levin, 55, 68, 76
Versailles, 33, 50
Victory Avenue (*Siegesallee*), 96
Victory Column (*Siegessäule*), 96–7
Vienna
   comparison with Berlin, 20
   Congress of (1815), 62

INDEX

Vienna (cont.)
  Friedrich von Cölln's comparison of Berlin with, 54
  Jews thrown out of (1671), 27
  unrest in (1848), 71
'villa quarter', 89
Volkspark Friedrichshain, 53
Voltaire, 50

Wahlberliner (Berliners by choice), 4, 19
Wall Street Crash (1929), 112, 131
Wandlitz, 194
Wannsee, 67, 90, 118, 125, 128, 222
Wannsee Conference, 157, 203, 233
Wars of Liberation, 62
  National Memorial, 63
  street names recalling, 64
Warsaw Pact (1955), 180
wartime bunker, 179
Wasserturm (water tower), Prenzlauer Berg, 92
waste management in Berlin, 65–6
Wauer, Hugo, 65–6
Weber, Carl Maria von, 67
Wedding, 87–8, 119, 189
Weigel, Helene, 126
Weill, Kurt, 126
Weimar era, visual representations, 8
Weimar Republic, birth of, 130
Weinstraße, 53
Weißensee, 90, 101
Wertheim department store, 100
Wessel, Horst, 132
West Berlin
  characteristics of the population, 189
  cultural investment, 190
  economic challenges, 189
  geographical separation from the Federal Republic, 178
  implications of generational shift towards social critique and activism, 192
  memorialisation and statuary, 203
  political conflicts, 190
  student unrest, 190–1
West Germany, acceptance of post-war borders in Eastern Europe, 194
Westphalia, Peace of, 21
White Rose resistance movement, 203
Wilder, Billy, 128
Wilhelm II, Kaiser (Emperor William II of Germany)
  abdication (1918), 17, 107, 112
  opposition to the Great Industrial Exposition, 80
Wilhelm Straße, 65, 146
Wilmersdorf, 89–90, 226
Wolf, Christa, 206
Wollenberger, Knud, 185–6, 215
Wollenberger, Vera (Vera Lengsfeld), 185–6, 214
women
  experiences at the hands of Red Army soldiers, 162
  increasingly drawn into the workforce, 125, 155
Work House, 65
Wowereit, Klaus, 227, 229
Wuhlheide, 199

Yalta conference, 165

Zehlendorf, 90, 119, 226
Zeughaus (arsenal), 33, 52, 74
Zille, Heinrich, 8, 88
Zion Church, Prenzlauer Berg, 186–7

For EU product safety concerns, contact us at Calle de José Abascal, 56–1°, 28003 Madrid, Spain or eugpsr@cambridge.org.

www.ingramcontent.com/pod-product-compliance
Lightning Source LLC
LaVergne TN
LVHW040613250326
834688LV00035B/542